Book Autobiography:

Data from the Education at a Glance in 2019 states that less than 2 percent of the United States' and world's population holds a doctorate degree. Germane to this fact, the National Center of Education statistics reported that, in the 2018-19 academic year, of the doctoral degrees awarded to women, only 10.9 percent were awarded to Black women compared to 63.6 percent awarded to White women in the U.S. Black women who are interested in pursuing a doctorate, already in doctoral programs, or in their field of doctoral work are in crucial need of resources, community, and support. For too long, Black women have faced many systemic barriers and various forms of racist exclusion and oppression in educational settings, which has often led to burnout, low sense of belonging, and low retention rates. This memoir, "Our Doctoral Journey: A collection of Black women's experiences," serves as a resource and toolkit for Black women doctors, future doctors, and professionals. Prepare yourselves to read transparent and ground-breaking stories from 24 co-authors, ranging from doctoral students to doctors to professionals, who, with great tenacity, have chosen to share their doctoral experiences. Undeniably, this memoir will give you hope, motivation, and determination to choose what is best for you and persist in your program or in your field of work. As the saying goes, "We're all that we've got."

Our Doctoral Journey

A Collection of Black Women's Experiences

Nicole A. Telfer

Copyright © 2022 by Nicole A. Telfer.

Library of Congress Control Number:		2022909918
ISBN:	Hardcover	978-1-6698-2710-8
	Softcover	978-1-6698-2709-2
	eBook	978-1-6698-2708-5

All rights reserved. No part of this book may be reproduced or transmitted in any form or by any means, electronic or mechanical, including photocopying, recording, or by any information storage and retrieval system, without permission in writing from the copyright owner.

Any people depicted in stock imagery provided by Getty Images are models, and such images are being used for illustrative purposes only. Certain stock imagery © Getty Images.

Print information available on the last page.

Rev. date: 05/27/2022

To order additional copies of this book, contact:
Xlibris
844-714-8691
www.Xlibris.com
Orders@Xlibris.com
833739

Contents

Foreword ix

Chapter 1	Nicole Telfer's Story 1
Chapter 2	Munazza Abraham's Story 14
Chapter 3	Sarah Adeyinka's Story 24
Chapter 4	Kenyatta Aldridge's Story 33
Chapter 5	Chanya Anderson's Story 42
Chapter 6	Toneille Bent's Story 48
Chapter 7	Angel Boulware's Story 55
Chapter 8	Juanita Crider's Story 63
Chapter 9	Dominique Garrett-Scott's Story 69
Chapter 10	Leeshe N. Grimes's Story 75
Chapter 11	N'Dea Irvin-Choy's Story 81
Chapter 12	Elisabeth Jeffrey's Story 87
Chapter 13	Tabitha Esther's Story 92
Chapter 14	Lisa Marie Lee's Story 101
Chapter 15	Keila Miles's Story 109
Chapter 16	Gaëlle Pierre's Story 118
Chapter 17	Ivy Rentz's Story 124
Chapter 18	Kristin Robair's Story 135
Chapter 19	Shanel Robinson's Story 142
Chapter 20	Briana Spivey's Story 148
Chapter 21	Emmanuela Stanislaus's Story 155
Chapter 22	Deja Trammell's Story 161
Chapter 23	Charity Watkins's Story 169
Chapter 24	Johniqua Williams's Story 179

For Black Women, Forever and Always 187
Acknowledgments 189

For our villages that made these stories possible
For all the little Black girls with big dreams who can't quite see their path
For Black womxn across the diaspora who are fearlessly present

We are here. And rising, still.

FOREWORD

Written by Dr. Rahmatu Kassimu

F ROM MID-APRIL TO mid-October of 2016, I cried every…single…day. Sometimes, it was only eyeball sweat, and other times, I made myself a blanket burrito and bawled like a baby. Three seasons that year saw me become a shell of myself. Internally, at least. Externally, no one could tell the difference. You see, I laughed when I was supposed to. I told jokes like I was supposed to. I showed up and supported my friends in various adventures. I threw caution to the wind and jumped off cliffs in Jamaica. I went to work each day, greeted roughly 150 students with a smile, and delivered learning experiences with passion, precision, and enthusiasm.

But internally…

I was cracking. Cracked even. Broken.

I had lost my passion for everything.

I didn't want to work.

I didn't want to go to school.

I wanted to do nothing but retreat to my blanket burrito and cry. Crying never actually made it better, but it was a release. I was perpetually exhausted. I woke up looking forward to my after-work nap. I wanted to do nothing, but I kept doing it because the weight of expectations spurred me on and told me that I had to.

I cried for almost half a year before I allowed myself to admit what was wrong with me.

I was in a high-functioning depression. Shame kept me from admitting it. A sense of ungratefulness gripped me the first time I said it aloud, as if someone was whispering in my spirit, "How dare you?" But there it was. I couldn't deny, hide, or intellectualize it away any longer. I was depressed. Funny thing, though, once I admitted it, I began to feel lighter. I took small actions each day to keep myself lifted and developed a system of care for myself that included social support, journaling, meditation, and prayer. It's not a perfect system, and there are often slumps, but I never allow myself to sink as far as I did that year and bounce back rooted in my purpose and identity, always looking to the future.

What brought this on, you say?

Well, it was a combination of things, but the primary thing was writing my dissertation. No one tells you, probably because they don't want to scare you, but writing a dissertation is a lonely process. No one understands what you're doing or why. You partly don't understand yourself. All you know for certain is that the question, "when are you graduating?" will cause an immediate anxiety spike. You simultaneously feel that you're doing too much but also not enough.

The cohort of peers that you had to bolster you through courses is gone, each person moving at different speeds to completion. You're floundering, but everyone keeps telling you that you have it and to keep it pushing. Well, I pushed until I hit a wall, and man, did the wall hit back. I had a conversation with my then advisor, and she basically told me that all the work I'd done, the work I felt was quality, was not enough. And well, that was the straw that broke my back, as it were—queue six months of fog.

When the fog began to clear, I intentionally approached my dissertation differently. I honestly approached life differently. I realized that I did not have to be "One Deep," as Z-Ro would say. I had supports; I merely needed to tap into them. I tapped, trapped, and cemented my support group, and they have stood the test of time. They rallied around me across the PhinisheD line and have been with me ever since.

Here's the thing.

My experience, while nuanced, is not unique. The experiences of Black women in graduate programs, particularly Doctoral programs, are often mired in challenges that equate to a mental health gauntlet. We're often the only or the few charged with carrying the weight of our race in class discussions, data, and expectations. We're inundated daily with biases, both explicit and implicit, and critical eyes forever assessing if we really deserve to be in these spaces. There's an inner push to prove, confirm, and justify ourselves.

It…is… exhausting.

But we do it. We do it because we seek higher knowledge so that we can elevate and empower. We do it so that we can achieve more, be more. We do it because once we read a shirt that said, "I am my ancestors' wildest dream," and we made it our personal mission to make sure that statement could not be contested. We do it because we want to break generational curses, setting our future families up to flourish in abundance. We do it for Sankofa and the need to go and bring it back to the village, lifting us all.

When Nicole Telfer posted on Instagram about wanting to write a compilation of Black women's experiences while completing their doctorates, I jumped at the chance. Through a series of fortunate events, I was given the opportunity to write this foreword. Not only that, but I've also been able to interact with a group of Black women whose stories will engage you, enrage you, entertain you, and inspire you. The stories that follow are tales of heartaches, trials, and triumphs. They are tales of women advocating for themselves unapologetically and walking in their excellence despite barriers placed in front of them. They are tales of Black women standing up and proclaiming that they will decolonize spaces with their voices, actions, and input because progress waits for no one. They speak to the indomitable spirit of Black women and the strength ingrained in our minds, bodies, and souls.

I hope that as you read these chapters, the strength, poise, grace, and tenacity of these women seep into your very marrow, encouraging you to pursue your wildest dreams.

Welcome to Our Doctoral Journey.

CHAPTER 1

Nicole Telfer's Story

NICOLE A. TELFER is currently a PhD candidate in Applied Developmental Psychology– with training in child and adolescent development– at the University of Maryland, Baltimore County (UMBC). Born in Brooklyn, New York, and raised on ackee and saltfish, Nicole is a proud daughter of Jamaican parents and takes pride in her heritage. She holds a Bachelor of Science degree in Human Development and Family Studies from Penn State University and a Master of Arts degree in Applied Developmental Psychology from UMBC. As a developmental scientist, Nicole's research focuses on ethnic-racial socialization practices, social determinants of health, the role of intersectionality, and finding ways to improve the educational experiences and developmental outcomes of Black youth. Ultimately, Nicole hopes to create preventive intervention programs and centers in inner-city neighborhoods for racially minoritized youth and their overall wellbeing. Outside of academia and research, Nicole loves to travel, enjoys listening to H.E.R and Jazmin Sullivan, finds pleasure in reading radical books, and spends ample time tending to her plants. She is a professional spoken-word artist and author and co-author of three books: Freed, A Black Woman's Guide to Earning a PhD, and Phoenix Phenomenon.

Introduction

It was approximately 2:43 AM when this book project idea came to mind. And in the early morning, when I thought about writing this book with other phenomenal Black women, I thought about how much I love us. I love us, for real. I am currently a fourth-year PhD candidate who should probably be devoting much of her time to writing research manuscripts and her dissertation, not guidebooks and memoirs. When I was writing down my ideas for this memoir in the note's app on my iPhone, I thought, "Lord, I do *too* much." But the thought that followed was, "If not me, then who?" Deep in my heart, I believe that I was called to do this work. I was called to create resources and be a gatekeeper for Black girls and women. Before I try to summarize bits and pieces of my doctoral experiences in a few pages, I must let you know that I will always ride for Black girls and women. I will always protect us. Black girls and women deserve the world, and I will always give them everything I've got. My story was written with Black girls and women in mind, and I am unapologetic about that. While reading the stories of other Black women doctors, future doctors, and professionals in this book, I must also let you know that this is not trauma porn for the soul. These stories were not written because we are in search of white academic saviors. If anything, these stories are a wake-up call for white academia. These stories are transparent, truthful, and vulnerable. These stories came from the heart of Black women who have survived and are surviving toxic, hyper-masculine, white spaces, such as the academy. We did not collectively write this memoir to defame anyone or any institution. We have written this book to share our experiences as Black women who have pursued doctorates or are/were in doctoral programs that have been stressful and triggering environments. We have written this book—for Black women and other Women of Color, by Black women.

Unapologetically for Black Girls and Women

It's ridiculous that some people think the simple phrase "Protect Black women" is controversial. We deserve to be protected as human beings. And we are entitled to our anger about a laundry list of mistreatment and neglect that we suffer. - Megan Thee Stallion

When my third year as a doctoral student began, I was in my aunt's living room in Brooklyn, NY. During the start of any other semester, I would have been in Baltimore, Maryland, on the UMBC campus, but COVID-19 had other plans for many–if not all–of us. The 2020-21 school year was a different experience as a graduate student for sure. *Everything* was virtual. Classes. Meetings. Events.

More often than not, it was incredibly difficult to stay focused and present. I was exhausted, as was everyone else. But my exhaustion began before the semester started because I was trying to picture what an academic year would look like amid this pandemic. In the first semester of my third year, I enrolled in two classes— primary prevention and methods of assessment— and dedicated my remaining time to my comprehensive exam portfolio. Despite the virtual setting, I enjoyed my graduate courses because there were always opportunities to interact, engage, and present meaningful work. In my primary prevention course, specifically, I had the opportunity to educate my colleagues on a topic that is very near and dear to my heart: the school-to-prison pipeline among Black girls. As I presented my findings and advocated for all the Black girls around the world, I reflected on my own experiences in the public school system. I reminisced on how there were teachers who physically assaulted me by grabbing my arm to drag me into detention. Educators who verbally abused me by telling me that I would never make it to graduation because I was not intelligent enough, which was why my standardized scores were low. Teachers whose behaviors kept me away from learning many times. I could not understand why I was a target and wasn't quite able to process my emotions then. However, I have come to understand that the mistreatment I've experienced on school grounds was a result of the long and untreated history of violence and hate towards Black folk, specifically toward Black girls and women.

Black girls are often hidden figures in conversations on school punitive practices and criminalization despite being pushed out of schools at an alarming rate. When we talk about the school-to-prison pipeline, Black girls *need* to be part of the conversation. I am grateful for my primary prevention course because it reminded me that I still have work to do in the fight and movement to dismantle the school-to-prison pipeline among Black girls and create more restorative justice practices. I know first-hand that Black girls are the least thought of in the public school system and society. When I think of protecting Black girls, I think of Ma'Khia Bryant. Oluwatoyin Salau. My nieces. My cousins. Myself.

Whenever we discuss the critical need to protect Black girls, the response should not be *Well, what about Black boys*? *Or Latina and Asian girls*? I have been asked those questions many times, especially when it comes to my research. Ain't it funny? When folks talk about creating and disseminating resources just for Black girls and women, there is an army of anti-Black girls and women fighting against this agenda because what good would this world be if we thought about Black girls and women for just a moment? Maybe if folks thought about me for just a moment, I would not have experienced prolonged child abuse. Or maybe, if I was on someone's mind for one second, the boy who punched me in the face in middle school would not have gotten away with it. Maybe, just maybe, if someone reached out to me because they randomly thought of a Black girl, suicide ideation would not have been at the forefront of my mind when I was sitting in my dorm room in college.

I believe that my calling to protect Black girls and women is earnest. It is not a joke or something for me to play about. There are wars we are fighting (that we didn't even ask to fight in) because of our intersecting identities of being Black and a girl or a woman or trans or fat or disabled or any other marginalized identity. I'm always going to fight for Black girls and women and make them my top priority in the liberation movement. My passion for protecting Black girls and women afforded me the opportunity to work directly with 49 Black girls who were seniors at the Baltimore Leadership School for Young Women for my doctoral practicum. After completion of my practicum, the CEO of the high school gifted me a shirt that said, "Remember your why." That simple gift truly meant the world to me because I do not always feel like I am doing enough as it relates to my calling, but my mentees reminded me every day of how grateful they were for my help. Serving as their mentor—by providing resources for college readiness and assisting with their senior research project—made me realize how important it is to simply be there for young Black girls.

A Black mentor who looked like me was what I wished for in middle school and high school. Perhaps I would have known more about historically Black colleges and universities (HBCUs). Or perhaps, I would have known about amazing undergraduate majors, like African American and Africana studies. Mentorship is so critical for our development. It shapes who we are and reminds us that we need help on this journey of life. We need people in our corner. I have never taken full credit for where I am today. I attribute my success and accomplishments to my village that stretches as far as the beautiful island of Jamaica to as close as Maryland and New York. As the legendary Bill Withers sang: *We all need somebody to lean on.* Black girls and women can surely lean on me.

A Shelter in the Time of Storm

The ache for home lives in all of us, the safe place where we can go as we are and not be questioned. -Maya Angelou

I've found myself cussing a lot lately. A few years ago, I couldn't get the f-word to roll off my tongue. Now, every little thing or person that irritates me is followed by a large word bank of cuss words. My aunt would always say, "If you find yourself more agitated than usual, then you need to check your space and do some Spring cleaning." I'm sure that her definition of Spring cleaning consisted of both mental and physical cleaning. Which negative people and what negative thoughts did I need to free myself from? What do I envision being a safe space for me? I immediately thought of safe spaces and people I had back at home in Brooklyn, NY. Like my elementary and middle school best friend, Abby, and my high school best friend, Temara. They were caring, warm, and expressed a soft kind of love that I didn't always know I needed. Because of them, I know what a safe space looks like for me. Then I thought about academia and realized that much of my cussing elevated when I started graduate school. I have not always felt safe, seen, and heard as a graduate student, which frustrated me.

Black women and other Women of Color often struggle to find safe spaces in the academy. I know this was my story for a very long time until I established the Black Graduate Student organization. This organization has brought me much peace, stability, and security, and I wanted other Black graduate students to share these same sentiments. However, connecting with UMBC Black graduate students and facilitating spaces presented some challenges as COVID-19 cases steadily increased. Still, I made significant efforts to keep folks connected to our organization by hosting online programs. One of our most memorable and successful online events was our Black history month celebration in February of 2020. We were honored to have Sybrina Fulton, the mother of Trayvon Martin, as our keynote speaker. Ms. Fulton shared many memories about her beloved son, Trayvon, with us, but the memory that most certainly warmed my heart was when she shared that Trayvon was "a momma's boy to the core." The same Trayvon that white America tried to depict as a thug and deserving of death was a gentle human who loved his momma. Trayvon Martin's murder was one that brought a movement back to life. Everyone around the world wore hoodies and bought skittles and a bottle of Arizona to honor him and stand in solidarity with his loved ones. Speaking with Ms. Fulton was such a humbling experience, and it reminded me of why Black mommas display so much tough love. That "make sure you're inside before the streetlights turn on" talk was never to punish us but to protect us. Our mommas carry so much wisdom, and they know that the streets won't always be kind to us.

And just like how Black mommas know that the streets won't always protect their babies, I know that our campus community won't always protect Black graduate students. I know that there will be first-year Black graduate students who will enter their programs and wonder why there is no one who resembles them. There will be Black graduate students who will experience racist discrimination from faculty, staff, and peers who try to undermine their capabilities in their respective fields. I know this because I have experienced these social harms in my first year of graduate school and struggled to find a safe space to run to. Many times, I would go home after class and look for new graduate programs to enroll in because of the severe discomfort I felt being the only Black student in many classes. Being called out in class for having *long hair one day and short hair the next* (as my professor described me to my peers, right in front of me) and being expected to always speak on behalf of the Black community was all too overwhelming, and I knew I couldn't survive in that kind of atmosphere without support. I later learned that, unfortunately, racist discrimination experiences and microaggressions exist and are pervasive throughout the academy. I learned that my experiences are not entirely unique. This is why the Black Graduate Student Organization was so important to me and to many other Black graduate students. It was our shelter, our safe space to decompress, share, reflect, and offer each other support.

We also made room for Black joy by hosting an Ebony ball and awards ceremony every year. Our 2022 annual event was the most recent, and it was truly remarkable. Our keynote speaker, Dr. Maya Rockeymoore Cummings, shared a powerful message, and there were amazing performances and delicious food. As I stood in the back of the event and stared at beautiful Black people laughing, dancing, and being free, my heart smiled. We deserve to be in spaces where we can breathe…and exist. In that room, I saw the collective experiences of trauma and pain but also triumph and perseverance. It reminded me that the ultimate goal is true liberation for all of us. But until then, finding your safe space is critical; it will keep you sane. If your safe space does not exist, I dare you to create it.

By the Still Waters

Caring for myself is not self-indulgence, it is self-preservation and that is an act of political warfare. -Audre Lorde

Every day at 6:00 PM, my alarm goes off and I am notified to "talk to God." During one of my casual conversations with God, I repeated Psalms 23 and expressed how grateful I was for the Sabbath. For Seventh Day Adventists, our belief in divine rest is deeply rooted in the fourth commandment, which tells us that God created six days for us to work and labor but the seventh day is our day of rest. I was reminded of the meaning of the Sabbath on a Friday when I felt depleted and overwhelmed. I did not feel like I accomplished much during the workweek and was tempted to continue working into Saturday and Sunday. To add to my exhaustion, one of my supervisors sent me a *time-sensitive* task to complete that Friday evening. Just when I was about to open my laptop, I heard a still, soft voice begging me to rest my weary eyes. This is, undoubtedly, the work and mission of the grind and toxic work cultures—to make us feel like we are undeserving of rest. That there is no time to sit or meditate for a few minutes. But I am grateful for the Sabbath because, at the age of 5, I was taught about the importance of rest which has led me on this journey of actively denouncing grind culture. I have seen what grind culture has done to some of my loved ones. It has made them feel like any time spent away from work— whether it be connecting with folks or watching an episode of their favorite show—will cost them significantly. This is also the work of capitalism, and I am so glad that I am free from these systems. Free all my brothas and sistahs. But Lord, please free my Black sistahs.

My good friend and colleague, Jabarey, invited me to his thesis defense, where he talked about *John Henryism*. I had no idea what that concept was and meant until I sat in on his presentation. The term John Henryism was birthed from a story about a man named John Henry, an American folk hero, who is said to have worked as a steel driver on railroads in the mid-1800s. According to legend, John Henry was challenged to a steel-driving contest with a rock-drilling machine. He won the contest but dropped dead right after. There is also another story about a man named John Henry Martin who worked hard to free himself and his children from the sharecropper system in North Carolina. Although John succeeded, he developed serious health problems in his 50s, including high blood pressure, arthritis, and stomach ulcers. After I learned of these stories, I sent a text message to my friend (a Black woman) and said, "I am John Henry, and John Henry is me." We chuckled for a moment but eventually realized the accuracy of my *joke*.

I admit that I am an advocate for rest but sometimes wrestle with putting down my laptop when I no longer have the capacity to contribute to academia for the remainder of the day. I wrestle with saying "no, I cannot take on this task" or "the workload is too much for me" to my advisors and mentors. I struggle with wanting to be an overachieving Black woman versus wanting to be a rest specialist. My fear of being depicted as incapable and lazy often outweighs my desire to lay my head and dream. This fear has led to many repercussions, like clinical depression, anxiety, and weight loss–all silent battles I did not want to overwhelm my loved ones. My folks never witnessed the depressed and anxious side of me. I made sure of it. My friends know me as the one *who does it all*. My mom, clueless and proud, would often describe me as the child who *has har head pon har body*, meaning that I have it all together. But I don't. And I have fallen apart many times while fighting these battles alone. I don't always feel competent or worthy. I don't always feel smart, and have felt lost, many times. I've encountered severely low days where I would question my life's purpose and entire existence.

I have written and said this numerous times; academia doesn't give a shit about us. The academy is not interested in the well-being of its professors, researchers, scholars, and especially its graduate students. I've learned this lesson the hard way when I was expected to produce quick yet quality work while trying to heal from all sorts of trauma, mourning the lives of my Black sisters who were murdered by police, and struggling with managing my anxiety and depression. In the midst of it all, I still felt like I could be doing and giving more. More time for my friends and loved ones. More time for a social life and dating. More time to research and manuscripts. Speaking of dating (I wish someone informed me of the ghetto), while juggling numerous academic responsibilities, I was also grieving a relationship loss that left me completely distraught and restless. I struggled with navigating this loss because, as an academic, grieving has often felt conditional and specific to a death of a loved one (although we are still expected to keep working even when we experience physical deaths).

How do I inform my mentors that I do not have any capacity to do work because the guy that I envisioned a future with broke up with me? I couldn't just *work the pain away*. I needed time to process and grieve. When I shared this painful breakup with a colleague, she said, "You may have lost him, but you know what you won't lose once you get it? That PhD!" I knew she meant well, but there was something inherently harmful about her response. The message was clear—leave no room for sadness. Move on and continue to focus on your career. Again, this was the work of grind culture and capitalism, of which I wanted no part. As one can imagine, I was immediately over my third year of graduate school within a matter of four weeks. Luckily, I had two safe spaces where I could take my worries: the Lord in prayer and my therapy sessions. One afternoon, I vented to my therapist about relationships and school, and she said:

1) Not every relationship that has ended—whether it be platonic or romantic—means that it has failed. Sometimes the connections we build with someone are only meant to last for a certain period. And when it ends, there is a lesson we are supposed to extract from that experience. Once I stopped viewing every relationship loss as a failed relationship, I began engaging in healthy grieving, which brought me peace and contributed to my journey to rest.

2) Rest is not earned nor given. It is a necessity. Period. We *need* to rest our bodies and souls, and when we are well-rested, we make great contributions to society. When we are well-rested, we are content and kind to one another, but most importantly, we are kind to ourselves.

Dear Black women and Women of Color: Prioritize your rest, health, and wellbeing.

Choose yourself first and academia later. There will *always* be work to do, deadlines to meet, and assignments to complete. But please, set your boundaries. Please know that saying *no* is acceptable. Sometimes we need to be still to free our space, soul, and mind. Academia has a way of bringing us through troubled waters, but peace, be still. You are not a machine. You deserve to rest and dream.

Accountability Looks Like…

Action springs not from thought, but from a readiness for responsibility. -Dietrich Bonhoeffer

Folks' thoughts on Martin Luther King Jr. on MLK day are always captivating—like Kimberlé Crenshaw, who stated that MLK Jr. was a critical race theorist before the term was coined. Yet, other thoughts remain concerning. On social media, one might see pictures of MLK Jr. giving his "I have a dream" speech with a caption that would say something along the lines of MLK being a peaceful protestor; may he rest in peace. Statements like these are the perfect example of America's failure to take accountability. And like many historical events that would expose the immorality of this country, we were conditioned to believe that MLK simply died without questioning his cause of death. MLK was not peaceful. In fact, he was considered the *Most Dangerous Man* in America. He was a radical, anti-capitalist, revolutionary Christian who was murdered as an enemy of the state (Hill, 2022). We will *only* learn about his "I have a dream" speech in middle school and high school history classes because America cannot bear to speak the truth and take responsibility for his murder. America and white people cannot bear to take responsibility for anything.

In October of 2021, I had the wonderful opportunity of meeting Nikole Hannah Jones at the Books in Bloom fest in Columbia, Maryland, where she talked about her book, the 1619 Project. After she gave her speech—which left me in complete awe—attendees were able to ask Ms. Jones questions about her past, present, and future work. I was the second attendee in line to ask a question, and when my turn came, I stood very close to the microphone with her co-authored book, *Four Hundred Souls*, in my hand. The first thing I said was, "Hey Nikole! My name is Nicole, too, but yours is spelled cooler" because that's just what you say as a fangirl. Then, I read a line from her chapter in the book which states, "If the *Mayflower* is advent of American freedom, then the *White Lion* is advent of American slavery" (p. 4). After reading that line, I proceeded to say:

> *This resonated with me because I learned about the Mayflower every year in my social studies courses, but I never once learned about the White Lion. Instead, I have learned about slavery as it relates to Black people's history and not White people's history. I acknowledge and have some respect for white folks who show up to these spaces and are ready to both learn and unlearn, but I often wonder what they do with the knowledge they receive. My question for you, Nikole, is how can we hold white people accountable? What could be some action items for white allies?*

After asking my questions, many people in the congregation clapped in agreement, and I was not prepared for such warm solidarity. Clearly, other folks shared the same point of view and had the same questions as me. What does accountability look like for white people? First, I think accountability looks like owning and accepting the truth for what it is. White people enslaved Black people for over four hundred years. Black people have been enslaved in this country longer than we have been freed, and because of that, there is a 400-year wealth and education gap. Until systems rooted in racist ideologies are abolished, Black people and other People of Color will never get the chance to live a free, restful, and content life.

On the one hand, folks still grapple with the idea of accountability. This is evident in one of the reviews I received on my last memoir, "A Black Woman's Guide to Earning a PhD," which states, "It seems these days nobody can just write an inspirational guide on how to achieve one's goals without resorting to woke-isms and blaming white people for reasons they can't succeed in life...you can't blame your way to the top." On the other hand, folks are acknowledging the past and present-day harm done to the Black community. The American Psychological Association (APA) made a public apology for its longstanding contributions to systemic racism. They have vowed to do better on behalf of marginalized groups moving forward. However, we know that an apology is simply not cutting it, and accountability rooted in action is urgent in all spaces, particularly in academia. I have often reflected on what accountability might look like in academic spaces for white people who perpetuate social harm. I believe accountability in the academy looks like 1) Believing graduate students, faculty, and staff of color when they share experiences of being micro aggressed, oppressed, or discriminated against, 2) Explicitly calling out the perpetrator (whether it be by phone or by email), and naming the harm they have caused, 3) Providing support to the victim and creating an action plan that will seek justice for and protect them, 4) Being effective bystanders, and 5) Unlearning lies and learning truths.

Some of us may never get justice, though. Backs may be turned, and eyes might be rolled to remind us that we are not worth white people being held accountable for. We are reminded that Black women, specifically, aren't worth anyone's sympathy and genuine apology. There are so many white academics in my graduate department who are still not being held accountable for the harm they have caused me. Yet, I must engage with them and pretend like they were not the reason why I spent nights crying in my bedroom, wondering if I am competent and capable enough to complete my program. I am so tired. And I'm tired of being tired. I'm tired of writing about all the things Black women deserve just for folks to skim past those pages. I'm tired of both witnessing and experiencing Black women-based verbal, physical, and emotional violence. When I think of perseverance in the face of violence, I think of Judge Ketanji Brown Jackson who had an unfair and racist experience while awaiting Senate confirmation as the nominee for the Supreme Court.

The dehumanization of this more-than-qualified Black woman reminded me that, after all these years of Civil rights-ing and feminist movement-ing and Black lives matter-ing, Black women are still fighting for respect, to be seen, and to be valued. I wish I was as strong as Judge Brown Jackson; or at least the *strength* she showed us on television. I believe her strength could have gotten me through my program when I was humiliated and belittled during class presentations for not having "basic academic etiquette"; when my competence as a teaching fellow was questioned by my supervisor, who told me my effort isn't as robust as it should be because I created a space where my students were not being lectured at and were given wellness days; a white professor I was a teaching assistant for told her undergraduate students that my writing was not the greatest and they should seek additional assistance from the writing center; when I was told to consider applying for other graduate psychology programs immediately after my advisor relocated in my first year because I would not "fit" in any other lab. In those times, I needed her strength. People love to discourage Black women from upholding the *Strong Black Women* schema, but what other choice do we even have? Are we ever given space to be anything other than strong? Don't they know that we are tired and would give up anything to free ourselves from this trope?

In order for Black women to truly be free from the *Strong Black Women* schema, we need to feel protected from perpetrators. It was quite visible that Judge Brown Jackson wanted to break down and cry during her confirmation hearings, but she held back her tears many times and chose strength instead. Some may applaud her for that, but only God and her family know about the tears she released on her pillow when the world was not watching. This is the story of many Black women and other Women of Color who dwell in spaces where white folks who perpetuate harm are not held accountable. We tough it out in person and cry it out at night just to be tough again in the morning. We no longer want this story for ourselves and the women who will come after us. We want to express the same softness that white women can freely express every day. We want to be supported and heard. We want *Protect Black Women* to be more than just a slogan. Let it also be action items. Let it be accountability.

Ecclesiastes 9:11

At the beginning of every year, I set aside a day to create a vision board that lists everything I hope to achieve both short-term and long-term. On my 2022 vision board, I pasted a picture of a Black woman doctor from a magazine and wrote "Dr. Telfer, 2023." Little did I know that in 2022, I would be in the final stages of my graduate program. When I turned in my comprehensive exam portfolio to my committee and passed in the summer of 2021, my mentor, Dr. EQ, said to me, "Not only are you meeting these milestones quickly, but you are also excelling in them." I wish I had told her, at the moment, how much her comment meant to me. I spent my entire graduate school career believing I was not good enough and did not belong because I was too young, too inexperienced, too Black, and too hood because I came from an inner-city and spoke using slang words. Four years later, I am still trying to find ways to free myself from those lies. My mentor's comment brought me to a space of reflection on my doctoral journey and how much I have done within just a few years. I then found myself in a space of gratitude and humility. I stayed in my own lane, *understood the assignment*, and by year four of graduate school, I began to work on my dissertation.

I spent the summer and fall semesters of 2021 writing my dissertation proposal, which examined the experiences of racially minoritized women in STEM undergraduate programs, running exploratory factor analyses on individual items to create my own scales, and cleaning my dataset and successfully defending it on December 3rd, 2021. I was immensely overjoyed and emotional and even cried at my proposal defense. However, I now had an important yet stressful decision to make: do I begin applying for jobs, or do I stay an additional year and develop a fifth-year plan? On the one hand, staying an additional year would mean that I could take more courses related to my specialization, but I would have to pay for student fees out-of-pocket. On the other hand, graduating after my fourth year would mean that I would have to seek a postdoctoral position that would provide me with additional training and "big girl" money to support myself. *Was I prepared to enter the job market? Was my curriculum vitae sufficient?* These were the questions that clouded my mind for months. The good ol' book tells me in Proverbs 19:20 to seek counsel and gain wisdom. I spoke with many people, which included my aunties, momma, mentors, and friends. I received two pieces of advice that resonated with me—the first being from my good friend, Dana. She shared a quote with me that said, "Your soul knows when it's time for a new beginning. Go forward and welcome it." The second piece of advice was from my high school mentor, who reminded me that learning is never-ending, and my learning does not end when I leave graduate school. She reminded me that graduating early does not make my training less rigorous and that I've received all that my program could offer me. The additional professional training that I longed for may be in another setting, and that is okay.

Despite the many reassurances, doubts still lingered and were especially salient on days when I felt stuck. My self-doubt was not a result of the Impostor Syndrome—I will no longer give power to that term—but a result of structural racism, white supremacy delusion, and western norms in the academy where quantitative experiences are more meaningful than qualitative experiences. That is, I was taught that the number of years I am enrolled in school will reflect my competency and knowledge and can outweigh what I have done, learned, and applied in a relatively short time. I did not share my four-year plan with many people, but the few academics who knew questioned how I completed my PhD milestones so quickly as opposed to congratulating me. Yet, in the face of doubt and having to make major decisions, I was sure of one thing—that I would continue to be an agent of change in my community. It took me a long time to get here, but I am confident in my calling and excited about the impactful work I will do as an applied developmental psychologist. My work will extend far beyond the doors of academia and its requirements, which include first-authored papers, ongoing research, conference presentations, and much more. My work will *always* center restorative justice, abolition, and collective healing, and these are all practices that consist of lifelong learning. I later learned that the stay-in-school-longer academics were wrong. My decision to graduate after my fourth year opened many doors, including a summer internship at a NICU follow-up clinic, many job interviews, and a postdoc offer from my number one choice: UNC-Chapel Hill. I find solace in knowing that I have done important and transformative work on my campus and in my community. From time to time, I may be tempted to wallow in the uncertainty, but my calling always reminds me of who I am and what I can accomplish. In the famous words of the down-to-ride woman featured on Dr. Phil – imma stick beside [her]. Her being me.

Dear Black women and Women of Color: Whether you've completed your doctorate in three years or in seven years, your work is meaningful. If you have decided to leave your program and begin your career, your work is still meaningful. Say it every day in the mirror if you must. You will make valuable contributions to your field. You will do great things. You will be the best of the best. So: 1) Focus on *your* journey. 2) Know that there is power in rest. Do not dream of labor; just simply dream. 3) Be sure to find your community. Lean on them and allow them to lean on you. 4) Always be gentle with and kind to yourself. It is okay if you do not have the capacity to give today. Just make sure you give yourself grace. 5) Remember your why. Sometimes your *why* can be found in the meaning of your name, and 6) Speak positive words over yourself and declare that you are more than enough. With or without a doctorate, you are valuable. And even if the vision has not been made plain yet, your purpose exists.

This race– whether it be your academic/professional career or journey to liberation and rest– is yours. Not the swift nor the strong, but yours, and I hope that you endure until the end.

Love always and forever,
        Nicole.

CHAPTER 2

Munazza Abraham's Story

MUNAZZA SAALIM ABRAHAM is a current PhD Candidate at the University of Maryland-Baltimore County (UMBC). She is a rising African-centered, Clinical and Community Psychologist whose work as a therapist and researcher aims to develop African-centered wealth and wellness programs that support the empowerment, healing, and freedom of Black communities in schools, low-income neighborhoods, and especially carceral facilities. Munazza also professionally performs spoken word to raise awareness on social justice issues and reflect on her personal experiences as a Black woman. Her first self-published chapbook is entitled Dear Vagina... Forgive Me. It is a collection of poems and confessions that welcome her readers into her raw and her ugly to see what healing really looks like. Her chapbook is available for purchase at Barnes and Nobles and Amazon.com. Munazza's exploration of healing and Black empowerment led her to this beautiful partnership between incredibly intelligent and driven Black women. Writing Our Doctoral Journey was the opportunity to engage in our African practices of relational storytelling to learn and pass on our lessons to future generations. This is how we ensure our collective success! Munazza Abraham can be found on YouTube (for poetry and future anti-oppression content) and can be followed on Instagram @nazz_shespeaks.

My name is Munazza Saalim Abraham, and as I am writing this, I am a 4th-year Clinical and Community Psychology PhD Candidate. Ever since I was a student, from grade school till now, I have been told what knowledge is and isn't, what intelligence is and isn't, and what success is and isn't. And every time those concepts have been defined for me, I always seem to fall short of "real" knowledge, "real" intelligence, and "real" success. This is likely because what was real was also defined for me. My reality was not mine.

The red ink of teachers told me everything I did wrong, little of what I did right, and left no room to reason another truth. And trust me, I often tried to reason my truth with puppy dog eyes and a district attorney's mouth to defend my intelligence to a person whose opinion superseded my own. A couple of times, I was victorious and felt proud of my self-advocacy. But most times, I lost and felt angry and helpless. In my grade schools, there was always only one answer, most questions felt like trick questions (like why would you want to trick me when I'm trying to learn), and there was no storytelling of relational ways of knowing. The goal was to simply memorize this or calculate that, but do it fast! Or else it wouldn't matter if I got the right answer after the bell rang.

In my youth and young adulthood, I never understood why time was so important until I learned about the lurkings of capitalism in my mid 20s. Capitalism is the system and subculture of white supremacy (Okun & Jones, 2000) that tells us to multi-task, despite the human brain's function to do one thing at a time. Capitalism tells us to work hard and work fast to produce, sell, and make a profit for "the man"; the corporation or to "keep up with the Joneses." And if we don't produce work a certain way at a certain time, then we are defective, disordered (mentally and/or physically), and not as valuable to society. Capitalism also spreads the myth that if you're resting, you're not productive (Schawb, 2021). And yes, this is a myth. How else do you restore the energy and mental clarity to work without rest? The profit motivations of capitalism mixed with the underpaid or unpaid labor of teachers and students in the education system tend to cause exhaustion, depression, and anxiety - which they will blame you for. But many mental health conditions are symptoms of a harmful system and not a reflection of your weakness or character flaw.

I may not have known much about capitalism, mental health, or systems back then, but I always knew something was wrong in grade school when homework started to puzzle my parents. I felt it viscerally. From middle school and beyond, I would get gnawing stomach aches and ugly cry over grades that wouldn't matter in increments of 4 years. I experienced anxiety in the form of somatic reactions to the piling academic assignments, timed tests, and permanent criticisms that I wasn't given much chance to apply or learn from. Essentially…school sucked…. and it literally hurt.

In my late 20s, I learned that the capitalistic and non-diunital forms of thinking that were impressed upon us in grade school and beyond were contradictory to traditional African values and ways of knowing. Non-diunital refers to either-or thinking like this is productive or not productive; you're in this category or that one; this is right or wrong; no in-between. Whereas diunital thinking or reasoning, in African-centered Psychology, acknowledges multiple truths can coexist (Myers, 1988). Back then and often now, I am only taught Western/European values and ways of knowing. I was taught to go against my very nature as a woman of African descent. I didn't know back then, but this unnatural and even harmful learning process rooted in capitalism and Western non-diunitalism was a major reason I felt less smart, anxious with every timed test, and severely unenthusiastic about school even though I loved to learn. I was an outcast wanting to belong where I wasn't supposed to fit. We are more aware of this now when we see Black people trying to blend into white spaces by code-switching. We code-switch our voices, our dress, our hair, and our mannerisms in order for white leadership to recognize us as professional; in order for them to make us successful. Code-switching is a survival strategy, but it is so dangerous when that switch gets stuck or when you don't know the switch happened.

In academia, I became a part of a reality that stifled my confidence in my intelligence, my appearance, and my skills. This is the power of white supremacy, to impose a reality that you come to believe; a reality in which you are inferior because you do not meet the white standard that was never meant for you. Of course, I had no idea back then. Alternate realities were Sci-Fi, after all...

But the more aware I become of who I am, who my people are, and the oppressive nature of these systems I navigate, the closer I get to redefining my reality and creating knowledge, as my ancestors have always done. My ancestors upheld the reality of abundance and collective well-being, contrary to the white supremacy paradigms of scarcity and individualism. So, as I reconstruct my reality in alignment with my ancestors, I aspire to build wealth and wellness programs with an African and Indigenous design that provides and inspires abundant living and collective healing. But how do I get to this future? Well, I take a look at my past. Also like my ancestors, who embodied Sankofa (a West African proverb meaning "Go back and get it"), I have to look back to move forward with wisdom. With this proverb in mind, I would like to delineate my lessons from my doctoral journey and how they lead to my new reality by first reflecting on three of my many past "failures" in academia.

"Failures" in Grad School

1. **I was the only one in my cohort to fail my PhD Qualifying Examination,** which was offered once a year. This meant that I could

not be a PhD Candidate, which is required for me to earn dissertation credit and graduate. So, of course, I cried as if I mourned the loss of my competence, that thing that always seems fleeting for Black academics. *But I knew from the jump that the Qualifying Exam of my program was inherently oppressive. The students who have failed my program's Qualifying Exam, in its entire history at my institution, have always been disproportionately students of color. So, prior to my "failure," I surveyed and organized with other students to advocate for an alternative exam that included a portfolio model similar to another psychology program in my department (our sister program). My ancestors must have known to stir my tongue before it was too late. I was the student representative, a trembling and muffled voice at the bottom of the totem pole. Every month, I spoke a little louder in a room full of faculty who, at the time, were too tenured and tired to change or too heavy with the burdens of attaining tenure to lift student voices. So, instead, the students lifted each other. We reached down our own throats and pulled out historical data, interviews, and research-backed protests that left our tongues dry. We identified our sister program's portfolio model, an exam that can be completed with both writing and experiential activities within the first two or so years of the program. This was contrary to the previous exam that necessitated at least four months of insecure studying, one week of typing six essays covering many topics we were not taught, and each essay with an arbitrary deadline and excruciating faculty critiques that easily incited heart palpitations. Contrary to the once-a-year previous exam, the alternative portfolio can be submitted anytime. It is composed of key milestones necessary to complete the PhD and relevant to post-graduation success, also unlike the previous exam. The portfolio included a conference research presentation, a first-authored manuscript, a career interest statement, and a biopsychosocial analysis of an individual's condition or a community problem. It wasn't perfect, but it was meaningful.

Of course, this proposed portfolio model was not instated by department faculty during my exam year (saving me no tears). I failed my first Qualifying Exam and endured a year of familiar yet painstaking self-doubt and the hushed shame of being alone in my "failure". The proposed alternative exam got stuck in the system. There was unnecessary bureaucracy from multiple faculty members in power who didn't know what to do with their power, refused to give any of it to students, claimed to not have the time to find alternative exam formats, then when students did the laborious research for them and provided faculty with viable exam options, many faculty members still didn't make time to raise a hand and vote on the damn thing! However, five years after the previous exam initially sparked concern (before I entered the grad program) and five suffering cohorts later (my cohort), the faculty moved the needle. And all it took was a hop and a skip down the hall to ask another program in our same psychology department, "What y'all doing?" Strange how communication was not a strong suit among so many psychologists. Anyways, they adopted the portfolio model, and I was the first to take the new exam and pass! Students celebrated via email due to our timely COVID-19 pandemic with silent "Yays" and sighs of "Thank Yous" for the long-awaited portfolio exam. #WeHappyButWeSalty #SlowBureacracyIsAlsoOppressive.

So, my initial "failure" of my PhD Qualifying Exam unintentionally added to the exam's racial disparity outcomes, further supporting student claims of its oppressive structure. And my later success in advocating for change and passing the new qualifying exam supported the relevance of the portfolio model as representative of academic rigor and PhD Candidacy. #Failure+Success=Still Success.

*Before we move on, I'd like to acknowledge that just because I "fail" at something, it doesn't inherently make that something oppressive. But when that something creates a set of "competencies" that test you on what you were never taught and/or doesn't reflect anything of substance about your ability to succeed, then that something only serves to hold you back, not lift you up. AND, when that something has a record of disproportionately failing people of color because our values, experiences, and ways of knowing and expressing don't fit the white standard…well, then that something is OPPRESSIVE.

2. **I was rejected from several fellowships**. The rejection from the highly competitive

Robert Wood Johnson Foundation (RWJF) public policy fellowship really hurt. I won't lie. I cried somethin' deep when I was rejected from this opportunity. The kind of cry that doesn't come out all at once. It lingers. A growing hotness beneath your face that comes closer to the surface with every congratulatory email that gets sent to your successful peers, yet you're stuck on the thread, a resentful witness to their rise. The RWJF fellowship would have paid for three years of graduate school on top of whatever funding my school gave me. This means that I would have earned "adult money" and avoided the typical exploitation that grad students endure overworking in faculty research labs.

I learned, much later, that just because I didn't receive the award, and just because my peers received and deserved it, did not mean that I didn't deserve it too. I made the mistake of associating the fellowship's monetary value and its high competitiveness with my own value and validation. Although the additional funding, network, and public policy training would have made my path much easier, it must not have been necessary for my path at that time. I have not had much pain and struggle in my life, so if this rejection is my "struggle" for the sake of building a better life for my people, then I accept it with overwhelming gratitude! My ancestors knew true suffering for me to call a lost fellowship a "struggle."

Further, this association between a fellowship and my intrinsic value was totally a result of the internalized inferiority I had developed since grade school. In my mind, at that time, being an RWJF fellow would have validated me. Of course, we shouldn't seek validation from anything outside of ourselves, but of course, we tend to. And I might do it again. But as I am writing this reminder to myself, I write it to you, too: When I don't win a thing, I assume I lose…and that's simply not true. When I don't win a thing, I have more space to accept new things.

After my "failure" with RWJF, I earned a $30K Community Health Fellowship, ironically, for the same amount of money as RWJF that year. I worked to develop a harm-reduction intervention plan supporting sex workers in a Baltimore community. So, boom! "When one door closes…"

3. **One month in at a prestigious clinical externship at a youth and family medical center, I had an identity crisis!** I felt so exhausted by the direct service work and the oppressive and restrictive standards of clinical psychology and medical policies. And I didn't even have to be there! Whether it was due to COVID-19 or oppression, I dreaded logging in for telehealth. I felt forced to assign life-changing diagnoses to children, some of whom needed extra support that, unfortunately, in our society, only labels can afford (insurance companies demand certain diagnoses to pay for health/mental health care). I also felt forced to give diagnoses to children who were just being children, but their divinely high energy was too much for some overburdened teacher or single parent. I felt overwhelmed by everything I was expected to do in that medical center, and I just did not want to be there anymore. I didn't want to be that person who didn't enjoy her work or that therapist who willingly perpetuated the oppressive system. I questioned whether I was harming families; I questioned who I was to do something like that against my people. Maybe I was thinking too extreme, but it was a thought spiral that created very real feelings. I legit cried in front of my clinical supervisor, then quit the prestigious externship. (You may have noticed my theme of crying under duress. I wholly support crying. We all need the release. Imagine what that pain could do to your body if you held it in).

After a good cry, I quit the whole Clinical Psychology track of my grad program to be a pure Community Psychology PhD student. After all, the Community Psychology track was aligned with my social justice values (Look it up! https://www.communitypsychology.com/). Quitting the clinical track gave me a weird feeling of both "failure" and relief. Knowing how very, very, very few Black clinical psychologists exist and knowing I was leaving an externship that also served Black families, I felt like I was letting Black people down. But I also felt relief that it didn't have to be me. I didn't have to carry the burden of healing my people in this way. But then, a couple of months later...

Enlightenment!

Through some peer encouragement, I spoke to other Black women who faced similar challenges in my Clinical and Community Psychology PhD program. These women challenged me to ask myself my original "why." Why was I here in this grad program; what was I set out to do, and for whom? My answers led me back to healing and building with my people, Black people. And I, again, reminded myself that my ancestors truly struggled for me to call anything in my privileged PhD experience a "struggle." I am privileged to choose a struggle, and for the ultimate vision of Black wellness and sovereignty, this is it.

The following semester, I rejoined the dual Clinical and Community Psychology track. Through all my "failures" and rejections and "identity crises," yet another door opened that I would not have seen otherwise. I found a private practice externship led by a licensed clinical social worker, a Black queer woman who specialized in healing practices for Identity-Based Trauma. Her clinical practice was the anti-oppressive environment I was looking for, which encouraged me to be creative and outspoken, and encouraged me to lead. She listened to my ideas and allowed me to use all of the talents that I deemed relevant to supporting wellness and expanding the practice. I didn't feel burdened here. I didn't feel misaligned with my values. I felt like this was where I was meant to be. And what an invigorating, deep breathing, soul-pleasing feeling that is!

I realized that I needed that mini-break from Clinical Psychology to lead me back to the Black women that led and supported me in reaffirming my values and goals. I later discovered that <u>my identity was never in crisis; it was in abrupt growth!</u>

My Message to You

To those in graduate programs wondering what you are doing there and whether you should stay, don't let them or their oppressive and arbitrary standards push you out. Choose to stay or leave on your own terms. Ask yourself first, what is my "why"; what is it that I want? Know that there are many paths to getting there. And you have the choice to walk whichever path is aligned with your values and spirit. To clarify, my clinical psychology graduate training thus far is not aligned with my values or spirit; however, further down this path, I will have this alignment because I'll shape the reality I want to see. What I want is to make clinical psychology aligned with my values and spirit by dismantling the white supremacy embedded in its traditional training and practices and, instead, centering African and Indigenous anti-oppression praxis. So, I am choosing this path and this struggle to create what I want to see.

However, your path may not necessitate struggle in this form. You may find a supportive and anti-oppressive training program or a series of life experiences in or outside of graduate school. And these experiences may teach you in a way that liberates your creativity and ambition and inspires a deeper commitment to return power, wealth, and healing to your people. You may not have to make this path; instead, it may find you. Either way, it is important to recognize it when it is here.

Below, I've listed some questions and original quotes along my doctoral journey that reminded me that I was on the right path, even when I couldn't see it:

- "What if you are exactly where you are supposed to be?"
- "Failing is still learning, and thus, not failing at all."
- "What if three steps forward and two steps backward is just your process?"...
- "Sometimes, you have to take a few steps backward to propel yourself forwards. How else will you clear your biggest hurdles?"
- In response to feelings of imposter syndrome and general struggles within academia: "When we see the system for what it is, intentional systemic oppression, then we can stop questioning our worth. When we know this system was designed for us to fall, we will celebrate every moment we stood and praise every ache it took to stand back up."

Now, How Do You Recognize Your Path and Purpose?

Talking to yourself with questions and affirmations is great and important to push through the struggle and uncertainty. *Yes, I talk to myself! What do you think your thoughts are? I talk to myself both inside and out loud if I need an extra* boost. *Even if I don't believe the affirmation at first (that "I am a healer"), I can at least feel the energy, the warm sound vibrating my throat and bones, tensing and relaxing my muscles. I may feel the truth before I believe it.* But to recognize my path and purpose, self-talk isn't enough. I learned that I needed to know who I am and who I am becoming. I needed to pray (talk to ancestors, the higher power, and my higher self) and meditate (listen to them) more often to recognize my inner voice, my intuition. I have learned through experience and the works of African descent scholars that blurring or suppressing your identity is a key objective of any oppressive system. Thus, a sense of identity, as well as a sense of community, are the necessary resistance. I had to find my tribe, people with common experiences, interests, or vision; people you feel energized to stand next to, talk and vent to about racist peers and professors; people you can laugh and learn with. There are many ways to find your tribe in or outside of schools, such as by searching for athletic clubs, book clubs; forming GroupMes and virtual or in-person study groups in challenging classes; joining Meetup.com, Facebook groups, Clubhouse, or other social media groups that share your values, gather for fun activities, and hold important conversations you want to be a part of.

Identity and community are central components to both healing and freedom from oppression and its associated symptoms (i.e., imposter syndrome, low self-esteem, social anxiety, depression, borderline personality disorder, etc.). In my personal research about African-centered psychotherapy (of course, not taught in my clinical psychotherapy training), I've learned that whether you plan to dismantle white supremacy and take on oppressive systems or you just want to go further in your personal development, self-esteem, relationships, and professional development - learning who you are should always be the first step and finding your tribe, the second.

Thus, if you are to take on oppressive systems or at least grow and heal from them, one of your initial steps would be to answer the following questions - as emphasized in African-centered Psychology:

- Who am I?
- How do I know?
- Who are my people?
- What have my people given me/done for me?
- What will I give my people/do for my people?

Now, your answers may change over time, and that's okay. Still, I challenge you to write down your answers in your journal or on a visible board in your personal room or office. Treat these answers as your affirmations, your purpose that you create. Recite them before prayers, meditations, and before making big decisions in your personal or professional paths. I promise, answering these questions and understanding who you are will grant you direction towards freedom, deeper healing, and a sense of power in knowing your purpose.

Although systemic oppression is all around us (for now), with this self-knowledge, you will know that your existence, on whichever path you stand, is resistance. And your success? Well, it's a F*ing revolution.

References:

Myers, L.J. (1988). Understanding an Afrocentric worldview: Introduction to optimal psychology. Dubuque, IA: Kendall/Hunt.

Okun, T., & Jones, K. (2000). *White supremacy culture. Dismantling racism: A workbook for social change groups.* Durham, NC: Change Work. Retrieved from http://www.

dismantlingracism. org/Dismantling_Racism/liNKs_files/whitesupcul09. pdf.

Schwab, L. (2021). *Rest to resist the grind: A critical rhetoric of Tricia Hersey's The Nap Ministry.*

CHAPTER 3

Sarah Adeyinka's Story

DR. SARAH ADEYINKA holds a PhD in Educational Science at Ghent University, Belgium, where she is part of the European Research Commission-funded ChildMove Project and is conducting research on the impact of transit experiences on the wellbeing of unaccompanied minors. Her part of the project is focused on young female, Nigerians who were trafficked into Italy for sexual exploitation. Alongside a colleague, Sarah also concluded a research project on the well-being of Nigerian and Ghanaian women working in prostitution in the Schaerbeek municipality of Brussels, a project which was funded by the municipality. The project findings resulted in a book publication by Routledge. Sarah is also the founder and board chair of CoCreate VZW (Belgium) and Cocreate Humanitarian Aid Foundation (Nigeria). She has worked in the field of humanitarian aid for over a decade with a focus on vulnerable populations such as refugees, asylum seekers, and survivors of human trafficking for sexual exploitation. She worked onboard two rescue vessels operated by Médecins Sans Frontières (Doctors Without Borders) involved in the rescue of migrants at sea. Her role included providing cultural mediation, identifying vulnerable women, and referring them to the right channels for assistance.

Some Glimpses into My Life.

Nostalgia

Growing up in Lagos, Nigeria, was quite an adventure. Thinking back to my childhood, it feels like there was never a dull moment. I remember lying in bed and listening to heavy thunderstorms that sounded like they would blow the roof off our house and the winds threatening to blow us away with it. Listening to the sounds of heavy raindrops that sounded more like pebbles drumming against the corrugated tin iron roof and smelling the sweet scent of rain as I lay in bed. Of course, the inevitability of a blackout during heavy rains also meant hearing my dad shuffle through the house in the middle of the night to find several lanterns and candles. I remember mum looking over us, candle or flashlight in hand, as we slept because she heard a mosquito buzzing and would not go to sleep until she had killed it. "No mosquito is biting my children or giving them malaria today!" is probably what my mum told herself as she "smack!" killed the mosquitoes who never stood a chance against her. Sometimes she would even burn them with a lit candle to ensure that they were truly dead.

The lanterns were lit and placed in corners around the house so that when we, the seven offspring of Debo and Foluke Adeyinka, got up to use the loo, we found our way easily. It was like clockwork, there was always a lit lantern when I got up to ease my defiant bladder, and no one ever sought credit for it or even mentioned it. I can still hear my mum saying, "don't let your left hand know what your right hand is doing; if you help someone, help them wholeheartedly and let God reward you, not man!"

I started this writing with memories from my childhood because those memories and the recognition of where I come from, influenced, and still influence me and my decision-making processes to this day. Even now, as I write this, I'm staring at the whiteboard in my board room on which these words "remember where you're coming from and going to!" My eldest brother, Deolu, still says to me when we say goodbye after a phone call "remember whose child you are." It's a reminder of my background, my roots, my home training, and my values. I see them in my decision-making processes, in my priorities, and in my personal and professional boundaries setting. Bear with me, I will start linking some of these to my experiences as a Black doctoral candidate, and as a Black woman who holds a PhD degree.

I have always had a passion for justice and for equity for as long as I can remember. Even as a child, I would rather be punished while standing firmly for what I believed to be true or just than give in and avoid punishment. My sisters and I still laugh about some of those stories today. One of the earlier memories I have of wanting to advocate for someone who was wronged (in this case, sexually violated) was in primary school. I must have been between 6 and 8 years old at the time. We were told that one of the girls (I still remember her name) in the same grade as I, had been molested in the bathroom. So, moving forward, all female pupils were to go to the bathroom in groups of two or more, never alone, for the foreseeable future. I remember that I was fuming and felt that I needed to do something about it but didn't know what. I even snuck to the bathroom alone with some rocks in my hands, hoping that the perpetrator would come and try to 'molest' me so I could teach him a lesson with the rocks. Never mind that I didn't even understand what molestation meant. I later found out that the perpetrators were three boys who also attended our school. I don't remember them being punished, but I do remember that the rules changed for the girls and not the boys. Ironic, given that the girl was the victim, but the rules changed for all the girls, not for the boys. There was no policy that boys were no longer allowed to play near the girls' toilet or that boys must always go to the toilet alone, nothing like that. Not much has changed.

In the two decades that followed, I fully immersed myself in studying and working with people in vulnerable situations and established myself and my reputation as an activist and a humanitarian. I was well-traveled, well-situated, what could go wrong? Well, in those twelve years, my father died, we had several major crises as a family, and I was a passenger in a bus hijack and shooting, to name a few. Yet, I have never questioned my mission in life to work with people in vulnerable conditions, do justly, and stand for truth. Little did I know how much those experiences of pain, loss, and suffering would impact my life but also how much pain, loss, and suffering Black women in academia experience! We will get to that soon!

Road Bump

Fast-forward to 2017, when I worked for Médecins Sans Frontières on the Vos Prudence Search And Rescue (SAR) ship as the Cultural Mediators' (CM) Supervisor. My role involved managing the CM team, providing psychological first aid, and identifying and referring victims (and potential victims of trafficking) to the necessary channels. I remember standing on the back deck one evening and telling my manager that, after 10+ years of humanitarian work and activism, I really wanted to pursue a PhD. One of the factors that led me to that decision was my witnessing the death (by hypothermia) of a Nigerian victim of trafficking. We did our absolute best to revive her, but she was gone. Something died in me that day as I held her, pleading as I continued CPR that she should wake up, until the doctor made the call for us to stop. Shortly after that, as I processed the event, it hit me that humanitarianism alone was not enough to stop the inhumane treatment of people traveling irregularly, the dehumanization of the "less fortunate other." I needed to combine my humanitarian heart with solid research knowledge and data to be more effective, I just knew it! That was what led me back to academia and to researching PhD opportunities that were funded, would sponsor my visa, and allow me to work on a topic that I was very passionate about addressing and studying more extensively, human trafficking.

I had one solid option at a United Kingdom (UK) university that I liked, but there was a woman in post-graduate admissions who seemed bent on making me miserable. She insisted that I needed to take an English test to prove that I could study in English. I, a Nigerian woman who had just graduated with her master's degree from that same university a few months earlier. I shared the full policy of the UK Home Office with her, which stated that if the applicant had studied at a UK or other "approved" English-speaking country within the past two years, a waiver could be applied. The woman refused and insisted that I pay for an English test before she would even give the professor (who was waiting) access to my files. At that point, I knew it was pointless to move forward there. I was not about to waste 300 Euros with the knowledge that the person handling my files could (and probably would) sabotage me, so I decided that it was time to look elsewhere, and I'm so glad I did. Dear academic staff, please do better, do not be like that person- a bump in the road that's there to slow others down, in this case, not for good.

I found another PhD vacancy online at Ghent University (UGent) in Belgium, applied for it, and was interviewed and shortlisted, but the professor went with another candidate, so I wasn't sure what to do. I will always remember the conversation with my manager, Stef, because he strongly encouraged me to find out from the professor if I could do the PhD as a self-sponsored candidate (which I didn't know was even possible) and what the cost would be; he said it might be a lot cheaper than I thought, and I could work part-time to pay for it. I emailed the professor to find out, and she said yes! She told me that she would love to work with me and would waive the bench fee, so all I would have to pay was the enrollment fee and tuition in the first year and the graduation fee at the end. Dear reader, the total amount was less than €2000!!! It gets better. About two months before moving to Belgium, she had some funds available and paid me part-time for a year and then full-time for the following three years. Information and necessary action always yield results. They may not always be the results we want, but they yield results, and we learn new things! Imagine if I hadn't sent that email, if I didn't push and just gave up? There was a way, not the way I had planned and hoped for, but there was a way, and it worked out perfectly for me! I wish I could say that from that moment on, everything was smooth sailing, but that would be a lie and a false representation of what the journey has been like for me.

Double Standards and Brain-Picking

Having lived abroad for 11 years prior to starting my PhD, I have worked consistently on multi-cultural teams and have been exposed to so many different world views and perspectives. What I was unprepared for, however, were the double standards that I would encounter so frequently that they were the norm in academia. The preference and respect automatically gotten by male, Caucasian professors in contrast to female professors stunned me. That goes on to the way Black and other non-Caucasian academics are treated. I have had my work and credibility questioned because I challenged something that was considered acceptable in my field of study. The issue is "acceptable by whom?" People being critical of my work doesn't bother me, I know how to defend my work because I do due diligence, and I am open to criticism that will help me grow and show me what I may have missed. What I cannot and will not tolerate is being criticized and told that I may have missed something because "things are done differently in Africa," "that's not how things are done here," or "you're too young in academia to be arguing x,y,z." I hold my head up, stand my ground, and damn the consequences. I didn't get to where I am in life by going along with the crowd and not shaking the table. Life hasn't been all cotton candy.

The equally nasty side of the "you're too young to be arguing x,y,z" situation is the "could we have a meeting so I can pick your brain about x,y,z?" That gets me every time! I still remember having a meeting which I reluctantly agreed to, during which the other person wanted me to explain step by step one of the major challenges in my field of study. She was writing down everything I said almost word for word, which I noticed quickly and inquired about. Eventually, she disclosed that a few people had been invited to teach on a topic that was not in their field of specialty at all. Instead of declining the invitation or referring the organizers to someone like me who specializes in that field, they wanted me to give them a crash course so that they could then give the presentation. I ended the conversation, livid. I was livid because I knew how long it took to acquire that knowledge, pay for education, work my Nigerian butt off and build credibility here as a Black woman working in humanitarianism and academia. I know the number of questions that I have been asked before being confirmed as a speaker at major events, the 'protocols' I must respect, etc. Yet, others are not treated the same way, and they're believed to be experts by virtue of their race, nationality, or in some cases, continent. Even worse was realizing how some people think that they can piggyback off that and teach it after a 30-minute conversation with me.

As I pondered the conversation with the person who wanted to "pick my brain," I realized that I didn't and still don't know any Black lecturers at my university. I don't know many Black female lecturers who are invited as keynote speakers at big academic events. They're often asked to give smaller lectures or asked to give presentations for free (remember Tiffany Haddish being asked to host the Grammy's pre-show ceremony for free? Same difference). They are invited to meetings so that people can "pick their brains" on certain issues, and those people go and share that knowledge as though it were theirs. The unbelievable reality which Berenstain (2016) discusses in Epistemic Exploitation:

I argue that epistemic exploitation is marked by unrecognized, uncompensated, emotionally taxing, coerced epistemic labor. The coercive and exploitative aspects of the phenomenon are exemplified by the unpaid nature of the educational labor and its associated opportunity costs, the double bind that marginalized persons must navigate when faced with the demand to educate, and the need for additional labor created by the default skepticism of the privileged. (pp.1).

So, I've learnt to be even more perceptive, frugal, and wiser with my time and my use of it. To distinguish between what I believe would be a good opportunity for me to present my work and educate others (whether paid or not) and what I shouldn't invest my time in. I've learnt to say no to some teaching opportunities, which is odd because if you know me, you will know that I love to teach. I enjoy engaging with people, having people disagree with me, and having very respectful arguments during which different perspectives are discussed. Discussions that lead to several outcomes, including:

- others seeing and maybe agreeing with my perspective
- us agreeing to disagree, or
- ending with absolutely no answers but with respect for each other and our arguments

However, I know the amount of time that goes into preparing for presentations because I want to give my best, and I value those who are setting aside time to listen to me. Therefore, I believe that it is only fair that I am justly remunerated for that. The hard work and diligence that I put into building my wealth of knowledge and credibility must be respected and honored. So now, I am very wary about requests to "pick my brain." I really dislike that phrase now.

Let me be clear, I believe in the importance of sharing knowledge and taking available opportunities to become a better public speaker, to accurately communicate my research, and to learn from the criticism and feedback of the audience. What I am saying is that as you hone your craft and get better and more confident in your field of expertise, remember that what you have and what you have learnt is valuable, and treat it as such. Credible research is important;

it is valuable and should be treated as such. However, data doesn't collect itself, do its own analysis, and present the findings; the researcher does. Therefore, the researcher should be treated with respect whether they're in the early stages of their work or have been conducting research for decades.

Valuable Lessons Learnt

They're many things I've learnt over the past couple of years as a PhD student, and I wish I could share them with you, but we don't have enough time or space. Honestly, there are some I would rather keep to myself and get a better grasp of first. However, I will share some of the key things that I learnt and that have always proved to be effective.

- **Be relentless**: remember where you've come from and how you got to where you are today. Despite the challenges, the hurdles, and the obstacles that you have overcome and others that you may still be battling, you're here. Don't give up. If you need to pause and fall apart, do so. Then get up and keep going.
- **Stand up to bullies:** there are different ways to do it. It could be through a formal complaint, an anonymous one, speaking up, or waiting till you have enough evidence to have a legal case. There are many ways to do so and would be unique to each one of us and our situations, but I have learnt not to cower before bullies, but to outsmart and deal with each one uniquely.
- **Be bold**: even when you don't feel like it, even when you struggle with yourself, don't cower. Don't drop your head. You're a queen, a king, put on this earth for a reason, a purpose that you are here to fulfill, lives that you will change for the better. Do not cast away your confidence, chin up!
- **Remember that you belong**: there is so much competition and condescension in academia. It may leave you feeling like you don't belong or that you are way out of your depth. Acknowledge that there are things you don't know, then remember that you are here right now because you have a zeal for knowledge. You want to study; you want to conduct research and be more of an expert in your field. You are a learner! That is something to be proud of. YOU BELONG!
- **Ask for help**: I know that some people are in situations where it seems like there are no allies or people you can turn to for help, and I hope that you find allies and colleagues in similar situations. Even if you find them online like I did in my Women Of Colour Writing Accountability Group

(WOCWAG), find them. They might not be where you're looking or who you think they will be, but there are allies out there. Be wise as you look for allies and people you can rely on. When you find them, or maybe you already have them, those trustworthy people, ask for help when needed. There is no shame in asking for help. Please ask for help when you need it. I can't say this enough. You are not alone.

- **Accept help**: I have noticed that it is one thing to finally ask for help but learning to accept help when it is offered is another thing. Learning to accept help without attempting to reciprocate because you feel like you owe the person who helped you is important. If you are offered help by someone who has your best intentions at heart, and you know that it comes with no strings, learn to accept it. That, dear one, is part of self-care.
- **Have fun**: It is so easy to get sucked into the work and the reading and to lose sight of the things that give you joy. Nurture those things, make time for what is important to you, have hobbies outside of academia, and truly enjoy them.
- **Spend time with loved ones**: they may not always understand your work or understand how you are not really a student but also not staff and fall somewhere in between. They are your loved ones, remember that. Nourish those relationships and even if you don't have as much time to spend with them as you would, have some designated time if that helps and cherish it.
- **Don't close your heart/the door to romantic love**: It is so easy to say that you don't have time because you're so busy working, but I have seen that work for so many others and for me. You make time for what/who is important to you. It is all about managing time and balancing schedules. It is possible and may lead to you finding a type of support that you never imagined was possible or one that you had always dreamed of.

Final Words of Encouragement

The power of words is something I will always acknowledge. Many cultures, including mine believe that words have power, that what you say is powerful as it may determine your actions. My mum used to have this sign in our home, it was on the inside of the toilet door, so every time we sat on the toilet, we had no choice but to read it until we eventually absorbed it. It said:

Words are like bullets
Once they are spoken, they can never be swallowed

The speaker may regret, weep, and mourn
But the damage done by the spoken words
Can never be recalled
So, think well before you speak.

Those words were on a sign in the bathroom of the home that I lived in over 20 years ago, but those words will always live in my heart and influence my life. Speak words of truth, of life, and of affirmation over yourself, and don't permit others to speak negative words over you or your work. You are uniquely you with so much to offer, believe that and don't allow anyone to tell you otherwise.

All my love and kind regards,

Sarah

References

1 Berenstain, N. (2016). Epistemic Exploitation. Ergo. An Open Access Journal of Philosophy. https://doi.org/10.3998/ergo.12405314.0003.022

CHAPTER 4

Kenyatta Aldridge's Story

DR. KENYATTA ALDRIDGE received her EdS from Piedmont College in Curriculum and Instruction and an EdD from Columbus State University in Curriculum, Instruction, and Leadership. Her research focused on the relationship between i-Ready intervention and Grade 8 mathematical achievement. Dr. Aldridge is currently serving as the 6-12 Science Instructional Coach for Macon County Schools. She has been employed in the K-12 sector for 12 years. As an educator, she has her online and gifted endorsements. She has taught English/Language Arts and Mathematics while employed as an educator. In her current position, she is a member of the leadership team and provides instructional strategies and feedback to teachers. Dr. Aldridge also continues to keep herself updated with the latest education to continue to improve student achievement.

Finished Before 40

Dr. Kenyatta Aldridge received her Master's degree from Georgia Southwestern State University in Education, an Educational Specialist degree (EdS) from Piedmont College in Curriculum and Instruction, and her Doctor of Education (EdD) from Columbus State University in Curriculum, Instruction, and Leadership. Her research focused on the relationship between i-Ready intervention and Grade 8 mathematical achievement.

Dr. Aldridge is currently serving as the 6 - 12 Science Instructional Coach for Macon County Schools. She has been employed in the K-12 sector for 12 years. Before her employment at Macon County Schools, she was employed at Sumter County Schools for 10 years. As an educator, she has her online and gifted endorsements. She has taught English/ Language Arts and Mathematics while employed as an educator.

In her current position, she is a member of the leadership team, and provides instructional strategies and feedback to teachers. Dr. Aldridge also continues to keep herself updated with the latest education to continue to improve student achievement.

I am the daughter of two amazing parents, the sister of one spontaneous brother, the mother of three outgoing daughters, and the wife of one patient husband. I grew up in a small southwest town of Americus, GA that is located 11 miles from the 39th president of the United States of America. To my childhood and high school friends, I am known as 'Yot'. To my students who I taught, I am known as Mrs. Aldridge, and after I completed my doctoral degree, my name changed again to Dr. Aldridge. Who would have thought a girl with tom-boyish ways, and sometimes adventurous, would grow up to be a Doctor of Education? When I speak of myself as Dr. Aldridge, it is not to be prideful or boasting but I hope you gain something from my experience. I hope in telling my story about my trials, tribulations, and triumphs, my ups and downs, will inspire and guide you to try to accomplish more than your mind thought you could or would do.

Early obstacles of achieving goals

Growing up my parents had two children, my eldest brother and myself. My parents always encouraged us to do our best at whatever we did. One day our lives drastically changed. My brother was involved in a car accident and died at the scene. This accident occurred one day after my ninth birthday, and I will always remember that day. From that day, my parents were more cautious when I was a passenger in someone's car, and always told me to be safe and they loved me.

With the loss of a family member, someone must shift their mindset and find their sense of gravity. For a long time, I used to cry and want him by my side and witness my accomplishments. Now, when I complete different milestones, I pray that my brother would be proud of me. For example, I would say this to myself "I am doing this for my brother" because he was not able to see me physically accomplish any goals. I also realized it is okay to miss a family member, but do not allow the depression to set in and it causes you to harm yourself. Have you ever thought that it would be better to die because you missed someone so much? Or that you don't deserve all of this success and someone so close to you was not able to witness your special moments? I had some of these thoughts and was thankful my husband and children were around to change my mindset to see how wonderful life is and will be.

As I continued through high school, I lost my focus on excelling in school and became pregnant. My parents were very disappointed in my choices, and I vowed to regain my educational focus and graduate high school. I also promised to become a great mother and role model for my daughter. While pregnant, I continued to complete my schoolwork and stayed focused on my goals. After having my daughter, I realized all the work of raising my daughter was going to fall on my shoulders. To finalize high school, I graduated in the top five of the graduating class of 2001. With this accomplishment, I knew once I put my mind towards completing a goal, I would succeed.

What a praying family can do for you? From these early obstacles in my life, I could have easily given up on myself and dropped out of school. My parents continued to stress the importance of gaining an education. They would not allow me to lose my focus, and always told me encouraging words. When I needed someone to take care of my daughter, my family always helped. I really believe "it takes a village to raise children."

Strengthening my support system

After high school, I knew I would need support to raise my daughter as I attended college. So, I attended the local university and worked part time at a fast-food chain. Based on where I started, I believe it's now how you start, it is how you finish. While working towards my first degree, I met my husband. My husband and parents were my biggest supporters as I graduated college with a bachelor's in business management. When I had to go to work, and my husband was working, my parents picked up my children from school or daycare. My parents also encouraged me to finish what I started. My husband was also supportive of me pursuing my goals. Whenever I told my husband, "I want to go to school to pursue a degree", he would say "go ahead and do it, we will be okay."

With this reassurance, I knew I wanted more for my family and myself. So, in 2007, I changed my career path from managing a restaurant to educating students.

The educational challenge

When I made the change to education, it was a challenging process. My family had to endure a decrease in pay, because I started off as a long-term substitute teacher. When my pay decreased, my husband worked more and assured me that we would be okay. After talking to the principal, who gave me a chance, I began the path to obtain my teaching certificate. When the principal allowed me to start my educational journey, I did not know what to expect or how to teach students. But that one person saw something in me, and knew I would make a difference in the lives of others.

I entered the education field with a goal to be the best at anything I start. I did not have an educational background to teach, so I entered the GaTAPP program. During this program, I had to learn how to write educational papers, and observe teachers from other school districts. In addition to completing the paperwork, I also had to take the take and pass the GACE assessments. I knew that I was not a good, standardized test taker and was very nervous when taking the tests. After completing the basics skills assessments (passed on the first try, THANK YOU JESUS!!), I registered for the middle grades' English assessment. After studying and preparing for the test, I passed the assessment on the first try. Although I passed the assessment, my passion was to be a mathematics teacher, not a Language Arts teacher. So, I registered for the test and completed the test. I did not pass the assessment. I didn't let that shake my spirit, so I registered again. When I received my scores back, I had FAILED again. I was upset and didn't know what happened. Before my third attempt, I purchased a book to prepare myself, and I printed off different practice problems to work through. Now, it was time to complete the mathematics assessment. On the third attempt, I PASSED the middle grades mathematics section. This goes to show you that although you fail at something, continue to try and do what you can do to succeed. If I would have given up after the second attempt, I would not have been a good example to my daughters and to the children I taught. As a mother, I always told my children to try their best at everything, and I would be proud of the outcome. As an educator, I always encouraged my students to never give up on a problem, and to always do their best.

After obtaining my teaching certificate, through the GaTAPP program, I continued to improve my educational knowledge and obtained my Master's degree in Education from Georgia Southwestern State University. While completing this degree, I knew I wanted more for my family. I wanted my daughters to see that with self-motivation and determination, that you can do anything. I expressed to my husband that I wanted to continue to future my educational knowledge, and he encouraged me to keep going. So, with my family's blessing, I entered the Specialist program at Piedmont college. This degree was challenging to complete, but I was able to obtain my Specialist in Curriculum in Instruction in 2017. As a full-time wife, mother, mathematics teacher, and softball coach, I weathered the storm and continued to make my family proud. I was determined to finish all my educational goals before I turned 40. As you are pushing through life, you should remember the purpose behind the journey. Once you know the purpose, you will take steps to ensure you are staying on course. If you lose focus on your course, it is okay, as long as you finish what you have sought out to accomplish. To help me stay on course, I asked some of these questions: Am I doing something for me? Am I doing it for my mother? Once you know why you are doing something, that should be your motivation to complete that task.

As you can see, it only takes one person to believe you are able to complete a job or task and they will give you an opportunity. So, as you are pursuing your dreams, continue to be a beacon of light and show everyone what talents you have to offer. You never know who is noticing your talents and will give you a once in a lifetime opportunity that will change your life.

Looking deep within myself

As I continued to educate students, I had to take a step back and look deep within myself to see if I wanted to make a change. During the process of teaching the students, I also learned how to direct adult learners to improve student achievement. When I was in the classroom, teachers would come to me and ask how to teach certain content and they utilized my suggestion in their classroom. When the teachers sought out my wisdom, I was originally surprised but was glad they valued my opinion. I was surprised because of where I started from in education. I did not go to college to be a teacher, and I went through an alternative program to become a teacher. But this is evidence that it does not matter how you started, it matters how you finish or work towards completing your goals. As I continued to guide students and teachers, I knew I wanted to get my leadership degree. So, I began the search for a program that did not require me to travel long distances, but could prepare me to become an effective leader. During this time, I also enrolled into a doctoral program with one of my friends. I always told my friend that she signed me up for this, and we will complete it together. In the program, I focused on curriculum and instruction and added Tier I leadership courses.

As I was teaching middle grades mathematics, wife, mother, and doctoral student, I began to doubt my teaching ability when the administrator stopped believing in me. I placed so much pressure on myself to be great at everything I start. In my previous school, the administrators continued to change, and they were not building relationships with their staff. I am a firm believer that a leader has to know who they are working with. One leader never communicated with me about the mathematics expectations, they always talked to the academic coach about me. When parents would express their concerns about my teaching style, the leader did not come to my classroom and observe what was happening in the class. So, this caused me to doubt if this was my true calling, because the leader was not defending what I was doing to educate the students. When the leader did not support my teaching style, I wanted to leave the school, because I did not feel she understood how I taught the students. I also felt the principal did not build a relationship with me, to know that I only wanted the best for the students and would do anything to help them learn the content. During this self-doubt, I continued to excel in the doctoral classes, and I was an excellent wife and mother. At the end of the school year, we had to analyze data, and over 30 students failed mathematics. With this data, I was very concerned about my placement next year with this leader. Then, students' end of grade assessment scores were sent to the school. Well, low and behold, the students who failed mathematics were the same students who scored a level one (beginning learner) on the assessment. From this data, the leader was able to see that the scores the students received in class were a true indication of their mathematical knowledge. The scores in my class also correlated with the students who knew the content, because several students scored a level four (distinguished learner). Although the data was evident that my teaching style was efficient, I was changed to a remedial mathematics teacher. With this change, it only caused more self-doubt, but I was determined to show the leader that even if I was placed in a remedial mathematics classroom, I was going to be able to help the students improve in mathematics.

From self-doubt to a new position

At the end of the school year that caused me to doubt my abilities, I gained a renewed sense when the end of grade assessment scores were sent to the school. Based on my practices, I knew I was an effective mathematics teacher, and I was able to help teachers educate students. I decided to leave the school system where I received my start in education. This was one of the hardest decisions I had to make, but I knew it was time to leave. When you are working somewhere, and they do not see your worth, don't be afraid to change what you are doing. In life, you have to know what you bring to any situation. If it is a job, what skills do you bring to the job? If it is a relationship, what qualities do you have to help the other person or yourself? But, if you do not feel that the job or person does not appreciate what you bring, do not stay in that relationship. The longer you stay, the more miserable you will become, and once you leave, they will see your worth. It is sad they see your value once you leave. I decided to apply for another job in another county. When I applied for the job, I didn't think I would be offered the job. That self-doubt started to ease its way back in my mind. After a couple of weeks, I received a phone call to see if I could interview for the job. I was so excited and nervous. So, I printed off my data from the past three years to show the leaders of the school how the students scored on the end of grade assessment after I taught them mathematics. Based on this data, students were learning the content, and I was able to decrease some of the gaps in their mathematical knowledge. It was time for my interview, and I was so nervous. I felt I was very prepared and answered all the questions the interviewers asked. After the interview, I received another call, and they asked if I could come for a second interview. At this point, I did not know what additional information they wanted to know. I called some of my educational peers and asked them what I should talk about for my second interview. I was not afraid to ask for help when I didn't know it was going to happen. As you continue on different journeys in life, do not be afraid to ask for assistance if you do not know what you are doing. From these conversations, I felt I was ready for my interview. During this interview, I was prepared and ready to elaborate on how I could be beneficial to school. About three weeks later, I received a phone call that would change my life. I GOT THE JOB!!! This new school saw my worth and wanted me to bring my talents to their school. From the different events that happened at my previous employer, I was able to throw that self-doubt out the window and get prepared for my new position as an instructional coach.

New school equals new roles

When I began my new job, I was nervous and a little timid. I was nervous because I was employed at my previous school for 11 years and loved the people whom I worked with. Now, I am at a new school and do not know the teachers or students. I was nervous going to work and felt like people were going to scrutinize my skills as a leader. I was employed as the Middle Grades Mathematics and Science Instructional Coach, and the new role provided a challenge to what I was comfortable doing. I knew how to teach students, but I had to learn how to teach teachers. Believe me, it is REALLY DIFFERENT. During this time, I continued my doctoral coursework, and knew I had a lot to learn to be successful at the job. When I was told that I was going to be the science coach, that nagging self-doubt started to creep in my mind because I had not taught the subject. So, what should

I do? I began learning about the content, because I was determined to do my best and provide the teachers some feedback they could use as they taught the students. I also asked for help from the other instructional coaches as I was doing something I had never done before. In life, if you are not comfortable or need assistance, do not be afraid to seek help. The assistance you receive from someone, will decrease your apprehension towards completing a task. Once I knew the content, I was able to provide the teachers with feedback on how to help students learn the content. As I prepared to provide teachers with feedback on their instruction, while learning a new content area, I continued working towards completing my doctoral journey. As I continued working with the administrators and staff, I started becoming more comfortable with doing my job. The leaders provided me guidance on how to observe teachers and provide them feedback on their lessons. As the teachers knew the purpose of my employment, they began to value the feedback I was providing them on their lessons. Originally, the teachers perceived me as someone who criticized their lessons and felt threatened when I entered their classrooms. Once the leaders and staff saw my growth as an instructional coach, I was told several times that I was an inspiration to some women. I never thought of myself as an inspiration to anyone outside of my family, and it brought me great joy to inspire someone else to complete a journey they started.

After a few months on my job, my title changed. I was removed as the middle grades' science and mathematics instructional coach to the middle and high school science instructional coach. When this change occurred, I was blindsided, and hurt. I was not given an explanation as to why I was changed to only science. I wondered if someone made a statement to my leader and said I was ineffective or if they did not believe I could not improve student achievement. When I was working my way through the self-doubt, my mind started going back in that direction. I began to think, "why do people always want to put someone down" or "not want them to succeed"? I was very upset that my leader did not have a conversation with me before they made the change. Because of this change, I had to think of the positive aspects that came from this change. I thought to myself, "I will be knowledgeable about middle grades mathematics, English/ Language Arts, and middle and high school science". I believe this change continued to make me a stronger person as I continued my doctoral journey. When you are completing a task, and someone does something that you do not agree with, take it in stride and give it your all each day. When I was changed to high school science, I had to study the content, and build relationships with teachers.

Doctoral journey and COVID-19

During my second year as the instructional coach, the global pandemic caused the world to stand still. Although the way we did things changed, I was still on my doctoral journey. In education, teachers had to teach virtually, and I had to provide assistance to teachers via an online platform. I had to learn how to effectively communicate with teachers online, and teachers had to learn how to provide instruction online. During this time, I was able to defend my dissertation completely online. Although the world was going through a pandemic, this allowed me to be in the comfort of my own home and defend my dissertation. During this time, I was also able to gather my data and interview participants. Once I had to return to work, I had successfully completed my dissertation and was waiting on a date to defend for the last time. Once I received that date, I was ecstatic and very very nervous. I knew the content, but I wanted to make sure I was providing the committee with all the information they asked. On May 12, 2021, I successfully defended my dissertation! Because of COVID, I was not able to graduate in the face-to-face graduation ceremony until December of 2021. Although it was seven months later, that was one of the best days of my life, when I changed my educational name from Mrs. Aldridge to Dr. Aldridge.

What's next for Dr. K. Aldridge

In my new role as Dr. Kenyatta Aldridge, I am continuing to learn. I am currently enrolled in Tier II leadership courses. In the world of education, I want to make sure I have all of the necessary documentation for whatever position I apply for. I also want to continue to impact teachers and students. At my current employment, I plan to continue to learn from my leaders so one day I could become an effective leader. As different opportunities come my way, I plan to apply for them. If I do not get selected the first time, I am going to continue to push forward. After completing my dissertation, I became very interested in the computer program i-Ready. I want to work for the company and learn more about the software. In life, people are faced with different challenges, but I am a living example that if you put your mind to completing a goal, you will overcome any obstacle placed in your life, and no one or anything will stop you from being successful.

CHAPTER 5

Chanya Anderson's Story

CHANYA ANDERSON IS a Data Analyst working in Baltimore, MD. She currently works to ensure Baltimore youth have access to quality education and opportunities in the city. Chanya holds a B.A. in Criminology from the Pennsylvania State University and an M.A. in Criminology from the University of Delaware. Her research has always been multi-dimensional and focused on three core areas: Black civil resistance and police violence, Black women's experiences with motherhood and incarceration/reentry, and state-sanctioned violence through the use of corporal punishment in Black southern schools. Halfway through her doctoral degree, Chanya decided to leave graduate school and enter the field of Data Analytics where she can make a lasting impact in her community. When she is not working, Chanya enjoys spending time with her favorite person: her son!

Dear Black Girl, Take a Break

To the woman reading this chapter, have you taken a break today? This week? Or even this month? If someone had asked me any of those questions just a few months before I had written this chapter, the answer would have been "of course not." And while I hope it is not true, the same is likely true for many of you reading this book. The truth is that though I had not taken a break, it certainly was not because I did not need one. Quite frankly, it was simply because there was just too much work to do and not nearly enough hours in the day. I felt like I just had no time to take a break. And more importantly, I felt like I had not done enough work to deserve a break. That was my mindset for a long time. It was that exact mindset, however, that left me feeling burned out, exhausted, and depressed by the beginning of my third year of graduate school.

It was the beginning of September, and the semester had just started. Yet, I was behind on every project I was working on, suffering from immense writer's block, taking hours to finish reading one paper (if I was able to finish at all), having to postpone my first comprehensive exam, and forgetting about meetings. It was not just my academic life that was suffering either. I was barely leaving my apartment, barely cleaning my apartment, unable to be actively present with my son, ignoring text messages and phone calls from my friends and family, not eating, not sleeping; the list goes on. Suddenly, I looked up and my dream of attaining my PhD, a dream I had envisioned for many years now, was very quickly slipping away. And the worst part about it was, in that moment of burnout, exhaustion, and depression, I was completely ready to let the dream go.

The story I hope to tell in this chapter, however, is not all bad. It did not take long before I looked up and realized that I was burned out and had nothing left to give. And in a moment of honesty with myself, I acknowledged that the burnout I was experiencing did not happen overnight. I had slowly watched as it built up for many months, and possibly, even years, all the while assuring myself that I would deal with it later. In the words of a previous professor, "If you do not deal with the stress, the stress will deal with you. And it will manifest itself physically until you have no choice but to recognize it." That is exactly what happened. It was not just my mind that broke down. It was my body too. The first moment of honesty I had to myself was just to acknowledge what I was experiencing. The second moment of honesty was a searing eye-opener: if I continued operating in the way that I was, it was not just grad school that was at risk but my long-term health and well-being as well.

So, I did the only thing that I could do. I committed to making a change. What was that change? Prioritizing rest like…*seriously* prioritizing it. Not like just squeezing in a nap here and there. I mean, like a major reset. My first step? I took a week off. I know it may sound crazy, particularly for the ladies reading this that already know the demands of grad school as a student, but I did it. Instead of reading, writing, answering emails, and studying, I took seven days to reset. During that time, I deep cleaned my home and binge-watched Netflix and Hulu shows. I spent time with my family and treated myself to nice restaurants. I lit my favorite candles while wearing my favorite face masks and journaled. Most importantly, I slept…a lot! Quite honestly, seventy percent of my week off was probably spent in bed. And I regret none of it. That one week was easily one of the best things I have done for myself in a really long time. Now it was not quite vacationing on an island surrounded by sand and blue waters, but between you and me, it was pretty close.

Once that week was over, I jumped back into grad school life, albeit with some changes:

1. I stopped making myself always available. That meant no meetings after 5 PM, and do not even think I am responding to an email after 7 PM.
2. I ate three full meals every day. Now that did not mean that they were the *healthiest* three meals, but they were three full meals, nonetheless. I created time to sit and eat in peace, i.e., no work while eating.
3. I stopped overloading my days. No more than two meetings a day, and I stopped writing daily task lists that would be impossible for anyone to complete.
4. I began planning out my weeks. This inevitably helped me to stop overloading my days, but it also allowed me to prepare for things that were coming up.
5. Most importantly– for me, at least– I stopped doing work on Sundays completely. Sundays, in my book, are now known as rest days.

So why am I telling you all of this? Well, because I genuinely believe that if someone had emphasized to me how demanding grad school would be and, thus, how important rest would need to be, I truly believe I could have avoided what happened to me just a few short months ago. Because the thing is (in the words of one of my favorite TikTokers, @terrykaye), "they can give you a lot of things, but rest is one of those things you have to give to yourself." See, grad school, unlike a lot of other jobs, does not have assigned clock in and clock out times. There are no scheduled days off or even paid time off. There's no boss telling you to go take a lunch break. There is not even really even real vacation time (yes, I'm looking at you, spring break and summer break, filled with publications, assignments, and more). In grad school, there will always be something to do and something that is due. And sometimes, well, most of the time, rest just becomes lost in all of it. Then you just become so used to the lack of rest that you trick yourself into believing that you do not need it. Or worse, if you are like me, you tell yourself you do not deserve it.

While writing this chapter, I could not help but think of one particular incident that happened right at the start of grad school. Now, to paint the scene, I was a young, eager, and energized first-year grad student heading off to the very first meeting I had that year with a professor. During our hour-long conversation, I remember telling him that my plan was to take Sundays off as a rest day. He laughed at me, and not even like a little snicker but full-on laughter. He found it extremely amusing that I had the audacity to propose such a thing for myself. Looking back, I realized that it should have been a warning sign. Like most new grad students, though, I just rubbed it off. It was not until more recently that I realized how much that part of the conversation stuck with me until I ended up in the exact situation I had been trying to avoid for over three years. I wish that young, eager, and energized me would have not only stood up for myself but also gone through with my plan of a rest day once a week. Instead, I let the demands of academia get to me.

As for that professor, I do not blame him for having that mentality toward my idea of a rest day. I do not believe that his laughter came from a place of being mean or even rude but, more simply, from a place of disbelief. For him, the idea of a rest day seemed impossible because of the demands of academia. That was his truth, and it is the truth of the overwhelming majority of those in academia, students and professors alike. But here's the thing, just because it is their truth does not mean it has to be my truth. Or yours, either.

Let's be real. There are a lot of demands in grad school, such as coursework, teaching, independent research, publishing, comprehensive exams, conferences, theses, and dissertations. That is not even all of it. So, when you factor all of those things together, it does not leave a whole lot of time. It can be very easy to fall into the trap of believing that if you are not doing all of these things and more, then there is no time for a break. It feels as though you have not done enough for a break. But here's the thing that I had to learn: rest is not a privilege. You do not have to earn rest. Let me say that again: *rest is not a privilege. You do not have to earn rest.* Dear Black girl, you are deserving of rest whether you did ten things today or nothing at all. You are deserving of rest whether you completed all of your to-do list, some of your to-do list, or none of your to-do list. Our truth does not have to be their truth. Give yourself the space, grace, and permission to take a break. Of course, a break can be a 30-minute nap or a 5-minute walk to get some fresh air. But, for as often as you need it, whether that be once a week or once a month, take a deeper break. One that really allows you to rest and reset. I promise your academic career and your health will be all the better for it.

I Promise, It's Okay

I was able to bounce back from my burnout by prioritizing rest in my life. I schedule rest into my week, but I will also randomly take a break in the middle of working on a paper if my body tells me that is what I need. Whether you're thinking about graduate school, starting your graduating school journey, or in the midst of one, I strongly encourage you to do the same. As I am writing this chapter to you, I feel so much better than I did just a few months ago. That one week off changed so much for me. And, though I did not realize it at the time, it gave me a level of clarity that I have not had in a long time. That clarity has allowed me to see that it is time for this chapter of my life to close.

Yes, you read that right. After three years in grad school, I have decided to leave academia in pursuit of my professional career. Do not get me wrong, this last year has been extremely successful for me, thanks, in large part, to learning how to prioritize rest in my life. I presented at my first in-person conference since the start of the pandemic, served on the graduate student council, and passed my comprehensive exams. And yet, I still crave more than grad school can give me right now. While rest is not the only thing that led me to this decision, it did play a large role. The demands of grad school and even academia, more generally, do not get easier. If anything, the more you progress, the more you are expected to do. I'd be rich if I could count the number of times I told a professor I was tired, and their response was, "well, this is the most rest you are ever going to get." My response always wants to be *how is that possible* considering how little rest grad students already get. Do you mean to tell me it actually gets worse, not better, when you become a professor?

In retrospect, I understand why my professor laughed about my Sunday rest days. It is not just him or a few professors in my department. It is the institution of academia. It is just the way it is, and it does not stop for anyone or anything, for that matter. Just a few days ago, I received an email from a professor saying she had not heard from me in a while. A while, being about a month. Now, for context, at the last meeting we had together, I had reminded her that I would be pretty off the grid because my first comprehensive exam was about two weeks after that meeting. So, when I responded, I reminded her that I had just finished up my exam and also that I was dealing with the loss of a family member only a few days before. Her response was first that she was sorry for my loss and second that we should schedule a meeting for the following week because we had lots of things to discuss.

Yeah, the demands of grad school do not stop for anything.

Though I had already made the decision to leave grad school by that point, that email exchange just reiterates my point. Even if I had not just lost a family member, was I not deserving of a break after completing my exam? I like to think that after completing a six-hour no notes exam, I was deserving of a few days off. Even one day off. But I was quickly reminded that that is just not the way academia works. And while that may be true, the truth is also that I do not have to deal with it. Quite frankly, I will not deal with it. So one door closes, and another one opens. I do not walk away from this with any ill will towards anyone I have encountered in academia. It is just quite simply a lifestyle they have chosen, one that I am not ready to choose. I also do not walk away from this with any feelings of disappointment or failure. I have accomplished more in the last three years than I ever could have imagined. Who would have ever thought that little old me from West Baltimore would grow up to get her master's degree? Well, maybe my mom did, but other than that, no one, not even me.

So, while my chapter may look a little different from others in this book, we all have a story to tell. At the beginning of my chapter, I mentioned how a dream I had, one I had for a long time, was beginning to slip away. For a long time, I thought it was because of exhaustion and that once I became better rested, the dream would come back. What I see now is that the dream slipped away not just because I was tired but also because I was unfulfilled. So, I guess the moral of my story is two-fold. First, to that Black woman reading this, your rest is of the utmost importance. Do not let anyone, academia or otherwise, tell you differently. Anyone that has any experience with grad school can tell you that taking a week off when you are supposed to be studying for comps is pretty wild, and I would agree. But at that moment, it was the best thing for me. I walked away all the better because of it. So, I end this chapter by reminding you of the second moral of my story: never be afraid to do what is best for you.

CHAPTER 6

Toneille Bent's Story

TONEILLE BENT IS a 3rd-year doctoral student at Oklahoma State University, pursuing a PhD in Social Foundations of Education. She holds a B.A. in Spanish from the University of Tulsa and a Master of Human Relations (MHR) from the University of Oklahoma. Toneille's research interests include Jamaican immigrant identity formation and music activism. While she does not plan to enter academia following completion of her degree, Toneille aspires to work that melds her passions for arts and culture, specifically music, social change, and education. Toneille began her career in the private sector and segued into education full-time over a decade ago as a middle school and adjunct Spanish instructor. She now works for a national education non-profit that places AmeriCorps members in urban schools to serve as "near-peer" mentors and tutors and is a certified life and executive coach.

A native of Jamaica, Toneille grew up in Tulsa, Oklahoma, and finds that this unique journey and experience as a "border crosser" in the most literal and figurative senses offers her a lens that informs her worldview and research. Besides learning, her greatest joys are her loved ones, travel, music and dancing, and good food!

Homeplace

First

I'm the first in everything. In my family, that is. The firstborn daughter of my parents. First grandchild of my grandparents, first niece/nephew/cousin, sister; first to journey this road to "PhinsheD." First, to pursue and, make no mistake, **earn** a doctoral degree. I'm also the first to tell you I'm clear that I'm here for no other reason than there's nowhere I've ever been more certain I need to be.

This isn't about a lofty pursuit that sets me up for prestige, approval, and access (although I'll gladly take them if I can offer said access to other Black and brown world changers). It's not about a conference of letters, titles, and self-import. This isn't a glamorous undertaking, no matter what those who are looking on may opine. This shit is hard. It is taxing and can be more isolating than being a Jamaican who says they don't love curry goat (I should know). This is not an exercise in validating my existence, nor is it about anything other than knowing: a) my innate worth informs the value of this PhD, not vice versa; b) learning spaces are my habitat, c) I'm necessary to the resistance and d) this pursuit is as much "me" as my name and the blood running through my veins. For the first time in a long time, as hard as this may be, I hold no question or confusion that of many things I've done, **this** is the most accurate.

Foundation

"If you waan' good yu nose haffi' run." Mommy's voice and one of her favorite and ever-ready Jamaican refrains run through my ears almost constantly, especially lately. In other words, it takes hard work and struggles to achieve. Blood, sweat, and tears, some may say. I concur that my endeavors and accomplishments have absolutely required investment and, in some cases, discomfort and deep sacrifice. Even with that, as it relates to my presence in formal learning spaces, any discomfort has always married with solid assurance that I'm exactly where I'm supposed to be. The moment I entered the doors of my first school, I felt at home. I knew I was in the right place, and as a dearly departed former minister of mine used to say, I took full opportunity to "stretch out in it." Thus, this reflection is not one of angst or struggle. It really is a statement about accuracy and assurance even in the face of challenges such as this purported ascent to elevated knowledge presents. This is my affirmation that when one holds clarity of purpose and placement, it is fine to rest in that and be relentless in their pursuit.

My Jamaican home in middle America was one where studying "yu book" was the obligation my brother and I held in our parents' and elders' eyes. In my early childhood, it seemed the top of every conversation during crackly overseas calls from Aunties, Uncles, Grandmas, and Grandpas in Jamaica always began with *"How is baby brotha' and how is school?"* No youthful concern or folly could challenge the expectation that we were to educate ourselves. My father was an avid reader and writer who shared his bold opinions on race, politics, and injustice regularly and readily to his spouse, family, friends, and of course, the local newspaper's Letters to the Editor. My mother affirmed my beauty and ability directly, read to my brother and me, and was ready to help us with homework, referring to information from her Student's Companion book and sharing any other deeply embedded learnings she'd gotten in her school years in Jamaica and Trinidad.

I lived in awe of my parents' ready intelligence and unwavering assurances that we were capable and headed for certain success in all things. I've not achieved every goal I strove for, certainly, but I don't feel I've really ever failed. Failure wasn't a notion in our home because the success was in the attempt and the acquired learning. My parents took the chance to move their young family to this seemingly safer land from a successful life in Jamaica, not knowing the struggle they would face in doing so. We looked on and learned what it meant to risk, experience loss, endure, and in time reap the rewards of many of those risks. I grew up with no notion that I was inferior or lacking. It never occurred to me that I could be anything besides powerful, unapologetic, and postured to challenge oppressive and illogical thought and structures. I knew my mind was my ticket, and from the first day I could recognize words on a page and sit at a school desk, I've felt my "place." Learning, whether I'm garnering it or guiding it, is my accuracy and my motivation. "Essence-tial" to my makeup.

This Is Our Business

"I always try and talk people out of it," she said unblinkingly. *"This was not something I wanted, and I kinda' got tricked into it. I didn't need to have this degree."* My stomach dropped. I felt completely stunned and somehow blindsided. Maybe this was her brand of mentoring?

Maybe she was saying these things because she knew how much this would cost me, but at this moment; I was not sure. I didn't let my surprise and internal recoil show at the moment, but I sensed that this White female professor was so easily able to say these things to me about my dearly-held dream because she had no notion that for many other more-melanated folks and me, this pursuit of "higher learning," while not mandatory, is **far** from optional. Our knowledge is power. What lives in our minds, we're taught, as Black people, no one can own, oppress, or steal. Ideally, there is no easily colonizing my consciousness, and if so, it's up to me, as Bob Marley said to "emancipate [myself] from mental slavery." It is up to me to perpetually resist. As she spoke, and as I tried to offer the benefit of my doubt that she was well-intentioned, I silently rejected every word she'd just said and proceeded to apply to graduate school.

In her 2019 book, *We Want To Do More Than Survive: Abolitionist Teaching And The Pursuit of Educational Freedom,* Dr. Bettina Love writes about "homeplace" and quotes the late bell hooks in describing "homeplace" as "a space where Black folx truly matter to each other, where souls are nurtured, comforted and fed. Homeplace is a community, typically led by women where White power and the damages done by it are healed by loving Blackness and restoring dignity." hooks, Love says, considers "homeplace" a place of resistance. As I silently resisted what that professor said to me, I recalled the abundant conversations I'd had over the years with my collective of over 10 PhD-holding friends, all of them women who are Black or of color. Each fully endorsed my plan to apply to a doctoral program.

Homeplace. None of them once poo-pooed their achievement as something they "never wanted" or were bamboozled into. These women held their heads and their support of me high and told me not to dare hesitate in going boldly about this, my business. Their business. OUR business of higher learning and my assuming my full place as a scholar, culture-contributor, shifter, and thinker. They saw me because they are me. *Homeplace.* I knew that it was providential and purposed that I'd been surrounded by their brilliance, could learn from their battle scars, and that they trusted me to conduct myself accordingly, to weather the storms of my studies and eventually join them in the ranks. I was assured that they never considered telling me to turn away from myself or to ignore my destiny's call. They continue to be my homeplace as they offer the restorative, supportive, loving energy that I needed leading to my entrance into my program and continue to need as I complete my studies. I can turn to them with any question, need or point of angst and I'm assured by their belief that I have the skill, ability, and the deservedness to stay the course.

What was so easy for that professor to say unflinchingly would be unfathomable for my collective to verbalize even with what they knew experientially and empirically, this doctoral deed would demand of me. I felt immediately defiant when the professor said, *"I always try to talk people out of it."* I felt shaken and resentful; I considered it all-too-easy for her to say, and I felt righteous in the immediate confirmation her statement offered me that I had no option NOT to leap fully into the deep end of this act of resistance and resilience. My stroke to a **strong** finish is the only response necessary. I guess I should extend gratitude to her as well since she offered me what I needed to affirm that I'm as necessary to this endeavor as it is to me. I'm needed to usher other brilliant, Black women like me to and through this process with truths told about the cost; to stand for them as they enter rooms with those who seek to silence them, turning resistant cheeks, blind eyes, and deaf ears to their undeniable statements of truth. I'm purposed to take up space and shake up those who presume Black voices anathema to "academia," and I'm here to obtain what's mine.

In Spite Of It

This path, with every soul-stifling, emotionally isolating, *"I can't do this shit," "Abolish ANOVA; is there no other data analysis way?!"* and *"Qualitative research IS actual research!"* moment is worth the stress and the stretch. Learning how to manage the political maneuvering, catering to professorial fragilities and fancies, learning who truly will advocate for their students, and maybe even more importantly, who sees us as threats, often outweighs any hefty and demanding coursework. The silencing and passive-aggressive regard for my contributions are a cost I'll stand because it would cost me more to stifle the truth. I sense that many Black PhD-holding, PhD-pursuant women agree that parts of this journey elude description and that even trying to verbalize the experience can, in and of itself, be damaging. I sense that there are parts of this that have to remain unspoken, likely for our own well-being as well as so those who come after and alongside us will not be deterred.

My long-graduated PhD friends just smile knowingly and say, "You've got this," almost like women who have given birth and hold membership to the mysterious all-but-secret society that crossing that painful threshold extended them. The only way to properly capture what this feels like is to participate in it. A close second is to observe someone in the middle of it and failing that, it's hard to grasp what this work demands, particularly of Black scholars. I often wonder what the true purpose of testing folx's mental wellbeing to such lengths might be. Is it requisite that mental health, our senses of self, and our capacity be so deeply challenged in order to say that we've arrived at evolved thinking and advanced critical skills? That we are stamped approved "qualified experts?" I wonder.

Pet And Threat

My Dr. Soror once made the statement that Black people in academia are a threat. I remember the invitation I received into this program and hearing that I was the sort of student desired in this program. A program where I thought we could and, in fact, should freely examine and critique social phenomena and ills as they impact and manifest in education specifically. It felt like every bit of wind and desire was knocked out of me when the professor who shared such a warm invitation later saw me as enough of a threat to, in my estimation, express their disdain indirectly but impactfully. I'd held the naïve notion that I was "safe" to share here as I'd been in most other educational spaces previously and that I was doing the right thing in speaking out against injustice and oppressive systems, critiquing and contributing. I considered my childhood learning by observation as I listened to my dad lift his voice. He was a Black immigrant man in America who was never nervous about naming the transgressions and violations so present here. I considered the reggae music he played incessantly that taught us to "Get up! Stan' up!" never stop the fight for our rights, nor hesitate to push back when our boundaries were crossed. It was that spirit and those of my ancestors I brought with me, namely as I'd been invited and, in fact, praised as a right fit for what I considered a course of study designed to speak truth to power. I was doing my job as a scholar! My insights and opinions are mine to offer; my voice is meant to be lifted. I've learned the price of exercising my empowerment. The same "pet to threat" phenomenon so many Black women face in professional spaces is very present in these places of "higher ed" and even higher insecurity, and it came to greet me. My voice and presence were superficially invited, and when I pushed too much, performed too well, spoke too critically, and challenged bigotry and racism on their face, I felt the aim became quieting me, albeit subtly.

The findings of my study show that more letters behind one's name do not necessarily correlate to less bias.

I value Homeplace so much more as I avoid the landmines and pitfalls, challenge censoring myself, and draw on those who know well the way I'm going to be my guides and my collective beacon. To observe Black women who've negotiated paths deeply similar to mine and to know that they've dissertated, defended, graduated, obtained jobs, have led departments and coordinated programs, published, and professed in spite of any manner of institutional bullshit or bullying is largely my fuel. They may not know that they are homeplace for me, but I'm putting it in so many words, and I commit to serving as one extension of Homeplace for another coming after and alongside me.

Highest Learning

Should the doctoral call sound for you, first make key considerations regarding your why, how, and where, and then seek warranted counsel. If you answer "yes," remember Homeplace. Reach out, be unashamed in seeking alliance and reinforcement from those like you who have the navigational skills that you'll need and that you'll acquire over time. Consider your application, enrollment, and scholarship all as acts of resistance. Take up ALL your space and keep in view that this work is righteous and necessary. Aim to take the learnings of self, analysis, and systems with you while you disrupt and handle OUR business. When they try to talk you out of it, go all the way in.

My truest, highest learning in these three years has not been in content, writing and research, and data analysis methods. It's not epistemology, nor is it ethnography. It isn't of theoretical frameworks or their masterminds. It's in the discovery of what lives in me. It's in the choice not to shrink or to cower and, at the same time, choosing when to use my voice. It's playing this game all the way to the endzone to collect my sheepskin. Through it, although this can feel lonely, that's challenged by my pride and clarity about this being my space; because of my familial and cultural foundation; because of the network of minds and hearts that are my Homeplace, and because I was made for this! There's no moment of fear or deflation that will make me turn back from my goal, for the ones who have gone before me, who walk with me, who carry me when I am tired, and who push me from behind do not deserve less than me doing my part in managing our business.

CHAPTER 7

Angel Boulware's Story

ANGEL BOULWARE IS a third-year PhD student in the Department of Comparative Human Development at the University of Chicago. She is studying the intersection of health, vulnerability, and culture. Her research interests are within the disciplines of sociology, public health, and psychology. Angel's personal experiences have provided her with the foundation to understand how research can be translated into structural and community-centered action. Her current work explores the impact community violence has on the psychosocial development of Black adolescents.

In addition to her independent projects, she serves as a researcher at a medical center focusing on reproductive health and contraceptive access, particularly in religious-affiliated hospitals. Additionally, she serves as a project coordinator for a community violence program.

Angel is driven and inspired by the power of health access, prevention, and collaboration with the community it's intended for.

Girl, Me Too…

The next few pages are the soundtrack to my experiences pursuing my doctoral degree. I am a music lover and rap connoisseur. If I was not in graduate school, I would be a ghostwriter or an A&R. Each section starts with a song that describes my mood and helped me push through each experience. I hope you enjoy it.

"Dreams and Nightmares," by Meek Mill

My decision to pursue a PhD was not innate, not because I lacked intellect but because I lacked exposure. No one tells Black girls from impoverished neighborhoods to pursue doctoral degrees. Being a first-generation college graduate was already an enormous milestone. I had already accomplished a goal that so many people in my family desired. I thought that I had reached the ceiling. However, my mentor, Dr. Bruce Wade, reminded me that there was no ceiling and that I should always shoot for the stars. Dr. Wade was the epitome of a phenomenal mentor because he saw what I did not see in myself. I struggled to fathom that a girl like me could achieve such a seemingly unreachable goal, but he helped me work through every insecurity and doubt and continuously pushed me beyond my comfort zone. Since I went to a smaller college with fewer research opportunities than many Research One institutions, I questioned whether I would be competitive enough for the top programs in my field. Dr. Wade helped me turn my intellectual curiosity into formal research by diversifying my research skills and helping me design my own projects. Sadly, before I could complete my applications, Dr. Wade passed away. I was instantly bombarded with heartbreak and grief. I felt lost and alone. Dr. Wade was not only my professor and mentor, but he was my family. He would check on me during the holidays and email me whenever I missed a class. He constantly reaffirmed me and pushed me to new heights. The whole idea of pursuing my PhD came solely from him. I had no idea how I was supposed to continue the journey without him.

About a week after his passing, I began meeting former students of his—a mix of Black women who were current doctoral students, research scientists, and professors. As I met these women, I explained the nature of my relationship with Dr. Wade and how I felt so lost without him. In his absence, these women came together to help me complete my research projects and PhD applications. At that moment, I learned what type of professor I aspired to be. Dr. Wade's legacy was so impactful and legendary that his former students from various stages in their careers desired to uplift and support me simply on the strength of their relationship with our professor. Their dedication to my success was indescribable;

from reading my personal statements, conducting mock interviews, and doing mental health check-ins; I was beyond grateful. My interactions with these Black women illustrated the power of Black women in academia. They were committed to their scholarship but also to breaking barriers to ensure the next generation of Black women scholars were academically, mentally, and emotionally prepared to excel in the academy.

Once the acceptances started arriving, I was overwhelmed with a wide range of emotions. I was elated because I felt I had expressed myself and my research interests well in my applications. I was adamant about only doing research that could directly support my community. My community helped me get to this point, so I wanted to ensure that the work I did in graduate school was relative and applicable to the place I call home. While I was overwhelmed and feeling very blessed with the immense number of opportunities I was receiving, I was also still struggling with the loss of Dr. Wade. It was hard to celebrate these accomplishments without the person who was so influential in helping me get to this point. I just tried to remain grateful, and I took pride in the fact that I was a part of his last class of students, and everything that I accomplish is tied to him.

"Superstar," by Lupe Fiasco

Before I started graduate school, I heard the term imposter syndrome a lot. Imposter syndrome is especially prevalent among students of color at Predominantly White Institutions. Many of my friends in graduate school would tell me that they felt like "frauds" in their PhD programs. My experiences with imposter syndrome started in the first few weeks of school. It was not immediate because I knew that, wholeheartedly, I worked so hard for everything that I have. All of my accomplishments come from many long days and hard nights. I did not doubt that I was in graduate school because of the strength of my own merit. My first encounter with imposter syndrome occurred during my first year in a theory class. Before graduate school, I had a nerdy love for theory. In undergrad, my professors taught us about the founding fathers in social science research but also made us aware of all the influential scholars of color who expanded upon these theories to include people from marginalized backgrounds. When I began graduate school, my love for theory changed drastically.

This particular theory course was reading intensive, and I had some challenges comprehending some of the readings. I remember going to my professor's office hours because I thought it was best to get help earlier in the quarter. I was not embarrassed about needing help because in my eyes that was the point of being a student. There is a common misassumption among many prospective and current graduate students that we are supposed to have all the answers. This ideology is so harmful and prohibits the learning process. The purpose of being a student is to ask questions and express when we are struggling so we have a chance to comprehend the content better. Essentially, we should all operate as students. We should never get to the point where we are above asking questions and learning more. Before the professor answered my question during office hours, he stated that he was surprised and concerned that I was not familiar with the theory, especially since it was something that I should have learned already as an undergraduate. My attempt to better understand the theory did not mean I was unfamiliar with the concept. I simply wanted clarity, and all students should be encouraged to openly express any trouble grasping the content.

Scholars such as W. E. B DuBois, Patricia Hill Collins, and Anna Julia Cooper were rarely mentioned in my graduate courses but were essential in my undergraduate training. This small incident with my professor impacted the way I approached my assignments, research, and theory and challenged the way I felt about myself. Anyone can feel imposter syndrome, but the severity and pressure is heightened for marginalized students. I was the only Black woman and HBCU student in the course and often the only Black person in most of my classes. I felt an extensive amount of pressure because my performance was not only a reflection of myself but also other Black people and HBCU graduates. My imposter syndrome was not something I initially felt, but it was exacerbated by my experiences with my professors and peers. I was often afraid to ask questions or add my perspective, especially because I knew that I was not just representing myself. The experiences in the theory class were just a starting point for my poor experiences in graduate school. I could write all day about every distasteful comment, microaggression, or blatant disrespect, but I want to be intentional about the space I have. I want to use these pages as an opportunity to express my emotions and experiences vulnerably, to connect with other Black women in similar spaces. As I write, I hope you read, connect, and say, "girl, me too."

"No Friends in the Industry," by Drake

I was tired, burnt out, and honestly sad by the end of the first quarter. I succumbed to grief and was overwhelmed with assignments, and just not sure who I was anymore. If I had to describe my first year of graduate school, I would describe it as lonely. I felt like I did not belong, so I started isolating myself. I only attended school events that I had to participate in, and I was not very engaged in my courses. If the class was over at noon, I packed up at 11:50 am. I missed the casual conversations among students about upcoming assignments and graduate school events because I went straight home after class. My lack of connections with my classmates impacted me academically because I did not feel comfortable asking questions or discussing assignments with them. Furthermore, it affected my ability to form interpersonal connections as there were weeks when I did not talk to anyone in person.

Before I started graduate school, all of my Black women mentors in academia constantly expressed the importance of forming a community. I would receive this advice constantly, but I did not fully understand its importance until school started and things became tougher. Naturally, I am introverted and did not think it was super important to find friends or community in graduate school. I had a robust support system back home, and I felt those connections would sustain me. Although I upheld the relationships with my friends and family, it was still very isolating to not have people to talk to in person. I did not expect distance to have such a significant impact on my well-being. I had a very reliable and secure support system in close proximity in undergrad. I could easily go to my best friends for a quick or very long vent session anytime during the day. Simple things like eating lunch or walking to class together made a huge impact on my day and positively affected my mood. I did not realize how significant these small interactions were until I was without them. Sisters, I greatly encourage you to find friends and community in your new city. Please find a way to keep a little piece of home with you or to access things and/or people that comfort you. The journey is tough.

"New Work Out Plan," by Kanye West

The Covid-19 Pandemic occurred during the second half of my first year of graduate school. As I was going home for spring break, the flights were canceled due to the pandemic. I decided to do remote classes from my hometown. Instantly, I noticed significant changes in my mental health upon returning home. I felt a greater sense of peace and support being closer to my family and community. During this time, I began doing virtual writing sessions with my friends in other PhD programs. What was intended to be supportive writing spaces often turned into emotional support groups. We spent hours each week discussing the challenges of being Black students in these programs and how it has greatly impacted our mental and physical health. It was refreshing to know my experiences were not unique, but I also recognized that this was not the life I wanted to live. I knew that I would have to make some severe adjustments in order to preserve my peace and well-being.

One random day I signed up for a workout class at a local gym in my hometown. At first, I was not sure how long I was going to keep up this new routine. I did not have high expectations for myself, but it was the best decision I have ever made. People think that the most rewarding benefits of working out are the physical body changes, but I continue to work out for what it does for my mental health. For an hour, about five times a week, I go to the gym and focus completely on myself. This hour is blocked out for me and me only. I do not read, I do not check emails, and I do not talk about research. I sweat a little, push my body to do new things, and listen to good music. I am a full-time PhD student with two jobs. Some days, I struggle to find uninterrupted time to eat a meal, and I never get a healthy amount of sleep. Forcing myself to go to the gym gave me an hour each day that was completely dedicated to myself and self-improvement.

I realized I needed to create stronger divides between my professional and personal life. The pandemic taught me to slow down, be patient, and listen to my body. We sacrifice so much for school; we deserve one thing that we will keep. The self-care and physical break from campus allowed me to recenter myself and regain the confidence that I felt was repeatedly stripped from me. Before the in-person school year started, I reminded myself that I was talented, well trained, and here for a reason. The year was still tough, and the microaggressions kept coming, but I knew my purpose was more significant than people's comments.

The gym became my non-negotiable. Under no circumstances will anything take me away from the gym because that has become my uninterrupted time for myself. I spend so much of my time working on things for other people that the least I can do is take a couple of hours a week to dedicate to my health and wellbeing. I would seriously encourage all Black women to find their "non-negotiable," the thing that makes you happy, fulfills you, and brings you peace of mind. As cliché as it sounds, you cannot pour from an empty cup.

"Nice," by The Carters

My plan was to leave academia and go into industry. I had such poor experiences within the academy as a student that I knew that I was not willing to return as a faculty member; plus, I really enjoyed research. My program has teaching requirements as a part of our curriculum. I was not sure what to expect once I started teaching my own sections, but it was better than I ever could have imagined. On the first day of class, I thanked my students for showing up in the midst of a global pandemic. Even though they are required to be here, I still wanted to recognize that life is happening outside of this class, and I am grateful for their attendance and engagement. I would also invite them to share any positive or exciting things that happened during the week before each class. I saw this as an opportunity for students to engage with each other as just humans instead of academic competitors. School is important, but we can also take five minutes to just do a simple life check-in. I was not sure how well this agenda was being received until one day, I did not immediately ask them to share something good about their week. When I did not ask, a student raised their hand and asked if they could share some good news they received that week. Unbeknownst to me, they had become accustomed to this routine and looked forward to this part of the class. The student shared that his parent was recovering from a significant health complication, and he wanted to share this good news with the class. This was probably one of my greatest moments to date, knowing that I was fostering such a welcoming environment where someone could share such personal news.

My teaching ideology is to simply be gracious and understanding. I am a human before I am a professor or instructor. I care way more about my student's well-being than their ability to turn in an assignment at 11:59 pm on the dot. As a social scientist, I was formally trained in sociology but had a lot of exposure to anthropology. I remember the week we were learning about anthropology, and my students had such a colonial and exploitive approach to the discipline. I was so disheartened but not surprised. Their exposure to these disciplines was the complete opposite of the way that I was taught. I returned to my syllabi and course readings from my HBCU and incorporated them into the readings for class. It was such a full-circle moment. These readings were so influential to my training, and I was grateful to pass these works on to the next generation. I was fueled by my experiences with coursework in graduate school because much of my curriculum while I was taking classes was centered on White men and excluded so many other influential scholars. Making these amendments and additions to the curriculum made me feel like I had finally found my place in academia. I was creating safe spaces for students to learn but also to breathe. I was also restructuring their exposure to social science by prioritizing Black and people of color who are indispensable but often forgotten in their respective fields. As I reflect, I am constantly reminded of all the people who helped me get to this point. I may not always be physically around my support system and community, but they are always within me. Ultimately my successes in teaching are a part of Dr. Wade's legacy because everything that I learned from him was then passed on to my students through me. I finished that class full of gratitude and appreciation.

"Alright," by Kendrick Lamar

The first few pages of this chapter described my journey into graduate school and my first few quarters as a graduate student. I wanted to use this space to be very explicit about a wide variety of challenges to hopefully resonate with other Black women in similar spaces. PhD programs are small and can often be isolating, so it can be hard to know if other people feel the way you do. There were many days I wanted to go home; I have called my friends and family very often about how I was done. As Black women, we are expected to do the impossible effortlessly. I struggled greatly with creating boundaries because I feared missing out on new experiences or opportunities. In my mind, I had to work more than twice as hard. I was always thinking of ways to improve my skills, research experience, and build my CV. I said yes to every opportunity that came my way, no matter how overwhelmed I was. I had to wake up early, stay up late, and work on the weekends even to be close to staying on track with my assignments. My calendar was my lifeline; I could do nothing without it. At one point, I was seriously concerned that something was going on with my memory because I was having an increasingly more difficult time remembering simple things. I realized that I had so much on my mind all the time that it was easy to forget stuff because my brain was at capacity. Academically and professionally, I was doing well. I had exceptional grades and a plethora of opportunities. Still, I felt like I was barely keeping my head above water. I was constantly sacrificing things that were really important to me, such as sleep, self-care, and time with my family and friends. One day I had to remind myself that the work would always be there. No one will reward you for your lack of sleep and not taking care of yourself. Those are not things you can put on your CV. I know the conversation of self-care seems trendy, but it is vital, and self-care looks different for everyone.

Sisters, do what it takes to find joy. Don't let these schools take your smile from you. I found joy in sisterhood, teaching, and the gym. Those are a few things that have made it a little easier to get up and try every day. I've described numerous encounters throughout this chapter where I felt my back was against the wall. Countless times I wanted to take a break or stop altogether. I watched a lot of my Black women friends leave their programs with tears in their eyes and smiles on their faces. Unpopular opinion, I do not see an issue with taking a break or deciding to leave. We are accomplishing such a big goal, and we are often the first person in our families to do so. With that being said, there is always an immense amount of pressure to persist. However, sometimes this unwavering persistence is dangerous. The degree is worthless if you come out broken and bruised. So, sisters, I have the utmost faith in you to do everything you desire, but I also wish you peace, relaxation, and serenity. If nothing else, I hope this chapter teaches you to choose yourself because you are really what matters.

CHAPTER 8

Juanita Crider's Story

JUANITA CRIDER SERVES as program advisor of the Purdue University Black Cultural Center. She is also currently a PhD candidate in American studies at Purdue University with a research concentration in Women, Gender and Sexuality Studies, and African American Studies. Her dissertation tentatively titled "Coming of Age Again: Menopausal Black Women and Black Feminist/Womanist Reawakening in Literature, Film, television and New Media" explores how Black women theorize menopause. Juanita's research explores whether Black menopausal women use Black feminist and womanist methods to address and construct the realities of aging. Crider asserts that these women do so, even though many fail to identify as feminists or womanists. Additionally, she argues that considering Black women in cultural gerontology scholarship provides opportunities to connect to larger theoretical and interdisciplinary correlations between fields. Therefore, her dissertation aims to address this gap and encourage Black feminist scholars to consider how their research might be more inclusive of eldering Black women but also endeavors to engage cultural gerontologists to further examine how cultural variables such as race/ethnicity, gender, and class fundamentally influence the aging experience. This research is very personal to Crider as a 60-year-old woman completing her doctoral journey!

From the Kitchen Table to the Classroom: A Post Traditional Graduate Student Ponders Where and When I enter [Black] Feminist Studies

At Mijiza's
Shifting landscapes of beauty
Braided together
By generations
Of simmering ebony folklore

Conjuring in kitchens
Crowns of natural glory
A graceful griot grandmother
A passionate poet warrior
A warmhearted womanist

Meshed together in love
Flowing in laughter
Like the strands of locs
Crying FREEDOM!
Or riotous natural ringlets

Twisting and turning
Sharing tales of kinship
From head-to-head
Sacred ebony science in each fingertip
Sistah triplets remember …
Village stylists

Clicking at stoves
Humming at sinks
Dancing between braiding
And beckoning
You to sit your soul still

At the altar of rituals
Roots to the Soil
Of Black Antiquity

This poem, written in 2008 when I was approaching my 47th birthday today, seems quite prescient. It perfectly traces what I describe as the genealogies of my nontraditional graduate school journey and my Black feminist passions while simultaneously encapsulating the inspiration for my current doctoral work. Why the kitchen table? As a Black woman reflecting on the Black women who came before me, the kitchen is at the center and not the margins of my memories. It is where I sit and ponder as I make life decisions and where I create ideas, edible or erudite, and it was where I filled out the applications once I made the decision to complete my college journey.

It's important to share some background. I began my college journey as a typical undergraduate student in the fall of 1979 at the tender age of 18. I had an academically successful freshman year. However, I became pregnant and did not return the following year, choosing instead to raise my son as a single parent. Yet, returning to school was always in the back of my mind. I was fortunate to get a job as a cook (there's the kitchen again) at a local university when my son was in elementary school. One of the benefits of working at the university was fee remission for employees. I was able to work and take classes to earn my undergraduate degree. During my undergraduate experience, a professor of African American history took me aside and said to me, " I hope you are considering graduate school. You write well, are a good student, and there is no reason you can't do it! I will help you through the process if you're interested." As a history major, I had taken several courses with this professor, and she knew my background: single mother, service staff worker, and student, yet she was supportive and encouraging. This type of mentoring will be a recurring and consistent theme throughout my academic journey up to this present moment as a doctoral candidate at 60 years old. I followed through with the aid and motivation of my mentor and was accepted into the master's program in history at the same university. Here I need to mention that since I worked full time and was raising a child, I was enrolled as a part-time student as an undergraduate and in the master's program and continue to do so as a doctoral student. As any good mentor does, I was encouraged to consider pursuing a higher-paying job within the university system once I earned my undergraduate degree. I tried to no avail. However, I did find a higher-paying job where I could use my university connections and continue my graduate work part-time. Although, I would lose the fee remission benefit. It was a very difficult decision, but I took the leap. Little did I know that this leap would directly lead me to where I am today.

Several experiences my mentor opened to me all through this process also are key to my doctoral journey: presenting at conferences as an undergraduate, publishing as an undergraduate, and serving on committees in the department when student involvement was requested. Reading this, you may be thinking, how on earth did I manage this while working 40 hours a week and raising a son? Well, first, I should say I was an unmarried parent versus a single parent because my son's father and I co-parented. So unlike some others, I had support; family, friends, and mentor support combined with maturity and the experience of being older was the gasoline for the engine of my dream of pursuing a doctoral degree. During my M.A. program, another opportunity opened for me, a job at a small private, Christian university. A professor from this university remembered me from a conference presentation and contacted me to encourage me to apply for the position as a staff person who would work on diversity programming and initiatives. The school was close enough that I would not have to move and would not disrupt my graduate program, and would also assist in paying my tuition fees. Interviewing for a university job at this level was a whole new experience for me. I had no idea of the various stages and meeting with multiple people and the expectation of making a presentation. My previous mentor was a valuable resource as I prepared for this new and, to me, intimidating experience. The process required three total visits to their campus. I was one of two finalists but did not get the offer. I was disappointed yet reminded by mentors that failure is often an opportunity to learn. Reflecting on this, I must admit that although I did not get the position, the process was a good experience, and I met wonderful, influential people who treated me well. This defeat would prove to ultimately be another ingredient in the fuel that propelled me to where I am today.

It's interesting how often we desire a change, but often it takes outside forces to place you in an uncomfortable situation to force you to make a move. The job that I was working had a change in board members, and the executive director was facing pressure to take the vision of the program in a new direction. This new direction would not make the best use of my skills. This was when a staff position at a research one university came to my attention from a network that one of my graduate professors suggested I join. This job would call for me to move two hours away to a community where I knew no one. I was no longer worried about my son; he was a young adult in college himself by this time. Perhaps it was time to take an even bigger vault into the unknown. I updated my resume and prepared a cover letter just as the posting required. When I received the call for a campus visit interview after going through an initial phone interview, I immediately recalled my previous experience. Going through that process and not getting the job, in essence, prepared me for this in two ways. First, the good experience and treatment of the staff, despite not getting an offer, gave me the confidence I needed to apply for this position. Secondly, the process of an intensive campus interview was under my belt. I knew how to prepare. Also, the possibility of working at a research one university with fee remission as an employee benefit opened the possibility of pursuing a doctoral degree after completing my M.A.

The campus visit went better than I expected, and several days later, I was offered the job which, as of this writing, I have had for 16 years. I began the job in the middle of my MA program at another university. However, the opportunity was too good to pass. I placed my master's degree on hold for a couple of years to adjust to a new city and learn the ins and outs of my new position as program advisor of a university Black Cultural Center. The dream of a PhD was still haunting me, and I was even more determined being on a research one campus and meeting students who were in pursuit of their doctoral degrees. It was time to make this happen. By this time, I knew that although I loved history, I was fascinated with the American Studies program at my current university. I made inquiries to the department head initially to see if any of my graduate credits from my previous master's program would transfer. After discovering that a minimal amount of my credits would transfer, I decided, after a recommendation from the department head, to enroll first as a non-degree seeking student and take just two courses to get reacclimated to being in school again. The school's policy is that if admitted to the program, these credit hours could be applied to my course of study. This is exactly what I did. Using my fee remission, I completed my M.A. in American Studies and was accepted into their doctoral program.

Thus far, it may seem like my doctoral journey was smooth despite it being intermittent. However, being in the classroom with students and professors who were younger than my son or my son's age proved challenging in some instances. For example, I often encountered ageist comments from students and occasionally a professor or two. I remember working on a curriculum vitae assignment in a graduate seminar. We had to bring our vitae to class with enough copies to share with our classmates and be prepared to discuss. After some brief discussion and Q&A about my vitae, the professor asked the following question," What else can we tell about Juanita from her vitae?" There were a few random comments but not what the professor was looking for, and so he responded, "we can tell she is not a spring chicken." I was taken aback a bit but quickly responded, "Well, if that's the case, what does that make you because you are older than I am!" The professor blushed profusely and later asked me to remain after class, and he apologized. In another case, a fellow student used the terms ancient and geezer when describing older people. I immediately spoke up. This was quite easy for me to do and truly very important to me because my research involves how Black women theorize menopause. I also look at how menopausal Black women are portrayed in popular media if they are portrayed at all.

After speaking up in class, it did not take long for my cohort and other classmates to be more cognizant of ageism. The highlight of my experience is when my peers come to me and share that they plan to include the issue of age in the courses they teach. Helping my colleagues to expand their intersectional analysis to be inclusive of age has been worth the ageist comments. Another difficulty I encountered by being an older student in the program and a full-time employee of the university is sometimes feeling disconnected from the social aspect of the program. By not having a grad assistantship and not having an office or cubicle in the department where graduate students gather and work, I didn't see many people in the program outside of class. This feeling was heightened when I was finished with coursework.

Although in my capacity as a university employee, I hired graduate students to work at the center, I still often felt disconnected. This disjointed feeling was exacerbated by the fact that I so desperately wanted a chance to teach.

I repeatedly expressed this to my department head, who was also on my dissertation committee, during our yearly meetings. I felt like I was in a very delicate position as a full-time employee of the university who was also a graduate student who was not receiving a graduate stipend or fellowship, which often came with teaching duties. How could I also enhance my vitae with teaching experience if never given the opportunity? Was I too old to even consider being on the job market in the traditional way most doctoral students are? These were questions that made me toss and turn some nights. Did my committee really understand how much of a dilemma this was for me, considering my age? When I was brave enough to be vulnerable with my dissertation chair, she said to me, " I think I can make it happen. I really did not know you were interested in teaching. Let me see what I can do." However, she also asked me, "What is it you really want to do once you're done?" I replied, "I would like to keep my present job or move to a higher level professional administrative position and also teach." I pointed to other people in the university who do both. As a full-time university employee to also serve as a graduate student instructor, I had to be approved for an overload. Once my supervisor and the head of the college where my department is approved, I was given the opportunity to teach an introduction to Women, Gender, and Sexuality Studies course. This was right in my wheelhouse since I had already earned the graduate certificate in the field offered by the university, and since my dissertation focus was on women, I was very familiar with the necessary literature and concepts.

As of this writing, I am finishing up my first semester of teaching the course. It has been wonderful for the most part. Having a chance to develop and practice my pedagogy to engage in a bilateral learning experience with students, many of whom have never had a Black teacher, has been exciting. Working and being a non-traditional student at PWI has taught me how to patiently coach and teach students to connect their personal narratives to the subjects and topics we are studying. As I reflect on the topic of this chapter, I would like to say the "where and when" I enter has been wherever the opportunity opens. Since I have been in the doctoral program, despite the moments of disconnection and losing my mom in my last year of coursework, I have also had the opportunity to present my research all over the world in places like Austria, Ireland, Poland, and Romania due to financial support from the university. In the aforementioned places, I was the only Black woman at the conferences. Being a member of the European Network of Aging Studies and the North American Network of Aging Studies has presented me with opportunities to publish and connect with people who are interested in my scholarship on Black women and menopause. I am eager to see what the next leg of the journey will be.

CHAPTER 9

Dominique Garrett-Scott's Story

DOM, SHORT FOR Dominique, Garrett-Scott (she/her) is a radically soft Black feminist poet-scholar, plus-size model, entrepreneur, and content creator hailing from Dallas, Texas. She holds a B.A. in Sociology with a concentration in African American Studies from the University of Mississippi and an M.A. in Sociology from the University of Texas. A former student, community, and labor organizer, Dom is currently a PhD student in the Sociology Department at the University of Texas at Austin. Her research investigates the relationship between misogynoir, fatphobia, and surveillance. Her dissertation research interrogates and theorizes fat, Black women's experiences with formal and informal surveillance pre-and post-bariatric surgery. You can follow her on all social media platforms @ domthefurious.

The Juggling Act: Undiagnosed, Untreated, and Going Under

"I just feel like I can't get my shit together." The words tumbled out of my mouth and sat on my chest as tears crawled down my face. I had never said it before, but the sentiment had been a shadow hanging around in corners for a while now. "It's not funny anymore. It's not cute or quirky. It's fucking up my life, and I don't know what to do."

Today was my initial assessment with a new psychiatrist to finally determine if I had ADHD or not. This was my first time meeting this psychiatrist, and I didn't like her. You know how people say, "they left a bad taste in my mouth?" Well, she left a sticky film on my teeth, like when you have sand on your feet and put your tennis shoes on. But here we were, sitting on a virtual call because I needed a diagnosis.

I had suspected that *something* was off years ago in college. I could never quite put my finger on it, but something about me was different. My obligations and responsibilities slipped through my fingers like snake oil, no matter how firmly I pressed them together and begged them to stay. My life was a juggling act – one I couldn't quite get the hang of.

In graduate school, things got worse. I was always dropping the ball on *something*. If I had to read a book for a class, I forgot the writing response. It would take hours and hours and hours to transcribe an interview because I couldn't sit and focus. And even when I finished, I couldn't celebrate too much because I would look up and discover that I had forgotten some meeting or appointment. I struggled with keeping up with the pace of my coursework. I waded through reading assignments, sometimes only being able to get through scraps of the book. I would be late to class because I couldn't find my keys, or I left my debit card; who knows where. I just couldn't get a handle on things.

I tried. I tried so hard to get it together. At first, I thought that I was just disorganized. It's not like I wanted to be so all over the place. It just kind of happened... and kept happening. I got planners, nice planners with thick, crisp, colorful stationery. Planners with thoughtfully crafted binding that housed stickers and habit trackers and bookmarks to keep me on track. You know the ones. The ones with an inspirational quote on every page. The planner that is guaranteed to set your life straight. With all the bells and whistles. I kept losing them or forgetting to write in them. Or I would leave them in who knows what tote that I put up who knows where. I set up calendar reminders for everything. Not just notifications, but I had Google send emails too. I still missed meetings, deadlines, and important appointments. I got the productivity apps. You know, the ones that track your habits or what you're doing with your time. I even paid for the Pro subscriptions! They were really only good for affirming that I needed more help than I could give myself.

In 2020, things really came to a head. I had started preparing for my comprehensive exams. With the end of my coursework, the juggling act got harder. Much harder. I was just left to my own devices, but I tried my best to come up with some semblance of a routine that would help me stay on top of studying. I was doing okay, not as well as my peers, but okay. I had a reading schedule that outlined what I would read and when. I had created a template for how to take notes. I changed the settings on my phone to block social media apps during the day to limit distraction. The juggling was clumsy, and I dropped the ball many a time, but I was juggling, nonetheless. Then the pandemic hit, and everything sort of fell apart, myself included.

I couldn't concentrate on anything. I was consumed by everything. There was a constant barrage of information about the spread of the virus and chaos at the grocery stores and the cases going up and school closures and the cases going up and travel restrictions and people dying and the cases going up. It all was just… too much. Every minute there was something new to know. And as the masochistic scholar that I am, I had to know all the things there were to know. I would pick up my phone every few seconds to doom scroll only to throw it down after being appalled or disgusted by some new insidious development, only to pick it right back up and do it all over again. Lather, rinse, and repeat.

I spent months isolated in my apartment as the days ran together. I can't tell you what I did in April or May, or June; that time is a blur to me now. The lack of structure did a number on my ADHD. I was not going to classes anymore. I couldn't go do work at coffee shops. The few accountability mechanisms that I had in place to help with my juggling act were gone. My apartment became the place where I was supposed to read, write, conduct interviews, take meetings, grade papers, attend lectures, send emails, cook my food, bathe, eat, sleep, and rest. It was difficult to transition from work mode to home mode when I had to sit on the same couch in the same apartment day after day. I would wake up with every intention of tackling a new task, but before I knew it, the day had slowly evaporated away – and I had nothing to show for it. I couldn't sit and work for any length of time before something snatched my attention. I could be in the thick of reading an article, and before I knew it, the dishes just had to be washed, or the laundry begged to be done. And beyond the untreated ADHD, the isolation and grief left a chill in the air. People were dying. The hospitals were at capacity. The police were still murdering us with impunity. My loved ones were getting sick. And here I was, still being expected to read a bunch of books and write a bunch of words…during a pandemic. It all felt so silly. I couldn't read. I couldn't write. I couldn't finish tasks, but I couldn't relax either. It was like being trapped in an endless cycle of guilt and defeat. I was just trying my best to stay whole as a person. My studenthood be damned.

But the world kept turning, and I still had exams. The date loomed closer and closer, and I couldn't get on top of it. My department had given everyone an extension on submitting their exams, and I didn't feel comfortable asking for another. How was it that they had given us two extra weeks to finish, and I couldn't even do that? I couldn't stomach the shame. So, I spat my exam responses on a Microsoft Word doc and submitted them. I passed. I waited and waited to feel different. I waited to feel pride and joy at overcoming such a major milestone.

But I felt no relief.

I was still spiraling.

Now I had my dissertation looking me in the eye, and I wasn't ready. I had barely gotten through my exams. The thought of writing a dissertation withered me down. Anxiety slithered in and nested in my bones. I began to doubt myself. *Maybe you're just not smart enough. It's not supposed to be this hard. Everyone else is publishing and presenting, and here you are. I really don't know how you even got into this program. You really finessed these folks. You're not even supposed to be here.* It is true what people say about comparison being the thief of joy. It tiptoed into my spirit and snatched away my self-confidence and certainty in myself. Two pillars that I had spent years building stone by stone began to weather in the wind. I was embarrassed at how hard it was for me to start and complete simple tasks. I was ashamed of how the advice "just write" just didn't work for me. For many, many, many moons, I did not look at anything dissertation-related. I went into autopilot, doing just enough to get by in my program but not really making any significant progress. I gave up on myself in a way that I didn't recognize. I was a skin of myself with no real body to me, my once mighty backbone now bent. The juggling act was no more. I dropped all the balls, and I didn't bother to care about picking them up.

During those months, I spent a lot of time on social media. Too much time on social media. So much time that I started to suspect that my ScreenTime notifications every Sunday were lying. But it was one of my few avenues to interact with other people. Like many other Americans, I started using TikTok. TikTok is a social media platform that hosts short-form videos in a variety of genres, including dances, tutorials, pranks, and daily vlogs. I came across a TikTok video about Black girls and ADHD. The topics in the video stepped all over my toes. In the video, the woman discussed how ADHD presented in Black girls and how and why it was commonly overlooked. It was like she was talking about me.

Things started to click into place. The hours and hours I spent in in-school suspension and detention for being too talkative. All of the times when my mind would wander away when people spoke. The mountain of tardy slips and truancy warnings for being chronically late to class. My 6-week stint in an alternative school in the 9th grade for "repetitive misconduct." Wait a minute. Did I... have ADHD? I thought, *naw*. A little voice said maybe.

I began looking into ADHD in women. I wasn't sure if it was just a string of coincidences or if I really had a neuroatypicality. *naw*. But as time progressed, the idea kept tickling the back of my brain. maybe. I went back and forth about it constantly. *naw*. I thought, am I just pathologizing my own laziness? maybe. Am I making a disorder out of my bad time management and lack of organization? *naw*. Am I self-diagnosing or should I trust myself and what I know? maybe. It went on for months. *nawmaybenawmaybenawmaybenawmaybenawmaybe*. Finally, after much research, maybe won. I decided to seek help from a psychiatrist for a formal evaluation. I figured the worst they could say was that I didn't have ADHD. And if I didn't, hopefully, they could help me with whatever the issue was.

I went through my insurance to find a psychiatrist who treats patients with adult ADHD. Thankfully, I have health insurance through my university. In order to take the test, one has to go through an initial evaluation with a psychiatrist, who will then refer you to take the test. I called a local mental health facility and set up the initial appointment.

On the day of the appointment, everything that could go wrong went wrong. The link to the virtual meeting would not connect. When it did connect, the psychiatrist and I could not hear each other. When we finally smoothed over the technical issues, the psychiatrist that I was assigned to was cold and aloof. This was not my first time encountering less than nice medical professionals in my life as a fat, Black woman. But I had handled her type before, and I knew that I had to advocate for myself regardless of her coldness. I needed help.

For the first time, I sat down and spoke candidly about the struggles I had experienced for years and how they had been exacerbated by the pandemic. As I strung the incidents together and laid out the consequences of constantly missing meetings and deadlines and appointments, I was struck by how deeply ADHD had affected me. It was a stain that leaked into every cranny and crevice of my life, and I hadn't even realized it. Before I knew it, I was sobbing in front of this cold woman, pouring myself out about how hard things had gotten for me. At the end of our appointment, she stated that she would go forward with the recommendation for the formal test. I was overjoyed. We scheduled the appointment, and the next week I took the test. I scheduled a follow-up with the psychiatrist for her to reveal the test results and talk to me about my options.

A week later, I opened the virtual window to the cold-faced psychiatrist and patiently waited for my results. As I expected, I had ADHD.

When I got my diagnosis, I felt like I had exhaled for the first time in months. I didn't even realize that I had been holding my breath. But the relief was short-lived, and the sweetness of discovery turned saccharine on my tongue. It was a relief to find that nothing was wrong with me. That I wasn't having so much trouble with everything because I was lazy or incompetent, but because I had a neurological disorder that made life different for me. I found myself mourning the chances missed and opportunities lost. I had fallen through the cracks so many times. I'm glad that I knew why, but it didn't change that it happened.

I wish that this was a story about triumph. I started to write it that way. But I didn't want to lie. Truthfully, I am still struggling with my ADHD. I want to be a success story; I really do. But I am not. Not yet (I hope). Getting access to my medication while caretaking out of state has been excruciatingly difficult (read: impossible). And figuring out my medication and dosage has been an absolute nightmare. Between insomnia and anxiety and heart palpitations, and loss of appetite, I am ready to throw up my hands. I wish I knew how many hoops I'd have to clamor through to get a decent treatment plan. I'm still not there. And I want to be there so bad. The truth is, if I don't get a handle on this monster, I won't finish my doctoral journey. I am in the 5th year of my program, and I still feel like I don't have much to show for it. I have given myself one more year to figure this out before I pack up and try to figure it out somewhere else. So, the journey continues. Stay tuned!

CHAPTER 10

Leeshe N. Grimes's Story

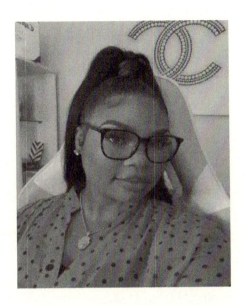

DR. LEESHE N. Grimes is a licensed professional counselor (LCPC), nationally certified counselor (NCC), registered play therapist (RPT), Psychotherapist, and Board-certified supervisor (LCPC-S). Dr. Grimes is the CEO/Founder of Elevated Minds, a private mental health practice in the DMV. Dr. Grimes is retired from the United States Army, which has afforded her the expertise in serving in many leadership positions. She has been in the mental health counseling field for over ten years. She leads various initiatives and has partnerships with several organizations to help break mental health barriers and ensure low-income Black and Brown communities and formerly incarcerated individuals have access to mental health services. Dr. Grimes received her B.A in Psychology from Hawaii Pacific University, M.S in Clinical Mental Health Counseling, Certification in Play Therapy, and PhD in Counselor Education and Supervision from Capella University. Dr. Grimes is an active member of Alpha Kappa Alpha Sorority Incorporated. She is very passionate about mental health and participates in numerous community service and outreach programs.

Girl, You Might Be Superwoman, but You're Still Human

Many days I look in the mirror and say, "Wow, little ole me from the hood in New York." Like girl, what?! You have a PhD! The reality is, I had been in survival mode starting at the age of four, and being successful still seemed foreign for a Black girl like me. Where I come from, a hood called "Cornhill," you're lucky not to get murdered by the time you turn 20. Being alive was a success in itself, so completing a Doctorate program often made me look at myself with surprise and doubt. "Nah, not me. I'm too hood. I'm not smart enough." School was something that always came easy for me. I was the student who never needed to study and would still be a straight-A student. I was the student who was literally at war in Iraq or would party all night long and still have a 4.0. Definitely a gift.

When I was in residency for my master's program, my professor at the time was a Black woman who had served in the military and was very inspirational. I remember getting upset when other students got feedback on what they needed to improve on, but she had none for me. This was a common thing amongst my professors. I remember telling her, "It has to be something; I am not perfect." Her words to me were, "Stop looking for the struggle. You are above where you currently need to be. Everything in life doesn't involve a struggle. It is okay to accept being successful. Your struggle may arise, but it hasn't yet. Get comfortable with this moment." When she said this to me, I was actually speechless. I never thought of myself as being successful. It was like a light went off. I was stuck and couldn't even move physically. I had never thought of myself as being successful, so mentally, this was mind-blowing. I looked at hard work as being a part of life. I just looked at myself as doing what I needed to do to survive in this world. That was one of my first mistakes. I had replaced the feeling of joy with the sense of being accomplished. Sprinkle in some perfectionism and not feeling good enough, yea, a recipe for imposter syndrome. At residency, this same professor told me, "You would be a great doctor in this field. We need more people like you." When she said this, I laughed! "Girl, what?! Not me. I'm done with school after this degree, ain't no way." Fast forward to two quarters later, I was asking that same professor, we'll call her Professor D, for a letter of recommendation to apply for a doctoral program. She was extremely excited. I think even more excited than me.

A few quarters later and I am now in my doctoral program. I am still on active duty in the Army and a senior leader, so my time was minimal. The first class was a breeze. It was so easy for me; I decided to take more than one class at a time. I remember saying, "man, why people be complaining about doctoral programs? It's so easy." I definitely ate those words. We'll get into that later. For this program, I had to complete three residencies. Imagine how excited I was to have Professor D as my first residency professor. Yes, the same Professor D from my master's residency and who had written my letter to get into the Doctorate program. Let me also mention Professor D was a strict professor, honestly the only professor to challenge me in all my schooling. I had an amazing time at that residency. During my second residency, not so much. I literally had 48hrs to rewrite my defense proposal, which required new research and a new topic because the school no longer approved my original proposal and topic. I broke down completely. I was in a frenzy. I literally left the classroom crying. I went to my room and cried for about an hour more as I packed my bags. This was it. I wasn't fit to be in a doctoral program. I was defeated, tired, disappointed, and exhausted. How in the world was I going to get months of research done in 48hrs and still be passionate about it. I even reached out to Professor D in tears. I explained to her what had happened. She helped me gather my thoughts, and I was able to refine my research without losing months of work. I promise Professor D was God-sent!

I had a few more classes to finish up, and boy, did I feel like I was just dumb. I didn't understand this one class at all. Nothing made sense to me. Again I told myself, "Man, I am not smart enough for this." I reached out to other colleagues, and to my surprise, they felt the exact same way about this course. Only God knows how I passed with an A because honey, sis was lost and confused just winging it.

I eventually finished up all my classes, and the only things left were a comprehensive exam, practicum, and two internships. All of these things I thought were going to be a breeze. Here's where I ate those words from earlier. I failed my comprehensive exam. I was distraught! I had a complete breakdown. I couldn't believe that I had failed it: I, a 4.0 student who had never failed anything in school. I had a panic attack. I called Professor D, who had become my mentor. She was able to calm me down, but I was defeated. From undergraduate to graduate school, this was the first time I failed. It was also school policy that failing this test was grounds for withdrawal from the program. Imposter syndrome was back. At that point, I said I was done with this doctoral degree. But that voice inside of me just couldn't give up.

I went over the requirements rigorously and decided to appeal the grade. I just wasn't convinced that I had failed this exam. The feedback from the professors contradicted themselves. You are only allowed to take the comprehensive exam two times in this program. I was convinced I wasn't treated fairly. While I appealed this grade, I wasn't in school for two quarters. The appeal came back, and I had lost. I had to decide to withdraw from school or retake the comprehensive exam. I decided to retake the exam. I received my compressive exam for the second time, and I received the same exact questions but with minor information added at the end of the questions. I should explain that this exam was three questions and amounted to 19 written pages. All I did was add the new information to the questions asked and resubmitted my exam. What do you know, it passed with no problems. This convinced me that I was just targeted the first time around because what was the other explanation? There wasn't one. I felt I was targeted because I was Black. Other colleagues who had the same issue were also Black. None of my white colleagues said they had failed comps the first time around.

I started asking other colleagues about their experience in the doctoral program and noticed only my Black colleagues were experiencing a lot of difficulties. Out of eight Black colleagues, only one passed the comprehensive exam the first time, and out of 12 white colleagues, only two had failed the comprehensive exam the first time around. We decided to create a group chat to compare our experiences and keep each other updated. This group chat would only enforce what many thought; Black students were treated very differently from white students.

We were now in our internship phase, where we would be paired with doctoral-level professors to teach the master-level students. Y'all, I wanted to fight one of my professors. I had gone over the expectations and what was required of us in the internship. I wanted to make sure I was prepared. This particular professor wanted me, and I say me because there were other white students who were also interning with this same professor. She wanted me to do a lot that was outside of the scope of the requirements. I asked the other white students, and they didn't get the same requirements as me. Some of her requirements were that I had to grade student papers in 24 hours while my white counterparts got four days! When I refused, she commented, "You people want everything handed to you. You don't want to work hard for it." First, it was the "You people," where I turned her off and wanted to fight. I wanted to fight this professor because I felt she disrespected me and was racist toward me. This fueled my anger. She refused to give me the hours I reported and insinuated I was lying. Without the hours, I couldn't pass the internship. I reported her to the school, and instead of being removed from her class, another professor allowed me to work with her and get the missing hours. I was livid this was happening and really had an "F these white people's standards" mindset. Again, I was over this doctoral program and wanted to quit. When I realized I wasn't the only Black student with this problem, that lit a fire under my a**. We grouped up and supported each other. We told each other that we all would finish no matter what. A sisterhood was formed, and a support system was developed.

Completing the internship was challenging; I started to hate the program but felt giving up would be giving up on those who may come after me. I found a new motivation to keep going. We were able to request our committee. Of course, I requested Professor D and two others I really wanted. I was nervous because no one was getting who they requested. When I saw Professor D was the chair of my dissertation committee, you couldn't tell me that wasn't God again. I didn't get the other two, but I got her.

I wrote my first two chapters very quickly with no issues at all. I told myself,

"This will be a breeze." My confidence was back. I felt amazing. But then, life happened. The world was changed forever. COVID-19 showed up, causing a pandemic. Due to COVID-19, I had to stop researching and wait to receive the Internal Review Board (IRB) approval again. Mentally, I was frustrated and upset. I had the "if it's not one thing, it's another" mindset. My motivation went right out the window. All of my protocols had to change. Once again, I was revamping and working against a clock. Going back and forth with IRB took two quarters to finally get my study approved again. During that process, I was tired of reading articles and looking at my study. By the time I started interviewing participants again, tragedy had struck. My cousin was murdered back home. This brought me to my knees. I would have told you there wasn't any air left to breathe. We were one month apart, and we had been close our entire lives. Unfortunately, dealing with murder was a common theme in my life.

Just when I thought I was back on track and motivated, I wasn't. My dissertation was the furthest thing from my mind. I was retired from the Army, working on a doctorate, running a successful private practice, living in the home I built ground up, and I didn't need or want for anything. But when this happened, I asked the question, "Do we ever really make it out of the hood? Yes, we are physically out, but mentally we're still there. So do we ever make it out?" I started questioning everything I was doing, like what was the point? What will change? I went into a deep depression dealing with grief. I was not meeting any of my school requirements. I actually tried to withdraw from that quarter, but it was too late.

Shortly after the murder of my cousin, I was in a bad car accident. My car was totaled, and I sustained a concussion, TMJ, lower back, right hip, and right arm injury. A car hit me at a red light. This all happened mid-quarter. I remember telling my mentor this just isn't for me. Everything that has happened has to be a sign that I am not meant to be in this doctoral program. I was constantly fighting to be in the program but felt I was drowning. My head was not above water. I was also fighting not to quit because I had never quit on anything I set out to do. So, while I felt my head wasn't above water, it also wasn't completely in the water. People were reaching out to me, and I was getting random messages about how I inspired them. I needed this. It gave me a little hope. A mantra that came from this to help increase hope was, "It's bigger than you." I wrote this on sticky notes and placed them in various locations. I couldn't quit.

I wasn't meeting any of my deadlines. Professor D knew this wasn't in my character. She reached out to me and told me to take some time off. I tried to convince her that I could still get things done before the end of the quarter. She told me, "No. You're done for this quarter. I know you're superwoman, but you're still human. You need to take care of yourself." Boy, did Professor D know how to get to me. I told her I couldn't afford not to pass the quarter, but she insisted I did enough work that would still allow me to pass even if I didn't submit anything else. At that moment, I asked myself, "Why was I rushing?" I told myself, "I am going to finish. I need to deal with the present moment. What's for me is for me. Take care of your mental health." That's precisely what I did. I took a break from school to take care of myself.

Over and over, I kept asking myself that same question, "What's the rush?" I no longer missed out on moments with my friends and family. While school was a priority, I found that work, school, and life balance, and guess what? I was finally happy. I no longer identified as a strong, resilient Black woman. While those describe me, I didn't want who I am to be associated with that. I felt it made me inhuman to others and myself. So many people were telling me I was inspirational, but I wanted them to know my life was nowhere near peaches and cream. I started becoming more vocal about the challenges in my life and school, from a survivor of attempted suicide, sexual and physical abuse, sexual assault, PTSD, depression, anxiety, grief, ADHD, and racism. No one had a clue of what it took to be me. I am the first Doctor in my family. Nothing was handed to me. It was a struggle; every odd you could think of was stacked against me. When I say I got it out of the mud, I got it out of the mud. But just because I had to doesn't mean you have to. I realized that this journey was bigger than me. I had to say F them people and go for what I wanted and add to the Black culture. We go through many things in life that are not for ourselves but for others.

As you can see, Professor D, a Black woman like me, encouraged this journey before I knew I would embark on it. A retired Black woman from the Army, like me, supported me when she wasn't even officially my mentor yet. A Black woman mental health clinician, like me, understood the superwoman complex of a Black woman and helped me find peace in resting. Professor D, a Black woman Doctor like me. She helped me from start to finish on this journey and was the first to call me Dr. Grimes. If God didn't send her, I don't know who did. But it all came full circle.

If I could leave you with a few things, I would say, don't quit. Take your time. You are smart enough. You deserve to be in the same room as your white counterparts. Speak up about what is happening to you, especially if you feel it is unjust. Reach out for help! We have to become the change we want. If we want to see more doctors who look like us and can understand us, we must become those doctors. It is a journey, a roller-coaster, and a horror film sometimes, but neither lasts always. Taking a break is not quitting. You deserve to rest! Get a support group that understands that current journey. You have the power to disrupt unjust systems for our Black and Brown community. You must first start within. You have to want it bad enough. It is not easy. Don't lose yourself. Take care of your mental health and understand that even though you are superwoman, you are still human!

CHAPTER II

N'Dea Irvin-Choy's Story

N'DEA IRVIN-CHOY IS a 4th-year PhD Candidate in Biomedical Engineering. Her current research focuses on the use of nanoparticle-based systems for maternal and fetal applications. N'Dea earned her B.S. in Biomedical Engineering, where she conducted research on the use of porous materials for orthopedic implants and discovered her interest in research.

N'Dea is passionate about diversifying the Science, Engineering, Technology, and Mathematics fields and encourages underrepresented students to pursue higher education through her social media platforms. Through her blog and various social media accounts, N'Dea aims to be a role model and representation for students who may not have traditional forms of access or exposure to the sciences. She serves as a mentor to first-year graduate students and undergraduate students of color and participates in many science-focused outreach programs in her community.

In her leisure time, N'Dea enjoys reading mysteries and memoirs at her favorite place, the beach. She is an avid yogi, loves sports, and exploring new creative projects.

The Black Biomedical Engineering Sheep

I trudged up the hill and glanced behind me to see how steep it was. It wasn't steep at all, but I was already out of breath. The parking lot at the bottom of the hill was packed, but somehow, by the grace of God, I found a spot not too far from the conference hall entrance. At the top of the hill stood the campus conference hall. Graduate student volunteers stood outside, all wearing university gear, and smiled as I walked past. I recognized one person from my department, gave a shy wave, then turned towards the door. Still out of breath, I got in line for orientation check-in. There was only one person in front of me, which gave me just enough time to check my phone for the time. 8:45 AM. I was 15 minutes early for orientation, but the check-in line was almost empty. Where was everyone?

After check-in, I moseyed over to the breakfast/coffee table. If I'm going to be here all day, I might as well get something good to eat, right? Wrong. All the morning pastries were gone. Bagels were nowhere to be found, and the only thing left of the fruit spread was honeydew melon.

I'm 15 minutes early! How could I be so late??

Realizing I was late to the party, I quickly made a cup of tea and headed to the conference room. Just as I suspected, the conference room was filled with eager first-year graduate students. The seats, maybe 400, were neatly lined up in rows, with an empty lane down the middle. The front rows were jammed-packed with students, with no empty seats in sight. Luckily, I entered the conference room near the back and could scan the room from behind.

Unsurprisingly, there were more blonde and brunette heads than coiled curls, but not to the ratio I expected. I knew I signed myself up for a doctoral program at a PWI, but I didn't expect the difference to be THIS stark. The volunteer usher must've picked up on the confusion on my face because she quickly found me a seat, which happened to be next to another Black girl. After a few dozen *Excuse me's* and *Pardon's*, I sat down and looked around to see where I could place my purse. "I think it's okay to put it on the floor this one time," chuckled the Black girl. "I don't know," I responded nervously. "I'll just hold it on my lap. We already get paid pennies as is." With a smile, she introduced herself as a first-year English doctoral student. She, too, was new to the area and hadn't met anyone from her cohort yet. I had never met anyone who was an English major, so out of curiosity, I asked about her program.

After answering all my questions (and there were a lot of them), she finally asked, "What's your major?" This was the moment I was avoiding and have always avoided during small talk. In undergrad, I quickly learned that most non-Black people didn't believe me when I told them my major or my class schedule. If I told them the truth, I'd have to prove I was enrolled and had classes in the engineering building. On the other hand, if I made up a lie, I'd be undercutting myself and all the hard work I'd done to stay in the program.

But with Black people, it was a completely different story. Telling the truth about my studies would suddenly make me the modern-day Mary Jackson or a Black Iron Woman. I would be badgered with questions about how freakishly smart I was or if I could build them a bionic limb, or how much money I made. In either case, it was just easier to avoid the topic altogether and ask the other person questions to make the time go by, but for whatever reason, I decided to answer. "I'm in the biomedical engineering program," I responded.

Immediately, her facial expression changed. "Oh, so you're like REALLY smart?"

"Uhm, I guess," I nervously laughed. "I've never met anyone in English, though. I love reading, but writing isn't really my strong suit. How can you write all the time and not run out of things to say?" Here I was defaulting to my normal method of asking them questions so they could talk about themselves again. Before she could answer, the speaker tapped the microphone to get our attention. They were beginning the orientation, so I was saved by the bell. The minute orientation started, I zoned out. Speakers came and went from the podium, but all I could think about was my name tag. My name was spelled correctly, thankfully, but I couldn't get over the title beneath it. *Doctoral Student.* How the hell did I, a Black girl from a small town in New Jersey, even get here?

Immediately, my mind went back to undergrad. I attended a small Division III university, where I played varsity field hockey while studying biomedical engineering. My graduation pictures were liked on Instagram, but my journey wasn't as picture-perfect as it seemed. The truth is, I didn't even know biomedical engineering existed until my sophomore year of college. I had been rejected from the chemical engineering program for the second time and was feeling lost. Luckily, I was offered a spot in the biomedical engineering program, and even though I had only done a quick Google search to learn about the major and possible job positions, I had no idea what I was truly getting myself into when I accepted the offer.

To my dismay, the classes were more difficult than I had anticipated. I, the former high school math whiz, was now in a class of math prodigies. My classmates had taken engineering classes in high school, scored flying colors on their AP exams, and went to science camps during the summer. Not only did I sell candy bars to pay for sports equipment and field hockey tournaments in high school, but I also hadn't been exposed to engineering concepts in school. I quickly learned that my high school weekends spent working at an assisted living center didn't compare to my classmates' weekends spent at design competitions. And now, here I was in college, trying to stay afloat in Calculus II while still attending practices during the week and traveling for games on the weekends.

College was rough, to say the least.

Now with graduate school, I was entering a new chapter in a whole new world, but this time at a bigger PWI. Everyone smiled at me and gave me their welcome, but it felt different. It felt foreign. And I was the obvious Black sheep. Overwhelmed and underfed, I left the graduate student orientation, and the next day I was introduced to my cohort. What I had feared had been confirmed: I was the only Black person. When I met the rest of the department, I was the only Black person there. And when the semester started, I was often the only Black person in my classes, although sometimes I would get lucky and be one of two to three Black people.

Everywhere I went, I was the "only," and although no one pointed it out or said it aloud, it was shown in the way I dressed, the music I listened to, and even my approach to problem-solving. I didn't fit in the bill of a typical biomedical engineer, and not seeing anyone that looked like me reinforced that fact every single day. The first couple of months of my first year flew by faster than I can remember. I spent the weekdays learning experiments in the lab, reading papers, and soaking up as much information as I could. In the evenings, I studied for my classes, prepared presentations, and read more papers until I fell asleep. My schedule barely afforded me time to eat or exercise, but when I found time, I almost always used it to sleep. Life went on like this through my first year, up until I had an anxiety attack.

I was preparing for my qualifying exam that was scheduled for the end of the summer and was incredibly nervous about it. The qualifying exam is the first milestone of a PhD program that tests your knowledge and understanding of your field or curriculum. In my program, that meant writing a seven-page paper and giving a 15-minute presentation with a 60-minute question and answer session with the committee.

Despite the qualifying exam being months away, I was terrified. I was also completely new to running wet-lab experiments and often spent time researching and practicing protocols that many of my other cohort members already knew. Not to mention, I had almost failed a class my first semester that my cohort raved was the easiest class they had ever taken. If it weren't for my professor giving me extra credit to bump my grade up by 3 points, I would've spent even more time retaking the class and less time learning in the lab. Considering how my first year went as a PhD student and how exhausted I was every day, I didn't feel prepared for the qualifying exam at all.

To ease what I didn't know was imposter syndrome and anxiety, I began reading and studying for my qualifying exam at the beginning of the summer. Although most people reassured me that I would do well, my anxiety had me questioning myself more than ever before. I would spend hours preparing slides for a ten-minute research update with my advisor, and I would take extensive notes when reading journal articles and seminars and pay extremely close attention to how people responded to me, my ideas, or even casual conversation. I was analyzing every moment of my workday while lying in bed at night, and because of it, I rarely had a full night of sleep. *What did that person mean when they said that? Do they know I almost failed that class? Do they pick up my mistakes more because I'm Black? What will I do if I don't pass my qualifying exam? Do I even belong here?*

These questions ran through my mind almost every morning for almost two weeks up until I had my first anxiety attack. I was stopped at a red light, minutes away from the lab, and was crying uncontrollably. My heart was racing, and because I didn't know what was happening, I became even more scared and cried even harder. The light turned green, but I was too busy trying to figure out what was going on with me to notice. There weren't any cars around me, probably because it was so early in the morning, so I sat at the light until I could collect myself.

By the time I pulled into the lab parking lot, I had calmed down enough to text my friend, "I think I'm going to try going to therapy."

Growing up in a predominantly Black and Latinx environment, therapy wasn't discussed. The only thing I knew about therapy was what I saw on tv shows, and from what I saw, people like me didn't go to therapy. Therapy was for rich, white girls, but not me. Luckily, my perception of therapy changed when it was openly discussed by other graduate students in my department. They spoke about the **free** options that were available for graduate students at my university and how they readily used them. Until graduate school, I didn't think therapy was something I would ever need, but my anxiety attack quickly changed my mind.

After my first session, I was set up with a therapist at the counseling center and began attending sessions weekly. For the first time since I had arrived at graduate school, I felt like my concerns and worries were heard and seen. It wasn't unusual that I felt isolated and unable to relate to my cohort and colleagues. It was, in fact, normal that I, a Black woman in a predominantly white male field, felt like I was constantly being analyzed and criticized for my mistakes. According to the NY Times Evaluation Bias Study, employees of color are disproportionately likely to receive lower ratings compared to white employees. This fact, among many others that applied to me, confirmed what I had already known and was feeling in the first year of my program.

With the help of my therapist, I began to learn about techniques and tools to keep me grounded and focused on my short-term goals of passing my qualifying exam, improving my sleep patterns, and changing my negative thoughts. Slowly, I started to see improvements in myself. I wasn't comparing myself to the members of my cohort anymore, nor was I overanalyzing other people's behavior or comments. I continued therapy through the summer and my qualifying exam, which I passed, and although I saw the improvements in my behavior, I didn't tell anyone I was in therapy except the friend I initially texted that day of my anxiety attack. I was still afraid of being labeled as "crazy" or "troubled," as I had heard family members and close friends say about those that sought external help for their mental health. But after several weeks of lying about where I was going or why I wasn't available during certain hours of the day, I finally started telling people I was in therapy and attending sessions at those times. I spoke about how it really helped me in managing my anxiety, improving my sleep patterns, and increasing my appetite. I told them how I was beginning to feel more stable and comfortable in graduate school and no longer feared other people's opinions or judgment.

In those moments, I had decided that if I were going to be judged by anyone, I would at least want to be judged for who I truly am. I had it hard enough being a PhD student in a challenging program surrounded by people that didn't look like me, so the added pressure of maintaining a fake persona that I "had it all together" was only adding more stress to my life. I knew staying in the PhD program would mean I would have to continue giving more than the average time, effort, and energy compared to my white counterparts, and if I wanted to do that, it would be best for me to eliminate unnecessary stressors in my life.

Reflecting on my first year of graduate school now, I am grateful for the people that broke the stigma around therapy and told me about the resources available on campus. While I made many mistakes in my first year of graduate school, I thank myself every day for having the courage to try therapy and show up as my whole self in those sessions. The transition to graduate school was not easy for me, but I am still here pursuing my doctoral degree and attending therapy. Despite any challenges or setbacks that come along with graduate school, one day, I will look back on those moments, then look at my degree on the wall or pictures in my cap and gown and be proud of the hardships I have overcome.

CHAPTER 12

Elisabeth Jeffrey's Story

ELISABETH JEFFREY IS a Ph.D. candidate in Biochemistry at the University of Miami Miller School of Medicine in Miami, Florida. After earning degrees in Art and STEM from Broome Community College, Elisabeth continued her education at SUNY Oneonta, where she conducted synthesis research, developed a fashion line, and earned a B.S. in Chemistry before transitioning to the University of Miami. Her current research focuses on the impact of the gut microbiome after spinal cord injury in collaboration with the United States Department of Defense and The Miami Project to Cure Paralysis.

Elisabeth is a member of Phi Theta Kappa, Iota Sigma Pi, and Chi Alpha Epsilon honor societies, a 2021 McKnight Dissertation Fellow, and serves on the Diversity, Equity, and Inclusion committee for Graduate Women in Science (GWIS). She uses vertical and horizontal mentorship to advocate for mental health, creative expression, and increased access to STEM education for communities of color.

Away from the bench, Elisabeth is a health consultant specializing in integrative wellness education to help people make evidence-based decisions about their health. She is passionate about utilizing microbiome-based research and education to support the health and life of historically underserved populations.

Opportunity, Perspective, and Taking Control

Life is usually not linear. Shared stories develop individuality; and help others find their path. When I heard about the opportunity to take part in this book, I knew it was my turn to share. For a long time, I struggled to find confidence in my future, because I wasn't represented in my environment. Looking back, it was often this uncertainty fueled by this lack of representation that made my path maybe a little less linear than it could have been. I'm grateful, as you'll see I learned, I am not alone.

I've accomplished a lot of things I didn't know were possible on the way to this PhD. I'd like others to know it's possible for them too. Especially those who have felt the fear of their dreams even before they could be defined. You don't have to know the "how" to get there. School wasn't hard as a kid, but I had very few distractions and a lot of resources. I grew up in a small town in upstate NY with religious Caribbean parents who homeschooled me for most of my primary education. The hands-on approach cemented my love of learning early on. After high school, an academic route felt natural. Partially because it was encouraged by my parents, but mostly because it was fun for me. Not once in the first 3 years and 2 degrees of college did I consider what might come after. I enjoyed school so much I had little issue focusing all my energy there and no mentors to guide me toward career exploration in college. So, I kept going to school (Don't be me y'all) Though I didn't know better at the time, the whole point of college is to support what you will do…. after college. There are lots of resources for this at most schools, seek them out.

What I did get to explore earlier in undergrad was independent research. I started working on inorganic synthesis to create stereo-specific carbon bonds that could be used to create pharmaceuticals. I already loved the classroom format, getting to break out on my own was an indescribable thrill. In the 2nd semester of junior year one of my other teachers mentioned a paid summer internship program called REU (Research Experiences for Undergraduates). I was late to the game with this one, most application deadlines had already passed, and these programs were notoriously competitive. So what? I was already excited to be getting course credit for research, now I could get some money too!? Despite having no time to prepare I applied for every program for which the deadline had not passed. I was accepted to ONE at a UC School on the other side of the country, but all I heard was "yes". This experience was my introduction to translational science and I LOVED IT! Senior year in New York was a continuation of research exposure culminating in multiple awards, fueled by my positive experience from the summer.

Opportunities.

Six months later, I walked across the stage to receive a B.S. in chemistry. I was happy about the achievement, but didn't really feel a sense of excitement to look forward to after graduation. I was walking across the stage knowing I wouldn't be continuing school in the fall. I didn't know what to do next.

I didn't always know I wanted to go to graduate school, because I didn't know what graduate school was. When I decided to apply I had very little guidance on how to do so. I looked for programs with good stipends and research including public health emphasis. Johns Hopkins was the only place I really wanted to go. If you're interested in grad school, the interview process is key. Typically, about 1-5% of applicants make it to this point, but since I had no idea what to expect, I got waitlisted.

I wasn't deterred for long. I wouldn't say the concept of a "gap year" was really introduced to me, it just happened. I chose not to settle, and to see the rejection as an opportunity. So, I got a job as a pharmacy technician at a 24hr pharmacy. I was about 4 months into the position when it was time to apply for grad school again. Despite enjoying pharmacy life, I missed research and the position was more fun than stimulating. This time around I had a better understanding of what to expect, to make sure I could get in where I wanted to go. I aced the interviews, packed up my gold Toyota Avalon and drove the 1354 miles to…Miami! (because, let's be real, Baltimore is still cold) Not getting into the grad school I wanted the first time sure felt like a failure at first. Have the confidence to see things that don't turn out as you plan for opportunities.

Perspective.

In the summer of 2014, after accepting that I wasn't going to grad school this year, I enrolled in a clinical lab tech program in my hometown. I was confident this was something I would enjoy, but 1 week into the program it became clear I was wrong. The foundation I had was academically beyond this program and I likely wouldn't be stimulated, to enjoy it long-term. This realization solidified my decision to attend graduate school. When I went to the director's office to tell her I would be withdrawing from the program her exact words were "this is the best opportunity you are going to get." In her mind this was a bad decision. Luckily, I had a different perspective.

Choose your perspective by focusing on your why and creating an environment for yourself that frames this purpose with certainty. A perspective shift can pull you from the deepest hole to the highest peak and keep you moving forward.

You are in control.

Sometimes life can make you feel like you're not in control and while it's true you can't control everything, You are in control of your perspective.

I came to Miami in July so I could start my PhD over the summer. That's how excited I was, after all I had waited a YEAR. Miami was a complete culture shock from the language to the traffic, unlike anything I had ever experienced. I wasn't just awestruck by palm trees, but also by million-dollar equipment, and top-level investigators. The first year of my program entailed classes, rotations, and ultimately choosing an advisor, the latter of which is considered a degree defining decision. It wasn't a smooth ride. At the end of my first rotation, I left the middle of my presentation in tears. The advisor constantly interrupted me with comments and questions which I couldn't seem to answer to their standards. I was later informed by other students in the program that this advisor was known for his abrasiveness. This was just the first of many challenges I found unique to grad school. From that point my priority shifted. Mentally, if I was going to succeed, I had to find someone I could trust and I found her. Once I joined the lab, I was completely immersed. I genuinely enjoyed the research and adapted well. I didn't register the building mental toll, or the fact that I invested little energy into maintaining a life outside of work to balance that pressure. I didn't know what burnout was and I didn't even really want to take breaks or work less than 10-hour days. I thought I was fine. I was not fine.

Spring semester, after flying back from my first presentation at an international conference, I noticed my ears bothering me. It wasn't always pain and never lasted long but about a month later I realized "my ears should have normalized from that flight by now". The following year provided a steady supply of nonspecific pain and deep exhaustion that rendered me unable to keep up appearances socially or drag myself to lab more than once a week. When I finally did seek medical attention, they ran tests, tried medications, and therapies, and ultimately left me with a list of diagnoses they described as physical manifestations of mental stress. I had no kind of framework, or support system to help deal with this. The psychologist used scary terms like "dark night of the soul", and "quarter-life crisis" but she was the first person to present me with genuine freedom of choice. I decided to leave the PhD. Without a solid "why", I was risking my mental health to continue in that state. More than 40% of PhD students in Science, Engineering, and Math do not complete their degree and graduate students are more than 6 times more likely to experience mental health issues compared to the general population.

After mastering out, the options were overwhelming, but I had to start somewhere. I tried teaching. I found this experience to be very rewarding as I was able to see a direct impact that I had on the kids, however I really didn't feel challenged and was starting to crave an aspect of science in my work. Then I found a job posting for a "wellness specialist". After 6 months of interviewing and clinical training, I was a wellness specialist. I had discovered a company that hired medical professionals and scientists to provide evidenced-based health information at no cost to the public.

This job connected all the dots for me. I had been missing the context and experience needed to visualize a marriage of my gained skills in research, and impact on public health. Thinking through the most logical ways to develop my platform while also getting to do research again. I landed on a PhD, ironically the same program I was in not too long ago. After expressing my goals with my former advisor, she agreed to help me re-enter her lab.

Going back to a PhD after mastering out wasn't something I knew to be possible when I made the decision. Now I know, just like everything else in life, anything is possible. Don't let my current confidence sway you, this was a difficult transition, and I felt crazy for most of it. I was taking a significant pay cut, and commuting well over 2 hours a day, not to mention the mental energy and time, plus I had a life partner to consider. And probably most terrifying of all, I had literally "been there, done that", so I knew a little too well what I would be getting myself into. I had so carefully considered my decision to leave, why would I go back?! I felt that fear in my bones. But it simply was not the same for me this time. The best way I can explain it as I've reflected, is that I could now visualize my purpose in the context of a PhD. And through the process I've learned to take a step, even when I can't see the next one, it's still there. For me this translated to a very deep sense of confidence that has allowed me to continue, because quite frankly the challenges of doing a PhD as Black woman haven't changed at all. Work-life balance and mental health are still not prioritized the way they should be. I often remind myself to ask for help, take a break, or simply refocus on my perspective. But having a clear vision of my purpose in this program is a special kind of motivation. This process has also taught me so much and I'm grateful for the privilege to share the ups and downs of my journey. My hope is to be an encouragement to little girls with big dreams. I would not be here had I not continued to show up for myself. Find the community that will support those dreams and you can do it. Let us be an example. You are not alone.

"If your dreams don't scare you, they aren't big enough."

CHAPTER 13

Tabitha Esther's Story

TABITHA IS A 5th-year PhD candidate in Epidemiology at the New York University Grossman of Medicine - Vilcek Institute. As a spatial & social epidemiologist, Tabitha understands the multi-level social-ecological framework that neighborhood & community has on health outcomes being raised in low-income neighborhoods. This passion has led her to work at the NYC Department of Health & Mental Hygiene and NYS Department of Health after completing her Master of Public Health from the SUNY Albany School of Public Health. Her current research focuses on understanding the role of modifiable behavioral and environmental respiratory drivers of accelerated aging in older adults to identify solutions that slow the progression of accelerated aging and reduce socioeconomic and racial aging disparities. Within the Department of Population Health (DPH) at NYU Langone, she is a member of the DPH Anti-Racism Coalition (ARC), whose mission is to identify, measure, and dismantle structural racism. When she is not analyzing disease trends, she is The #BodyConfident Coach and creator of the #UnshakeableBodyConfidence movement. A movement where your body finds acceptance and your unique brand of beauty finds confidence. As a woman who suffered from body dysmorphia, underwent weight loss surgery, and multiple plastic surgery procedures, she created #BodyCon

University to support women who are considering the same route she took. As a purpose-driven project #BodyCon University is a coaching program to help women heal body image issues pre-and post surgery while educating them on their personal body science to maintain surgical results.

A Broken Heart, A Journey Pivoted.

"Public Health broke my heart." I expressed to my doctoral advisor of four years during the peak of the COVID-19 pandemic in May 2020. My reflection on my computer screen during this week's Zoom session reflected the floodgates of the tears of my West Indian community in Crown Heights, Brooklyn, New York. The community who raised me, a daughter of immigrants from St. Martin & Guyana... was dying. Shoot, my father almost passed. "Ping!" Yet another WhatsApp notification of a funeral announcement from one of my family members. I put my phone on mute.

What is life? I thought as I closed my laptop computer screen. Nothing made sense. I started this doctoral journey with a vision of wearing that deep violet New York University graduation gown while walking across that graduation stage. My million-dollar smile is beaming as I hold my doctorate from the prestigious NYU Grossman School of Medicine (NYU GSOM) within 4.5 years. *Yeah, I was that bish*. A culmination of dreams coming true after walking with an empty bag of self-worth that at times felt heavier than floor-length faux locs. Trying to find my place in the research world over the last ten years had its own direct line to the demolition of my self-confidence.

How could it be that a pandemic that seemingly came out of the script of Contagion deter the plan I set forth? In the blink of an eye, I had become a 4th-year doctoral student without a defended dissertation proposal and no clear vision of what was to come. I sat in my apartment with my eyes focused upward. The force of my body-shaking sigh triggered yet another wave of tears. I was frozen in time with waves of pain, confusion, and anxiety.

What do I even do now? I'm lost. The foundation of my identity also seemed in question. *Who is Tabitha without science?*

God provided the answer throughout the next year. I found her through intimate talks with God, sensual escapades, and finding my voice. I guess you can say I found my purpose through the gravel of COVID19.

This is my story. It is a story of transitions, endings, and new beginnings that led to finding my purpose.

Welcome.

Allow me to introduce myself and give a brief rundown of my professional and academic history just for context. My name is Tabitha Esther, and I am a 5th-year doctoral student at the NYU GSOM within the Department of Population Health. Prior to joining NYU, I was a Research Scientist at the New York City Department of Mental Health & Hygiene (NYCDOHMH) and the New York State Department of Health (NYSDOH). I received my Master of Public Health (MPH) with a concentration in Epidemiology from the State University of New York (SUNY) Albany School of Public Health. I attended the City University of

New York (CUNY) Brooklyn College and was a part of the National Institute of Health-funded Minority Access to Research Careers (MARC) program. MARC is a two-year honors undergraduate program that aims to increase the number of underrepresented scientists in biomedical and behavioral fields while preparing them to pursue a PhD in basic science. Now the perks of the MARC program were that it paid your tuition and provided a stipend of $985 a month. That was a lot back in 2009.

Doctoral Journey Tip #1: "Mommy, somebody gonna pay me to go to school." There is ALWAYS a FREE route to education. Find a program (doctoral, master's, or undergrad) that pays for your tuition and provides a stipend. The more you can avoid going into debt while pursuing your passions, the better. I would not be at NYU GSOM if they did not pay for my tuition and provide a stipend ($38k). My mother still reminds me today of that statement I made after graduating high school. Okay, so now y'all know my academic history, let's get to the tea.

Who am I?

April 2020

"Thank you for your dissertation update, Joanne. Tabitha, what is the status of your dissertation proposal? How are things coming along for you?" I froze and felt a ball of heat from my gut to my throat. I wasn't prepared for this question on a Zoom call with 35 pairs of ears of my classmates and faculty all waiting for my response. I still hadn't accepted that the project I had been working on for the past 1.5 years had come to a screeching halt due to COVID-19. I'd been split between 3 sites to complete my dissertation proposal for the past three years. Borough hopping and traveling daily from my home in Brooklyn to my office at 34th Street-Times Square in Manhattan to the NYC DOHMH in Long Island City in Queens. I took a deep breath and tried to pick out one of the 1,000 responses that popped into my head while swallowing the ball of heat and uncertainty in my throat. "… Well, my dissertation proposal is in an interesting space. I don't wanna talk about it." *Really Tabitha? That's all you could say?*

I didn't stay long to hear my other classmates' updates. I silently pressed the red "End" button on my Zoom call. That ball of heat now transformed into an outburst followed by a river of tears. My classmates' reports of escaping the pandemic in NYC by heading for their homes outside of the city for an oasis of relief from the frantic energy of COVID-19 was the common theme. An example of the racial and socioeconomic disparities between myself and my classmates. As I listened, my eyes surveyed my rent-stabilized apartment that was over 15 years due for a renovation. I closed my eyes and imagined myself anywhere other than my low-income neighborhood that had been abandoned by my colleagues and city officials in public health.

I sat down in my journal the next morning and pleaded to God for answers. *Life wasn't supposed to be this way.* I questioned God about this journey. I was angry. Over the next three months, God would provide guidance through his word, friends, signs, and messages. I began to develop my own personal love language with God. Each morning in meditation, I met with Him in a sunny field full of lavender flowers. Under a tree, I'd hug Him and tell Him how much I didn't think I could make it through the program. How much I thought He'd selected the wrong woman for this challenge because I didn't believe in my voice or my original thoughts and ideas.

God listened. Some days all I'd receive was…silence. Even as a pastor's kid, I didn't know what God's voice was supposed to sound like. Growing up, I'd imagine He'd sound like Morgan Freeman or James Earl Jones. But most times, all I heard was my own voice. Who knew that was God speaking to me? I started to pay attention in the silence and heard God's voice (in the voice of myself) reassure me that He is able to do more than all that I dare ask or think, beyond my greatest prayers, hopes, or dreams (Ephesians 3:20).

My daily morning crying sessions with God built my emotional strength and faith to levels I never knew existed. I learned to believe beyond my current standing in my program. I began to believe in the impossible. My diligence in meditating with God daily was the source of my strength.

Doctoral Journey Tip #2: Have an active relationship with God, the anxiety reliever. God is very active. Sometimes He may be even too responsive. I remember my neighbor saw me in the hallway of my apartment building and gifted me three packs of salmon just right after I told God I didn't have dinner and I'd go hungry another night. Yes, chile, He's that active. Each and every promise written in the Bible is intentional and has a purpose no matter the problem you're facing. You don't have to be a bible scholar. All you need is prayer, meditation, and daily repetition of these three verses:

> When you pass through the waters, I will be with you; And through the rivers, they will not overwhelm you. When you walk through fire, you will not be scorched, Nor will the flame burn you. (Isaiah 43:2)

> For I know the plans I have for you," declares the Lord, "plans to prosper you and not to harm you, plans to give you hope and a future. (Jeremiah 29:11).
> The Lord will fight for you; you need only to be still. (Exodus 14:14)

Watch Me Unfold

"Production Saturday Nights," I devilishly described to my two homegirls as their mouths dropped open as I displayed the lingerie pictures on my phone.

"Girl, you should submit these pics to SAVAGE Fenty."

About two years ago, I had the idea of doing a personal "boudoir" photo shoot. I tend to be attracted and drawn to raw authenticity and natural beauty in art and in my life. Through my #BodyConfident journey in the past few years, I was gradually becoming infatuated with the woman I saw in the mirror. The raw reality of me, after all I've been through. And honestly... I was impressed. From being 267lbs in 2011 at my undergraduate graduation to now being a size 8/10 and proud of the hard work and dedication I put into my body, I couldn't help but want to honor myself.

After a breakup in January 2019, I was given the opportunity to explore Tabitha again. And so the creation of "Production Saturday Nights" was birthed in full effect. Honoring myself each and every Saturday night, dressed in lingerie, I put the camera on to the most valuable and ride-or-die person in my life: myself. Dancing, singing, and making videos for no intended audience was my therapy throughout this doctoral journey. Never had I taken such dedicated time to dissect the nuances of me. I discovered angles, curves, and, most importantly, full acceptance and love for myself. This type of body confidence couldn't be outsourced externally. Sensuality saved me.

Doctoral Journey Tip #3: Stay sensual. It is your anxiety relief, confidence sustainer, peace provider, and men snatcher. *How do you romance you?* You learn her intimately. No judgment. Create space for her to be. What type of fabric makes her skin glow? What texture sheets make her night softer? Does her scent demand attention? Or is it subtle & smooth? What music makes her red-lipped smile stretch from ear to ear? What songs make her hips dig deeper? Try This: Visualize her. Name her. Pick 2 outfits (day & night). Take her out this weekend & learn her. She'll surprise you every time.

For the rest of 2020 and 2021, there wouldn't be much activity on my dissertation proposal. I went through multiple cycles of brainstorming, literature searching, and writing, only to find another bump in the road that would deter me to a new path. At this point, I was tired and decided to let go and let God. "What are you trying to show me, God? You know I don't like to feel idle. If I'm not supposed to be focused on school, what are my next steps?"

"Tell your body confident story and how sensuality saved you," God replied.

Ummm... excuse me? You want me to tell the world how and why I was obese by the time I finished undergrad in 2011, had lap-band surgery, and a tummy tuck with a breast lift and implants (that I later removed)? How I experienced medical malpractice and a permanent change in body shape that fueled and uncovered another level of body dysmorphia and body image issues? Then you want me to invite the world into my intimate sensual moments with myself? The intentional private moments I created just for me to celebrate my body? You want me to show the "Production Saturday Night" pics too? For why? A woman named Alizarin would have the answer for me the next day.

"Tabitha, have you ever considered surgery? Plastic surgery?" a 25-year-old gorgeous Hispanic woman asked me at my parent's school the next day. In conversation, Alizarin expressed her want to have a breast reduction and liposuction because of her family's distaste for the curves she'd developed. *God, is this your answer?* I thought. As I continued to listen to Alizarin through tears in my eyes, I knew it was time to tell my Body Confident story publicly. A story of how emotional trauma and a lack of self-love led me down a road of weight loss and plastic surgery. On November 1, 2020, I wrote a love letter to all of the women who struggled with loving every curve, crevice, and feature of their body and published it on my Instagram @IamTabithaEsther.

That same month I started hosting the #BodyConfidentConfidential series, where other women and I told our stories of how the influence of society, social media, and our lack of self-love led us down a road to somehow believing that our bodies were less than anything but a masterpiece. It was a safe space for me, the ladies, and our unheard voices. With my dissertation proposal at a standstill, in 2021, I became The #BodyConfident Coach. I became an advocate and the person I needed back in 2011. I helped women who are unsatisfied with their bodies develop unshakeable #bodyconfidence through body science, self-awareness, and mindset hacks. After each Wednesday group coaching session, I'd have so much energy that I'd stay up all night and dance the night away.

March 2022

After almost two years of my dissertation proposal being shut down, I realized that God kept placing roadblocks in my doctoral journey and was leading me towards a career based on my passions. *"You really want me to leave science after 15+ years? This is a big change; send me three signs."* And that he did. On my 33rd birthday, I made the decision to take a 1 year leave from my doctoral program and pursue body confidence coaching full-time with the creation of #BodyCon University. A program created for women to avoid the challenging and life-altering aspects of my plastic surgery journey. It is a coaching program to help women heal body image issues pre-and post surgery while educating them on their personal body science to maintain surgical results.

I guess my doctoral journey IS a journey back to myself. My truest self. That pandemic was the storm that uncovered the diamond in me, an advocate for the quietest voice in the room waiting to be seen and heard. I realized that I have so much more to offer the world than novel observational studies. I had passion and drive more than I had ever seen in an academic or government setting. *I found purpose.* Listen, girl, just like the Esther in the Bible, you were made for a time like this (Esther 4:14). You may not see the road ahead, but God does. Trust your voice, trust your gifts, and trust God.

Love, Tabitha Esther

Tabitha Esther's Acknowledgements

Firstly, I'd like to thank God for guiding me on the road less traveled. I always say that school deepens my relationship with God and my doctoral journey has proved that to be true 1 million times over. You are my greatest blessing and my forever friend. This doctoral journey has been nothing less than a spiritual one. I am honored to be called your child.

My family, my Julien tribe that never fails to support me but also gathers me together when necessary. Mommy & Daddy, thank you for saving my life more times than I can count. I may be your wildest child, but I promise it's going to be all worth it. This is just the beginning. Abigail, Timothy, Chantal, Margarita, Marisah - I am the product of your never ending love as your sibling. Thank you for never letting me wander too far off into the deep end and being a reflection of God's love. You guys are my home.

To my Aunt Felecia Connor, your life and legacy live on through me. You will always be my greatest inspiration, motivation, and best friend.

To my riders, Lucie & Rayvon, thank you for listening to my fiftyeleven WhatsApp voice notes about my doctoral journey, my internal battles, and my tears. Your emotional support is what dreams are made of and keeps me grounded. Thank you for the experiences that we create that will ultimately become the stories we tell our kids and grandkids. I'm looking forward to more girls trips when we're 80 complete with Wray & Nephew, afrobeats, and experiences we'll never forget.

To my prayer partner Dr. Melissa Noel, thank you for praying with and over me. You are my spiritual sister for life. Your support has held me holding on when I didn't feel like I could hold on anymore.

To my advisor Dr. Lorna Thorpe, you are my academic mother. Thank you for holding me through the twists and turns of these past 5 years of my doctoral journey. Your patience, understanding, and support is what is needed in academia. You are stuck with me for life.

To the ladies of the #UnshakeableBodyConfidence Facebook group, we just getting started! You've watched me grow and make mistakes while still staying resilient. I have plans for us and with your support, I know all things are possible.

CHAPTER 14

Lisa Marie Lee's Story

DR. LISA MARIE Lee is a People, Culture, and Operations Solutionist who founded Linked Results, LLC. First developing her career in the United States Navy, she learned her passion for solving workplace issues. She earned her PhD in Education, specializing in Training and Performance Improvement, from Capella University. Her study focused on how supervisors influenced trainees' willingness to effectively perform on the job based on various factors. Research results contributed to improving how the research site hired, trained, and supervised employees to maximize performance and ensure a positive impact from training initiatives. Dr. Lee utilizes her research skills to investigate and ensure that abusive and incompetent individuals and cultures are held accountable to prevent future workplace trauma and empower new cultures that are more inclusive and accountable. She collaborates with organizations to educate and empower teens and young adults about their employment rights so that they are able to self-advocate and implement change within the workplace. Her consulting and executive coaching services are designed to determine solutions to performance issues and evaluate initiatives to ensure actual behavioral change occurs. She is also working to enhance the veteran transition and hiring process through collaborative efforts with various organizations.

Empowered by Incompetent Privilege

I began my doctoral journey with a vision to change the face of corporate America through research by holding corporations that instill and empower toxic cultures accountable. It has been known for decades and continues to be accepted that Black women are significantly underrepresented in leadership roles, are less likely to receive support and access to advance in their careers, are significantly underpaid, and face day-to-day discrimination as they navigate the corporate workplace to achieve their professional goals. I hoped that researching and using my consulting business would help to empower change from within. I felt it was vital to initiate change since, like millions before me, I was denied an opportunity because I understood and loved myself.

Specifically, I am a Black woman who has always embraced her natural self. I have never dressed or wore my hair to appease others or ensure I looked the part, except when in the military. I found out early after transitioning from the military that this was a hindrance if I wanted to succeed in corporate America. I hit roadblock after roadblock trying to enter the corporate world. I was constantly told I wasn't the right fit but never what the right fit meant when I was just as or even more qualified than those hired for positions while given the "thank you for your military service" smirk. Constant feelings of failure actually almost deterred me from wanting to succeed in the field. It was hard to understand how I could be viewed as an exceptional talent in the military at the age of 17 and given responsibilities to oversee over 50 individuals and manage a budget of over $250,000, but in the civilian world, I was deemed an unworthy talent. It was hurtful to be viewed as valuable in defending the United States but unworthy enough for a corporate job.

I was blessed not to fall victim to negative thoughts that plague many veterans, but society lacks true appreciation for the service and sacrifice of military veterans. Instead of begging for acceptance or considering lower-level positions that I was overqualified for, I began contracting as an HR consultant. Pissed off but focused, I wanted to prevent others from receiving the same denials and further trauma after finally gaining access to corporate positions, only to later fall victim to microaggression, discrimination, and hostile policies. My goal was to increase the number of HR professionals who actually investigate performance from 30% to 100% to ensure inclusivity was a priority and that cultures and policies focused on safe, fair, and diverse work environments that held all individuals accountable.

I was determined to prevent individuals from fearing what made them great: their individuality, which would hinder them from receiving a job, promotion, fair pay, or the chance to get ahead in corporate America. It was time to create an empire that would highlight the demand for an end to the corporate desire for a glass room with a secluded table of dying ideas. Taking on this great task was a goal for me because I knew what it felt like to be deemed unworthy. I also understood that corporations don't care about people, only money. Pursuing my Doctorate in Education, specializing in Training and Performance Improvement, was the key to developing my understanding of performance psychology to determine effective solutions and new opportunities for improving how corporate America functioned. I could then interpret that information into why quotas, goals, and a return on investment were not occurring. I knew the sacrifices would be great as a single mother struggling to build a successful consulting business, but significant change was needed.

Foundation for Success

Of course, I was used to being the only Black woman, so sadly, taking this position during my doctoral process was nothing new. Coming from a background of always being the only Black girl to now being the only Black woman strengthened me to know I am destined to take my place amongst others who do not look like me, think like me, or share my experiences. These previous experiences sadly prepared me to deal with the nuisance of being subjected to others' inability to accept that differences exist in the world.

Thankfully, during the beginning of my doctoral coursework, being the only Black woman would not be an issue, although I did struggle with the learning process. I came from a business-minded background that focused on the science of business and maximizing profits. Transitioning to the field of education, which focused on the psychology of behaviors, was a huge shift in thinking. Of course, it was not what I was expecting, and I struggled in a world of new jargon, theories, and perspectives. Switching my understanding to why and how versus what and when was extremely challenging. At times, I felt I may have picked the wrong field because of so many differences in reason, terminology, and the use of a "scholarly voice." There were so many times I would cry in frustration as to why words had to be so complex. I truly hated everything regarding the academia of the process because it was too wordy and, in my opinion, unnecessary.

My ability to prepare prior to situations allowed me to expect these feelings of being overwhelmed, although it didn't prevent them. Many would argue that I was suffering from imposter syndrome, which was not the case. I didn't feel inadequate or as if I was not worthy, but I didn't want to conform. I did not always agree with best practices and accepted thinking, which was okay, but at the time, it was very frustrating for me. In retrospect, I always needed to justify my ideas, which in hindsight is the purpose of a scholarly program, but at the time, I was always on the defensive. I had to learn to take time and meditate on what really mattered, and that was my voice. My voice and ability to explain my thoughts and beliefs using research was the key to finding my scholarly voice;

it was a representation of me. It didn't matter if I aligned or agreed with what people were saying; I deserved to be present and heard as long as I was able to justify my thinking.

It took me almost six months to become comfortable with researching and justifying my ideas. I had to learn to look from the perspective of a lawyer or marketer. My persistence and willingness to never give up definitely came from my past experiences of learning to figure things out on my own. Regardless of my frustrations, I never embraced negative thinking and maintained a positive mindset. This is what helped me to accept that it is okay to stand out from the societal expectation of conforming, which helped me to refocus on my goals. We are taught at a young age that there is only one answer, but later learn as we grow that there is actually no right answer and only your perception of a situation. I was learning and growing into embracing the understanding of how perception determines your understanding of right or wrong.

I believe my decision to select an online higher education platform with a strong military support system versus brick and mortar to avoid issues of microaggression and other forms of abuse based on my past experiences also contributed to my success. Many would argue that online is more difficult, but not for me since I was used to attending distance education programs during deployments. Also, many training programs are designed based on a distance learning format. Not to mention, schools with a strong military support system are more likely to operate within the guidelines when it comes to holding individuals accountable and ensuring support during the learning process.

Although residencies were a requirement, the experience of meeting individuals was eased since relationships were established prior to establishing face-to-face communication. Online offered me a sense of freedom and control over my personal space, time, and unnecessary assumptions based on biases and differences that can be seen versus the actual need for discussion that occurs many times without visual descriptors. Current research has suggested that my feelings corroborate with many women of color within the corporate workspace and explains the rise in retention, career shifts, and the demand for remote work to become a staple in the modern workplace.

Additionally, my previous military experience allowed me to connect and build relationships with peers and professors with similar backgrounds and struggles. Taking the time to determine the necessary decisions that would support me throughout my doctoral journey is what helped me to create a foundation for success during the learning process and contributed to my ability to maintain a presence on the President's List throughout.

For example, as a single mother, I knew I needed to build a foundation that would champion me to success. I drafted contracts with my family members that ensured they would help with watching my daughter for set amounts of time if

I needed help. This allowed me to remain present with my family, hold myself accountable to complete goals, ensure my family would support me through my journey, and allowed me to make time for myself. Thank God I thought ahead! I would not have survived all those long nights of Googling and researching databases for studies, analyzing and synthesizing data, and the writing process. Lord, the sleepless nights of reading and writing to only reread and rewrite the following day were sometimes maddening and felt never-ending. I know that some may not have that type of support system, but something similar can be considered to ensure a stable structure that would work for you. I know for me, it helped me to maintain balance and allow time for myself, which is the most important factor of the journey.

Weeds Can Grow Through Any Foundation

One thing I forgot to consider when establishing a foundation is that even weeds can grow. One of the undesirable issues that would plague me throughout the remainder of my degree process was discovered during my comprehensive examination. Of course, it happened when I was on cloud nine and riding the wave of successfully completing all course requirements. During the review of my submissions, I learned that my greatest weakness would be my writing skills, which was something I expected because I am not a natural writer. However, I didn't expect that my tone would be perceived negatively and even as threatening within the world of academia. When certain individuals of other hues read my interpretations and ideas, they perceived them as harsh and accusatory instead of suggestions or implications, even though they were justified by scholarly research. I was stumped and confused because my tone was never an issue before, but I must admit I learned my approach from a white male perspective. Assuming they were never given the same criticism, Interestingly, the criticism was not something that would hinder my grade; it definitely stung because it wouldn't be the last time I would hear it from certain individuals. I used ignorance and unneeded criticism as motivation and continued to charge forward on my journey.

As I carried the burden of constantly struggling with my writing, I decided to invest in grammar software to strengthen my technique and prepare for my dissertation milestones ahead. During this time, I was also faced with my second and most disappointing hurdle, my inability to relate with my mentor. Once again, my expectations were crushed by reality. I was looking forward to having a mentor and expected that it would help me complete the process quickly. Sadly, that was not the case and actually cost a year of wasted time and money.

The relationship started with an understanding that I wanted my studies to focus on military transition and how a lack of support has hindered successful transfer to the civilian workforce. In hindsight, I understand that my mentor had no understanding of how to assist me with transforming this focus into a study that focused on my field of study. I actually spent almost a year trying to get my topic approved by the dissertation committee because there was no cohesion between myself and my mentor. In hindsight, I understand that not every scholar is able or willing to understand how to assist you. I blindly and foolishly assumed that I would be fully supported when, in actuality, I was led astray by inept understanding that was masked as support. My inability to be successful was hindered by the lack of qualifications of someone else. To this day, I still wonder if it was intentional and why? Of course, because of my past issues with others, I assume it was a way to ensure that I failed, while some may assume that it just wasn't meant to be. Regardless, my mentor's inability to step aside when it was understood that there was no pathway to ensure my success and that the lack of connection and understanding was a hindrance during my first year in the process was inexcusable.

When I finally confronted my mentor, there was no real explanation given except to say, "I don't know how to help you." I was shocked and pissed the F off. The only response I could muster through my quivering lips with a stern voice was, "thanks for wasting my time and costing me thousands." I never considered myself a victim but one that perseveres. This experience was proof that my talents are needed to ensure accountability within the workplace. I was not swayed by the bull---- and moved along and requested new assistance. Of course, this time, I ensured it was someone that was direct and skilled at ensuring learners could complete their dissertation within at least a year since I was not trying to spend extra money on incompetence. Once matched with my new mentor, we connected immediately. We had similar backgrounds and experiences, even though we were of different demographics. I was able to restructure my approach and have my topic completed and approved within a month, and later my research study within five months. Hilariously enough, my study focused on how the support provided by supervisors influences newly hired employees' self-efficacy and motivation to transfer learning to successful performance on the job. My focus was a nod to my previous experience and how the lack of support hindered my confidence. However, I had the motivation to complete the PhD process successfully.

To ensure I was supported throughout the writing process, I decided to hire an editor, per my mentor's advice. I was thankful I took that suggestion because my topic focused on a large amount of scholarly literature and qualitative information. In the end, my final dissertation totaled 250 pages. It would not have been a success without the help of a keen literary eye. As planned, I completed my dissertation process within a year and successfully defended my dissertation after completing my degree program after four years.

Whew, even with all my precautions for success, I still was faced with major challenges. To even relive my past through writing has opened my eyes to how the journey has shaped me as a woman. I am thankful but glad it is over. There are many lessons and takeaways that can be learned from my greatest struggles. I have synthesized them into the following lessons:

Lessons for Others

✓ *Always stay ready*

It is essential to plan and establish a strong foundation to ensure that you are supported through your doctoral process. Only then will you be prepared to handle unforeseen issues, challenges, and growth opportunities. Align with others like yourself, look for opportunities to grow your circle of influence, and stay connected with those that truly support you. Focus on building a strong foundation is the key to remaining focused, understood, and even challenged as you level up in your thinking and master your field.

✓ *Never conform but compromise*

It's **OKAY** to be **YOU**! It's **OKAY** to disagree with others. The goal is to justify your thinking with scholarly information. When presenting your knowledge, you are in the role of an expert, not a friend. Your goal is to demonstrate your competencies, which can infuriate others and even result in unneeded criticism and insecurities that are masked as feedback. It is **OKAY** to take in the information as a compromise, but you do not need to conform to appease others. Your scholarly voice is your own and not mimicked or a replica of others. Focus on ways to strengthen your presentation of facts to ensure your messages are not lost but reinforced by your capabilities. The goal is to pitch your ideas as if you are marketing to generate billions in sales or as if you are a high-profile attorney defending a client on a death row case! Stand ten toes down in your justified beliefs and confidently present your intelligence to the world. Remember, if there is a probability, then there is a possibility.

✓ *Always put yourself first*

It's important to understand that the privilege of teaching or being in a leadership position doesn't mean that every individual is competent and able to utilize the best practices that qualify them to be an expert. To ensure that you are successful throughout your journey and afterward, it is essential to always put yourself first as you practice within the field. Cover your A--by avoiding expectations and only focusing on results. Only then will you know when to walk away when objectives have not been met and not rely on the inconsistencies and inabilities of others. Also, it's important to ensure you are building a strong support system. Include others in your planning process. Find ways to remain balanced, whether through food prep, assistance with childcare, hiring a housekeeper, including a workout regime, or whatever will help to keep you centered and aligned to reach your goals.

✓ *Follow your passion*

Your research should be based on a personal area of interest or a desire to understand. This approach will keep you motivated throughout the process, especially during challenging times. I hope that my story is able to inspire others and empower them to flow through their journey effortlessly.

CHAPTER 15

Keila Miles's Story

DR. MILES IS the first Black woman to earn a PhD in Neuroscience from the University of Cincinnati College of Medicine. Her dissertation research focused on the use of a ketogenic diet as a potential treatment for a rare metabolic disorder, Creatine Transporter Deficiency, that causes intellectual disability. As a doctoral candidate, she wrote a successfully funded NIH grant application, installed a diversity and inclusion organization for shaping STEM leaders, contributed research for policy initiatives at the Cincinnati Health Department, and engaged the community through outreach. After graduating, Dr. Miles completed a science policy fellowship at Research!America, a non-profit that specializes in research advocacy. There, she provided expert advice on translating scientific findings to compelling messaging for congressional outreach. Notably, she facilitated collaboration with the National Science Policy Network's #BlackInSciPolWeek on Twitter, curating a collection of videos that featured preeminent Black science policy professionals. Dr. Miles hopes that these examples of visual representation will inspire the next generation of science policy leaders. Currently, Dr. Miles is an 8th-grade math teacher and special education case manager for Montgomery County Public Schools in Maryland. This position provides a unique vantage point for influencing STEM education policies and legislation in the future that will hopefully improve retention rates for underrepresented populations in higher education STEM programs. In alignment with this goal, Dr. Miles has recently accepted the position of Learning Impact Fellow with the Federation of American Scientists housed within the Institute of Education Sciences at the Department of Education. In addition, Dr. Miles maintains a passion for informal learning and museum education through her role as a museum associate at the Glenstone Museum, an inquiry-based contemporary art museum located in Potomac, MD. In her free time, Dr. Miles enjoys learning about Black history, pursuing her fashion interest through thrifting, and experiencing art.

Sharing stories from what felt like my seven-year "internment" as a doctoral candidate frightens me even as I type. I have little desire to revisit the psychological warfare and physical trauma I put myself through to earn these three letters behind my name. I question most days if what I went through was truly worth it. I know it was because I know that sharing what I went through means the next Black woman (or non-binary person) interested in pursuing a higher education degree in STEM will gain more insight and perhaps a "cheat-code" on how to better navigate academic spaces that were never designed for us to traverse. Naming the struggles I faced, both imposed and self-inflicted, is just what I need to heal. Further, finding the words to celebrate me for achieving the impossible dream my ancestors prayed for is the legacy I want for myself.

Aight, So BOOM!

I am elated, nervous, excited, and (mostly) scared to (finally) have an opportunity to pen my graduate school experience as a Black woman at a predominantly white institution. I would like to thank Dr. Lucy Oxley for trailblazing this path for me.

To be completely honest: I went to graduate school not on the strength of my personal beliefs in myself that I could succeed but on the never-ending encouragement of the faculty at my undergraduate HBCU, Oakwood University. When I enrolled in college, I was convinced I was going to be a medical doctor. Not realizing I was following the dreams and passions of my close friends, I majored in biomedical science. I ignored my love for Black History and dropped my African American Studies minor after one semester. Why? Because of dollars and cents. I was socialized to believe and had accepted that my academic endeavors must amount to tangible success, success being defined as six-figure salaries and recognition. My thinking was limited to only believing medical doctors could access this aforementioned success. But then…I failed my first biology exam (or at least it was what I considered failing; I probably got a seventy-something). In a meeting with my biology professor, they asked if I had ever shadowed a medical doctor. I had not. They arranged for me to shadow a physician who was also an Oakwood alum (FYI: My undergraduate alma mater ranks fifth in producing Black students for medical school enrollments). That day changed my career trajectory. Not only was I tired of them having to remind patients to care for themselves by remembering to take medications that had already been prescribed, but I was also uncomfortable with the thought of being responsible for physical exams and engaging with strangers about their personal lives. For example, a patient we rounded on was an elderly gentleman with recurring kidney stones. After the physician completed the exam and shared treatment options, his wife piped up to ask, "Are his kidney stones the cause of his erectile dysfunction?" My G, I was too through after that. Following my decision not to pursue medical school, I was given the opportunity to join a summer research program, and this ultimately led me to apply for a PhD program.

Aight

Throughout undergrad, I participated in summer research. Once more, I have to credit my HBCU for arranging these opportunities by securing grants. Summer research taught me a few things about doctoral pursuit in a STEM space: 1) Graduate students are the lifeblood of the lab. Without them, there is no lab. 2) Don't NOBODY look like me unless we arrived for the same program geared towards increasing minority scholars in all-white spaces. 3) The definition of productivity is (unfortunately) peer-reviewed publications. You would THINK I would have seen these as warning signs to do anything but enroll in a PhD program, but like my ancestors (specifically the ones from Princess Anne, MD) used to tell me as a youth, *I'm hard-headed* (this was typically followed by "a hard head makes for a soft behind." Rest in Peace Granny aka Francis Dix Miles). My summer research experiences did what it was supposed to do: encouraged me to apply to a PhD program. Although I still question my motivations for pursuing a PhD (as is my right), I know that my steps were ordered (subtle reference to my continued belief in God, despite my faith not outgrowing the size of a mustard seed most days).

In regards to how I selected my PhD program, (ONCE MORE) shout out to my HBCU, Oakwood University. My alma mater has pipeline relationships with several prestigious universities that come to our campus and recruit, often doing mock interviews. On the day the University of Cincinnati rep came to campus, I was sleep SLEEP. My slumber was interrupted by a phone call from Dr. Rand, who called to ask where I was and why I was not in line for mock interviews with UC. It's professors like this that really make the HBCU experience unlike anything else. I arrived at the interview looking like I was at the intersection of disheveled and professional. Nevertheless, the meeting went WELL. (FYI, I thought my GRE scores were too low. Ms. Hildreth, the UC recruiter at the time, said they were just right. A special thank you to her. In my graduate and professional experiences, it was rare that I felt a white woman (WW) genuinely believed in my success, let alone verbalize it to me. From the day I met Ms. Hildreth and maintained her encouragement for my completing the program because I was capable).

So

At the time of my admission in 2013, the average timeline for completing a STEM doctoral degree was 5.5 years. The timeline breakdown consisted of two years of coursework followed by three-plus years of thesis research. During this time, newly enrolled students are to select a lab for their doctoral candidacy and thesis. Around the two-year mark, graduate students complete a candidacy or qualification exam. For my program, the exam consists of conceptualizing a unique research question that you will ultimately defend using no tangible data—just evidence-based inferences. The written deliverable is comparable to an NIH-style grant application that details the relevance of the question and literary evidence that supports proposed outcomes. Y'all, this exam requires mental acrobatics.

I had just completed my pre-qualification exam for doctoral candidacy. My committee lowkey ripped my Specific Aims page to shreds. In my opinion, the committee asked that I write far more about methods and projected results than my classmates. (I really tried to make it a "not race-related reason," but… these are the types of "hoops" that give me pause.) Anywho, after making the edits, I passed to the next stage of the hunger games, that is doctoral candidacy: Preparing for the candidacy exam. To reiterate, candidacy is what separates graduate students from doctoral candidates. Graduate students are lab flunkies that take classes. Doctoral candidates are lab flunkies that take classes and can withstand a verbal firing squad composed of tenured PhD's who may or may not believe that their research is THE ONLY research that matters.

I read, wrote, typed, back-spaced, deleted, and cried on a loop for four weeks. I did not get past writing two sentences until week three. But it wasn't enduring the candidacy process that was the turning point for me, a turning point as in truly believing that I could complete the program. The turning point came when after *independently* developing my research question and successfully defending my candidacy exam, the post-doc (WW) made a jaunting statement that, to this day, I still can't believe. The post-doc called me into their office (FYI, I did the majority of the writing for my candidacy exam in their "office." I would stay after lab until 3 or 4 AM and cry-write until I couldn't fight off the sleep any longer). They began this impromptu meeting by saying, "I noticed there seems to be a change with you." They weren't wrong. I had indeed adjusted how I interacted with people in my immediate lab space. And by adjusted, I mean I stopped trying to talk and get to know everyone because I didn't feel it to be a genuine interaction. I say this because no one really talked to ME in lab. People talked AROUND me, and I would interject where I could. (There are a few exceptions.)

The conversation continues, and she says: "You know, Keila, just because you started doesn't mean you have to finish." I was stunned at this statement. How could they be so daft as to ask me, the ONLY Black woman enrolled in the program, to QUIT? Moreso, they were asking this after I reached a monumental milestone of passing the candidacy exam. I could rationalize now that perhaps they felt this was sound advice. But the fact remains that they told me to quit before asking if I was okay or in need of help in any way. Also, to suggest I discontinue pursuing a doctoral degree on the strength of me not engaging in lab small talk is WILD. As my doctoral journey continued, I began to realize, only through validating conversations with my Black women peers, that my work environment was hostile and toxic. Note that a hostile work environment does NOT have to look like overt racism. Rather it can present as covert racism or so-called "unintentional" microaggressions and selective ignorance from the majority population.

Examples of this from my experience include, but are not limited to:

1. Being accused of work avoidance by a (WW) classmate while at my grandfather's funeral because I had not responded to an email/= or added to a Google Doc for an assignment that was due five days after I returned from the funeral. Like, she really "reported" me to the director of the course without bothering to send me an email about her "concerns." I found out about this because the course director interrupted me while taking a 17-page exam (not kidding about that page number) by stating, "Your group has some concerns with your lack of contribution to the project."
    0   The same course director said in response to learning of my Grandfather's death: "Well, at least you knew your grandfather."
2. My PI used the N-word in my presence while reading posts on Reddit.
3. My postdoc stated they struggled to get their own work done because they were too busy doing my candidacy exam.
4. A labmate touched my hair without permission and remarked how shocked they were at its soft texture.
5. My PI told me that Sandra Bland would still be alive if she had only complied and showed me a Chris Rock video on how Black people should act when they are pulled over.
6. My PI and a lab tech discussed how the Confederate flag is simply a historical symbol, as is the Nazi symbol.
7. My PI asked if I was from Africa or the Caribbean during our first meeting because I wore a headwrap.
8. The third reviewer of my NIH F-31 Diversity Grant Application commented, "Applicant has several awards, however, they are all related to diversity." As if receiving recognition for STEM accomplishments is sub-par because the awarding entity highlights minority scholars'

achievements. BE THAT AS IT MAY, YA GIRL WAS AWARDED THE NIH GRANT!
9. My postdoc suggested I try flirting with the only other Black man in the gym after I jokingly mentioned I was attracted to a white man at the gym.
10. I never had consistent one-on-one meetings with my PI to discuss/strategize my thesis until year four of my program. If you're reading this and enrolled in a graduate program, make sure you have these types of meetings scheduled (embedded in your calendar). It's these types of meetings that add to your overall development as a doctoral candidate.
11. The program formalized the publication requirement in year four of my journey. This meant that a peer-reviewed publication was REQUIRED in order to be considered for doctoral defense. Prior to this, it was strongly suggested. When I inquired about being grandfathered in, given that I was not close to publishing, they pretty much said, "Nah, you good." (Note: The publication process can take up to 2 years as manuscripts are rarely accepted without the request of revisions by reviewers. Do the math: The rule changed in my 4th year. I was "expected" to apply for my doctoral defense in my 5th year. I finished in 7. Refer to #10).

I had no clue that when I was admitted to the Neuroscience Graduate Program at the University of Cincinnati College of Medicine that I was the FIRST Black woman admitted. Had I known prior, I probably would not have attended. I didn't learn of this until I was two years into the program. A couple of things puzzle me about this revelation: 1) Why didn't someone tell me?

2) If y'all knew and ain't say nothin…*side eye* 3) HOW in the 30+ years of the program's existence had no one thought to recruit a Black woman?

The pressure to perform and produce at the graduate level is already enough. This added to the feeling that I had to represent all Black scientists because my institution had never thought to recruit or admit someone from my demographic. Chile, Twas A LOT. Oftentimes, I found myself so overwhelmed that I didn't even want to try all together. The fear of outright failing or letting down other Black (women) scientists by performing poorly or not going the extra mile haunted me daily. Imagine coming from an environment where everyone looks like you and you know just about everyone in your class cause your school just reached an enrollment of 2,000, and there was an ice cream social to celebrate it. Not to mention, I am moving to a midwest city that neighbors a southern state.

I think the anxiety and impending depression caused by grad school were first masked by my desire to be independent and start fresh. My depression and anxiety sat down and had a meeting without my sanity, and it turns out…things were "worse" than I thought. In my third year in graduate school, I landed myself in the emergency department at the university hospital. I was diagnosed with mild depression and anxiety. Each year after that, I faced some form of a health crisis. Most infamously, needing a blood transfusion because my hemoglobin level was seven due to my period lasting for more than a month (possibly triggered by the stress of coming into lab every day to learn that my PI and post-doc were discussing my science without me and then instructing me on what to do as if I was an undergraduate trainee).

I am exceedingly grateful for the Black women scientists I was privileged to converse with and share academic space with. Had it not been for them, I would not be breathing. Black women scientists saved my life in grad school. They validated my experience by sharing their own. They challenged my negative (and suicidal) thoughts when I lacked the strength and courage to do it myself.

Jessica, Chrystelle, Juwen, Paige, Markaisia, Fayth, Sharon, Wendy, Dominique, Brandy, Ashley, Marguerite, Chanel, Kristen, Tia, Matia, Maddie, Monica …I want to use this platform to publicly speak and acknowledge the women PhD's that took time to uplift and encourage me to sojourn.

BOOM!

My private defense was the most embarrassing presentation I have given to date. I couldn't answer a single question. At the conclusion of the presentation, I was given the infamous "conditional pass," which meant I would need to return to my written dissertation to address all the questions I could not answer. I wept in my car in the parking lot for a minimum of an hour after this meeting. I remember blaming myself for not advocating for myself more with regard to how unprepared I felt prior to the meeting. But honestly, I didn't have the energy to. Most of my energy during the final writing phase went to combating suicidal thoughts. I was and am still exhausted. My lowest point in graduate school was writing and editing my dissertation during the onset of a global pandemic and being diagnosed with a chronic illness exacerbated by stress from graduate school. I called the suicide hotline at least three times during this stage of my doctoral journey.

BE THAT AS IT MAY…the point is: I made it out. Alive. Nothing could have prepared me for the amount of adverse lived experiences I would encounter in graduate school nor the amount of inner work I would have to complete just to build the mental fortitude and stamina to withstand such academic acrobatics. Rather than spend time harping on what I could have done differently, I want to congratulate myself for the things I did—waking up each morning, getting dressed, and making a plan to conquer what felt like the impossible. The number of positive thoughts and decisions it takes to wake up and get moving deserves accolades, especially when my mindset at the time was rooted in the (fortune-told) idea that I would fail. My point here is there is nothing wrong with celebrating yourself. No matter the scale, show yourself kindness by celebrating yourself.

For me, this looked like throwing myself a graduation and a graduation party. A year AFTER I defended, I finally had the energy and the cognitive awareness that I had accomplished something worth celebrating. I planned an entire commencement service seeing as how I did not participate in the virtual commencement or go back to my institution the following year. I did see a point in "celebrating" in a space that caused me such mental turmoil. I wanted to celebrate myself on my own terms. My commencement was everything I needed it to be. It was held at a Black History Museum in my home state of MD (because I was Black History! The first Black woman to earn a degree from the Neuroscience graduate program at the University of Cincinnati College of Medicine), the commencement address was given by THE Dr. Wes Bellamy (shout out to networking!), and my hooding and degree conferral was done by Drs. Jessica Dade and Juwen DuBois. After receiving my degree, I got to embrace each of my mentors, an extremely powerful moment for me. I struggled to find the words to adequately thank them. I was surrounded by friends and family who had lent support during my doctoral journey and continue to do so.

Aight, so BOOM: I PhinisheD. No, I am not healed from the trauma of graduate school. But, without the doctoral journey, I would not have known that I possess the tools to heal, persist, and thrive.

CHAPTER 16

Gaëlle Pierre's Story

GAËLLE PIERRE IS currently embarking on her second year of her Women's Health Nurse Practitioner/Doctorate in Nursing Practice program. Professionally, Gaëlle works as a Travel ER nurse and has substantial experience in Emergency Medicine and Women's Health.

Within both settings, Gaëlle has always noticed the ongoing barriers that impact women of color and their access to varying healthcare services. Utilizing a multifaceted approach, she aims to formulate evaluative mechanisms that aid clinicians in recognizing their own implicit biases and develop hospital-based policies that address inconsistencies in the scope of practice. Through compassion, education, and the implementation of evidence-based practice, Gaëlle's ultimate goal is to curate environments that foster patient-centered care that caters to the needs of women of color. She recognizes that there is an overwhelming need for Black female scholarship within the realm of healthcare and is ecstatic to be a part of this book to empower Black women to do just that.

Part I: A Weary Soul

I found myself pacing as I anxiously waited for a reply from a recent "SOS" message that I sent to a group chat. As I came upon my fourth lap around my apartment complex that warm Sunday afternoon, my legs grew tired. Looking down at my phone, I impatiently realized that the distressed text message did not summon the assistance and immediate support that I had hoped for. Noticing the time, I raced back towards my apartment building. As I pushed through my front door, I nearly tripped over a sea of moving boxes that were sprawled all over my apartment floor. After barely catching my breath, I turned on my computer and prepared to deliver the message of defeat. With 10 minutes to spare, I began to eloquently rehearse my speech. "Despite my best efforts, I don't think I can move forward," I whispered to myself. "Unfortunately, this may not be the right time..." I had set up a virtual meeting with one of my professors to inform her of my official decision to withdraw from her course and subsequently withdraw from my dual program. "I enjoyed this course and your instruction; however, I've ultimately decided..." I continued to practice in hush tones. Even in the midst of panic, my need for perfection still wanted this news to be delivered flawlessly. Going through a divorce, being an essential worker through a pandemic, planning a big move, initiating my travel nurse journey, and starting a master's/doctoral program all within the span of three months started to take a toll on me significantly. I essentially convinced myself that this was impossible, that my overall grade of a B was a means to an end, and that I had no business in a program like this. Far be it, though I tend to be very melodramatic in nature, this program (and most nursing programs) considered a B- to essentially be a failing grade. Despite this program having a two-strike rule, the enormity of stress, the chokehold of imposter syndrome, the emotional fatigue, and doubt started to rear their ugly head. So, there I was, sitting in front of my computer, prepared to quit. As my professor finally jumped on Zoom, we proceeded to talk about my progress thus far. With heaviness in my chest, and a burning sensation in my throat, I managed to utter, "Professor, I honestly don't think I'm capable of completing this course." Puzzled, she paused and began scanning her computer screen. "What?! Gaelle, I can't let you do that. You can't quit! Your grades are not terrible, and you are an amazing student. Don't quit now; the world of nursing still needs you."

Part II: Period of Transitions

As I contemplated what to write about in regard to my rollercoaster of a doctoral journey thus far, I couldn't help but be reminded of how my path towards a doctoral degree looked vastly different from most of my fellow co-authors.

Attaining a Doctorate in Nursing Practice (DNP) degree will essentially prepare me for the highest level of nursing practice with the intention of translating scientific research into everyday clinical practice. Amid this being a degree and not a role, DNP programs are often attached to additional coursework that would help prepare one to fulfill an actual role in advanced nursing practice. Specifically, my role would be a Women's Health Nurse Practitioner. Parallel to any other registered nurse, I contemplated the novel idea of leaving the bedside for a while. I've dabbled in my fair share of settings, but Emergency Medicine was like an on-again, off-again relationship that I kept going back to. As you can imagine, the organized chaos had its fair share of stress, challenges, and devastation. Some shifts consisted of the relentless request of turkey sandwiches from the flippant homeless man, who couldn't seem to stop flashing his crotch to the entire department, to rooms where we would be administering rounds of CPR to the lifeless body of someone who was battling COVID-19.

Every shift in this fast-paced environment carried a new challenge.

But, in the same breath, the ER carried its own addicting adrenaline rush. Sometimes it even offered the gift of gratification when you were able to, as my favorite ER physician used to say, 'fix' someone. Even so, with all the varying gifts the ER offered, burnout was by far the greatest one. After a few years within its grasp, I started my transition into Women's Health. Aside from this path being a stark difference from Emergency Medicine, the world of Women's Health offered a different form of fulfillment. Unbeknownst to me, it was a step toward greater meaning and, ultimately, a new avenue to fulfill my purpose.

My yearning to work in the realm of Women's Health was birthed when I decided to pursue my nursing career. Though life brought me into the ER, I knew deep down I could never stay there. Over time, experiences in both areas stirred up a deep desire for change. Every time I noted the dismissal of a Black woman's pain level from a clinician, the unethical handling and treatment of a Black inmate within the confines of the ER, the consistent condescending tones dripping with disdain, or any other maltreatment that was deeply rooted in structural racism and racial stereotyping, it fed my God-given responsibility to protect my sisters. This responsibility grew the more I interacted with Black women, and they shared the maddening stories of their experiences within our healthcare system. Early on, I understood that there were systemic barriers put in place that assisted in silencing women of color. So, as a Haitian American nurse, I made it my best practice to try and foster environments that allowed these women to tell their stories and share their worries or concerns. As I cared for these women, I made sure I was the soft hand and relentless advocate for their needs. All the time. Every single time. But my heart knew, long before my brain realized, that there was so much more that could be done. As a nurse, I felt there was only, but so much my reach was able to actually alter. The more I watered this seed, the more I realized that

I needed to transition into a role that could create tangible changes to the racism embedded in hospital protocols and that would help in creating equitable care for Black women. Little did I know, life's painful transitions would essentially keep me anchored and push me closer to my dreams.

Part III: The Paradigm shift

At some blurred stage in my doctoral journey, I got to a point where daily tasks around my new place and homework assignments kept me distracted enough to keep me from crying. Shower: check, work on DNP paper: check, eat: blank, workout: blank. I'm a checklist type of gal, so I quickly obliged when my therapist encouraged this method to keep me functioning during this time period. I know these were seemingly simplistic tasks, but it took me days before even working up to accomplish one thing from that list. So, two out of four meant this indeed was a good day for me. If tackling imposter syndrome while navigating uncharted DNP waters wasn't enough, life added situational depression as an added bonus that I needed to work through. "Keep your everyday tasks simple. Small progress is still progress," my therapist often reminded me during our weekly sessions. Though many friends knew of my life's new circumstances, very few understood the reality of the varying emotions I battled during that time period. Divorce and major life transitions are tricky things, as they often open a pandora's box of emotions that I, at the time, so desperately wanted to keep shut. Paired with my doctoral journey, those dark days seemed vastly overwhelming. Everyday tasks were daunting, and I started to experience uncomfortable interactions with my classmates. There were times I was the only

African American in the course and had the unpleasant honor of facing indirect questioning from peers during discussions about disparities that Black women faced. These interactions often ignited my anger but truly fatigued my soul. *"Is this even worth it?" "Will I even make an impact with this degree?" "Why did I put myself through this?"* These pesky thoughts often lingered as my sleep-deprived brain didn't have the strength to push them away.

Between the frustrating exchanges with classmates and my own personal struggles, imposter syndrome often got the best of me. It wasn't until we had to curate videos of ourselves, presenting subject matter relating to our DNP papers, that my vision finally began to shift. Under my video submission, another African American classmate applauded my topic choice and noted that I was genuinely tackling a gap in nursing that needed to be filled. She proceeded to pour out accolades and celebrated the passion she noted while watching my video. After further paralleling her own experience with my topic, she closed out her commentary with a lovely compliment about my sister locks. Her praise didn't go unnoticed, and her comments gave way to a sense of solidarity. Her experience as a Black woman in healthcare and her public affirmations reminded me of why I decided to embark on this journey in the first place. Her comment eventually led to many offline discussions filled with support, conversations sharing similar frustrations regarding our doctoral journey, and encouragement. That classmate and many others became foundations of support that gave me the clarity I needed during that time.

Days flew by, and weeks all meshed together, but I managed to work up enough fortitude to complete more tasks around my new place each day. Though I still had days where I grappled with my varying emotions and still tackled frustrating conversations with classmates, my perspective was shifting. I started approaching my emotions from the divorce, my imposter syndrome, and my emotional fatigue head-on. I even took full advantage of my flexible nursing shifts and scheduled any crying sessions on my days off. Did I really schedule my breakdowns? Oh, absolutely. Okay, please don't give me that judgmental look. I am indeed a very on-brand Type A individual; trust me, I know. But honestly, there is nothing like a good cry to release any pent-up emotions! So, with intentional action plans, I spent less time in the fetal position, crying, and spent more time walking in my purpose.

Obviously, I didn't quit that day during my Zoom meeting with my professor. In a near barren apartment, with tears in my eyes, my professor spoke life into me that day. I'm sure she wasn't prepared for a 45-minute Zoom meeting that was essentially me pouring my heart out, but she still virtually held my hand with grace. She kept reiterating during our conversation that the world of nursing needed me as if to blatantly remind me that this path that I was on was far greater than me. I didn't realize that those words acted as imaginary hands that encouraged, guided, and safeguarded me as I paced through my doctoral journey.

Every time I couldn't get a grip on the flood of emotions I had for the day or even when I faced the subtle undertones of disregard and the constant battle to 'prove' my intelligence amongst my peers, "the world of nursing needs you" were the words that continuously rekindled my light. Like many of my fellow co-authors, pushing many of these experiences to the outskirts of my mind has been common practice during this journey. Like many of them, there were days I felt confident that my seat at the table was well deserved, but there were also days that this constant burden of microaggression fed my imposter syndrome. This is why I've continued to find great value in tapping into various communities of like-minded people and forming groups of solidarity amongst other Black women on similar journeys. I realized that fostering these therapeutic environments with other Black women was always honestly restorative. Being around other successful women whose stories mirrored my own allowed me to stay anchored to my goal.

Part IV: Full Bloom

As I continue to gain the education and experience, the hope is that my new role as a DNP-prepared Women's Health Nurse Practitioner will allow me the ability to be an active advocate and change agent in how the care of African American women is managed. Gaining this doctoral degree solidifies my pursuit of gaining expertise in a specific area of teaching but also gives me the opportunity to improve diversity in a realm that is severely lacking. DNP degrees in the hands of African American women is a rarity that I hope changes. I want to shift the paradigm of healthcare within my community, especially for the vulnerable populations around me. I'm committed to improving patient outcomes for Black women, developing health care policies that cultivate better environments for Black women, creating better access to resources and innovative technology for Black women, and ultimately diversifying leadership positions across different practice settings to better represent, you guessed it: All. Black. Women.

With my professor's prompting ringing through my head and a newfound sense of strength, I proudly continue to push forward with my doctoral journey. Despite having to navigate through my own traumatic life transitions whilst on this journey, I realized that actively piloting through those moments only deepened my sense of compassion and empathy for others. It opened a door for authenticity and solidified my desire to not just aid Black women through suffering and injustice, but truly walk with them through it. My portion of this book is to pass on this same gracious hand that walked with me during the most crippling portion of my life. The world of ___ needs you. Fill that blank portion with whatever realm or area of work that God brings to your mind. Take up that space and overwhelm that void with the overflow of Blackness that this world so desperately needs. Society often attempts to challenge us as Black women and often questions what value we bring. But this, my dear, is your gentle reminder that you ARE the value. We, as Black women, especially in the world of academia, tend to face these challenges more compared to others. But let my life be an example of how hardship has a very humorous way of shaping us for our ministry and, honestly, how your most powerful assignments may actually be propelled by your deepest pains. You reading this book is no accident. So, trust the careful orchestration of your life and lean into what has been pushing you to this point. There are rooms, patients, students, and communities assigned to your story and are waiting for you to take a leap. Let these words walk with you as you take a step toward your own doctoral journey:

"The world of ___ needs you."

CHAPTER 17

Ivy Rentz's Story

DR. IVY RENTZ has been a licensed occupational therapist for 23 years. Additionally, she is the owner of Kidz Korner childcare centers in Westchester County, New York. She also owns ITI Therapy Services and has contracts with the Westchester County Department of Health, New York City Department of Education, and the City School District of New Rochelle to provide therapeutic services to children three to 21 years of age. Dr. Rentz has also been a member of the New York State Black Occupational Therapy Caucus for over two decades. She has recently been appointed to the Roster of Accreditation Evaluators (RAE) on behalf of the Accreditation Council for Occupational Therapy Education (ACOTE) starting in January 2021. Previously, Dr. Rentz was the Academic Fieldwork Coordinator and taught various pediatric treatment courses at York College, CUNY, and an adjunct at LaGuardia Community College, CUNY. Currently, she is an Assistant Professor/ Doctoral Capstone Coordinator in the Occupational Therapy Doctoral Program at Quinnipiac University. Dr. Rentz attends New York Covenant Church in New Rochelle, NY. She is currently the Director of Children's Church and the administrator for Youth Ministries. Dr.

Rentz currently serves on the Executive Board of Adelbrook Inc.'s residential and educational programs for children as the Chairperson and is a youth mentor with the City of New Rochelle Court System. Dr. Rentz is married to Damon Rentz and has six children.

Faith

"Now faith is confidence in what we hope for and assurance about what we do not see." (Hebrews 11:1).

"Congratulations, Dr. Ivy Tilson Rentz," Dr. Susan Iverson said as she opened the wooden door. As I stepped through the threshold of the doorway, I glanced around the room and saw my doctoral committee, Dr. Nikki Joseph, and Dr. Joseph Phillip clapping and my husband cheering for me. I successfully defended my dissertation on August 28, 2019. I was no longer "All but Dissertation (ABD)." I was "All but Defeated." I was in shock! I had worked so hard, overcome so much, and all I wanted to do was grab my purse and get out of there. As I reached for my purse, Dr. Iverson placed her hand on top of mine and said, "Wait, we need to take some pictures for Renee." Renee Gargano was the Assistant Director for the Doctoral Program and one of my biggest cheerleaders. As we all stood there taking pictures, my mind began to flashback to everything I had gone through to be in that very spot. Everyone who has been through the *Journey* of completing a doctoral degree has a story. Mine had so many obstacles it had to be God's plan for me. I am Enough!

As a child, I often felt invisible, abandoned, and like I didn't belong anywhere. The adults in my life seem to be always dealing with their adult **STUFF**! Throughout my childhood, I wondered why I felt like that? Why no one seemed to know how I was feeling or why it wasn't important to them? As I got older and began what young people refer to now as "adulting," I gained some perspective and insight on human behavior. I began to understand that people can't give you what they don't have. We are all a collection of our beliefs and experiences, living out our destiny. My maternal grandmother was the primary caregiver for my sister and I growing up. Wilma Moss was the daughter of a sharecropper. She gave us what she could and planted in us whatever she knew how to do. She told me that she wasn't allowed to go to school after the ninth grade in Statesboro, Georgia. There were no high schools for Black children. She would have to wait most of her adult life before she could earn her GED.

My grandmother had a strong belief in education. She wanted us to have the education she didn't have. My grandmother would tell everyone that my sister would be a doctor and I would be a lawyer. She praised us highly for our academic achievements. She also taught me to be responsible, diligent, hardworking, and to have love for my family, no matter what! She once told me, "The world won't stop for your pain. You gotta keep going." I would carry those lessons and her dreams for my success with me to this very day.

I always did well in school, and it became my safe space, one of the few places I felt I belonged. I won a lot of awards as a child for all kinds of subjects and perfect attendance. I had a dream of going to Spelman College, but that would be a dream I would never be able to fulfill. During my senior year at Hillcrest High School, which was in Jamaica (Queens), New York, I found out I was pregnant. I really wanted to go to college but wasn't sure how I could. I remember meeting with my guidance counselor (I don't even remember her name). I can still see her looking through my file, with all my grades (mostly A's, a B here and there). She turned and looked at me with a blank face. "How do you think you are going to go to college with a baby?" she asked. I said, "I don't know. That's why I am asking." "The best advice I can give you is to transfer to Ida B. Wells. They have a program for pregnant teens, and you can get your GED, then you can get a job and support your child," she said. I was pissed, to say the least. I began thinking she was another adult that didn't even see me! I hid my tears, as I often did. I didn't want to give her the satisfaction that she had hurt me. She had written me off that very moment. I stood up and said, "I already have a job. Thanks for nothing!" I walked out of her office and slammed the door behind me. I was 18 with only three more months of high school left. I was only taking one class, economics, from 7:45-to 8:30 AM. That's all I needed to graduate. I had been in an honors program since I was in elementary school. I had taken a lot of regent courses in junior high school and only needed economics in the second half of my senior year.

My guidance counselor tried to get me kicked out of school because I refused to voluntarily transfer to Ida B Wells. I had to go all the way to the superintendent to get permission to stay and graduate with my senior class. I gave birth to my first son Justin on March 7, 1991, and I missed three days of school before I returned. His paternal grandmother kept him so I could finish. My guidance counselor's words hurt! Maybe because a small part of me thought she was right! I was so scared to mess up my son's life and drag him through what I had been through. I wanted something better for him. I wanted someone, anyone, to say I could do it. I still cry to this day for the young girl who needed someone to speak hope into my life, and like almost all the adults in my life, she had made me feel invisible, alone, and like I didn't belong with my peers. But God! "Let us hold unswervingly to the hope we profess, for he who promised is faithful." (Hebrews 10:23).

Something inside of me said not to believe her, not to trust what I was seeing, hearing, or experiencing at the time. So, I pushed forward and went to Queensborough Community College with the hope of becoming a nurse. By this time, I lived in a two-bedroom apartment in Queens Village. My sister Wilma, who was 17 years old at the time, lived with me because my grandparents had moved back to Savannah, GA. I don't know how we made it, but we did. I worked at Pathmark, and she worked on the weekends at a catering hall. It was only for five or six months, and then she left on a full academic scholarship to Emory University in Atlanta, GA. I was so proud of her.

During my first year at Queensborough Community College, I had an

Educational Opportunity (EOP) advisor Dr. Gladys Aponte. EOP was for students that needed supportive services academically or financially. She was amazing, one of the few adults in my life that saw me. She told me I didn't belong in community college and that I could go to a four-year college. She helped me find and apply for a scholarship. I received the New York State Higher Education Scholarship. It paid my tuition in full. I then applied and got accepted to Stonybrook University. They had campus housing for families and a daycare.

I thought I had solved all my problems. However, there was a waitlist for both housing and daycare. I thought I could commute until a spot opened for housing and childcare, but four weeks into my first semester, I realized, financially, that it was going to be impossible. It cost $20 a day to commute back and forth to Stonybrook. I was only making $ 7.00 per hour part-time at Pathmark, and my rent was $600 dollars a month. I remember the embarrassment of having to explain my financial situation to each of my professors. I could only afford to come to class once a week. So, all my professors allowed me to pick up and hand in my assignments once a week. There was no Zoom or email in those days; everything was in person.

It was tough for me. Justin's dad was in the military. I decided to go back to community college and move into my Auntie Pam's basement. My Uncle Hugh converted it into a one-bedroom apartment. It was small, but it served the purpose. The bathroom was inside the boiler room, and the kitchen was so small I could stand in the middle and touch both walls if I extended my arms. I didn't care. She was only charging me $250 a month, and I started braiding hair to earn a little extra money. I didn't have a checking account, but I had a savings account at Emigrant Savings Bank. I did what my grandmother taught me, and I can hear her voice now saying, "Save what you won't miss. That way, you won't go back and get it." At 16, I started putting $5.00 every Friday into my account, and I gradually increased over the years. I wanted to buy a house. The rest of the money I would put in envelopes. I would label each envelope with the bill that needed to be paid (rent, groceries, savings) and put them under my mattress. It appeared I had gotten my life back on track finally! During the fall semester of 1993, Justin's dad proposed, and we got married in January of 1994.

Time seemed to move so quickly after that. I graduated from Queensborough Community in June of that year and transferred to York College in Jamaica, Queens. We did a SouSou and, with the money I had saved, bought a two-bedroom home in Elmont. Shortly after we moved into the house, my grandmother reached out to me and asked me to take care of my little brother John (he was only one at the time). I was pregnant with my second child and working at a group home on the weekends. I remember John came to live with us on a Wednesday, and I gave birth to my daughter Ashley on Friday. It was a lot! I went from having one child to three, all in the same week. I would dress them alike, and I really enjoyed being a mom.

I got accepted into the Occupational therapy program the following year, in the Fall of 1995, and finally graduated with my Bachelor of Science in Occupational Therapy in June 1998. Two years later, I separated from my husband. During that time from 2000 to 2003, I went to graduate school for a Master of Science Administration. Central Michigan University had an off-campus program at the Fort Hamilton Army base on the weekends. I began working for myself as an independent contractor with the New York City Department of Education and opened an in-home daycare. My life was back on track again, or so I thought. Life would throw me yet another curveball. I remained close with my in-laws after the divorce. I had two sisters-in-law, Wendy and Natalie. Wendy was the oldest. Both of them had sons, Andrew and Kimo jr. The boys attended my in-home daycare.

One morning Natalie dropped the boys off and said she was going to work, and Wendy was home with the flu. Natalie had just come back from the hospital with Wendy. I was with the children in the daycare most of the day, and the next thing I remember is Natalie calling me, screaming on the phone, saying she had found Wendy dead in the house. I don't know how I got to the hospital, but I remember seeing Wendy's body lying in a hospital bed, dead, as family and friends walked in and out of the room. As a family, we would never be the same. It was so heartbreaking. She didn't have the flu. She had meningitis. She was so young, 25 years old, and it still feels like a dream. Three months later, my best friend since kindergarten died. Her heart just gave out after years of having sleep apnea. That would be the hardest thing I had ever been through. Eighteen years later and I still fight back the tears. I still can't go to her grave without falling apart. She was someone who never judged me. She always loved me. I could call her at 2 o'clock in the morning and tell her I needed something, and she would just come. We did everything together. She was the heartbeat of our friend group. I miss her so much every day. I can't even put real words to it. It just felt like I was drowning. I remember feeling really down during that time. It just seemed everything was going wrong. The divorce would be final in early 2004.

My little sister Wilma was attending a PhD program in Organizational Leadership at the University of Maryland Eastern Shore. She encouraged me to apply, and I did. School had always been a safe space for me. Being newly single, everyone was setting me up with all kinds of dates. I met a guy, Damon Rentz, at my friend Gail's game night party. We hit it off very quickly and got engaged in January of 2005. I got accepted into the program, got married, and found out I was pregnant. I was so happy! In my twenties, I found out I had endometriosis and was told I had a 14% chance of getting pregnant naturally. I showed up to the first day of class nine months pregnant. I couldn't help but notice everyone's stares. I knew what they were thinking. How was she going to do this program pregnant and commuting from New York?

It was a weekend program. The program director politely came over and basically asked what everyone was thinking. The program was designed for working professionals. Each semester consisted of three courses that were five weeks in length. Basically, a 15-week semester was divided into three courses. I completed the first course and withdrew from the other two courses so I could give birth to my daughter, Anyssa. I came back in the spring and doubled up on my classes in the fall to catch up. By the following spring, I was pregnant again with Alyssa. I was super surprised as I thought I was just lucky the last time. I finished the coursework in two years. I waited for the following year to take my comprehensive exam, which I passed. Two months later, my ex-husband died of cancer-related to volunteering as a first responder during 911. It was such a sad time. He found out he had cancer one week and died the next week. I took my children every morning for a 6 AM prayer. My divorce was hard for them, and co-parenting them had just gotten to a place where it was manageable. I didn't know what to say or do to comfort them.

Over the next few years, I would try to complete my dissertation, but it just seemed impossible. My endometriosis returned, and I had hidradenitis suppurativa and fibromyalgia. I was in and out of the hospital. Pain became my life. This was a very hard time for me. I often didn't feel well. I went to so many doctors that really couldn't even tell me what was wrong. I would sit by myself and cry. I don't know why it has always been so difficult for me to let people see my hurt. My grandmother told me a story of how she would hide in the bathroom at work and cry. I would remember my grandmothers' words, "The world would not stop for your pain." So, I just kept pushing.

I also had two miscarriages and ectopic pregnancy. I think this was the most difficult thing I have experienced thus far. The miscarriages were back-to-back. I was wearing maternity clothes. I had already begun to tell people I was pregnant. It was the same thing both times. I didn't know how to feel. People would say things like, "Well, at least you have other children." I wanted to just scream, "those are not comforting words" a loss is a loss, period. I felt so alone, and I couldn't even bring myself to talk about it with my husband. I just cried in private, as I always did. Just when I thought it could not be any worse, the very next year, I had an ectopic pregnancy. I was told I had to take Methotrexate to stop the growth of the baby, or I would die.

While I knew this was not a viable pregnancy, I couldn't help but feel like I was killing my own child to save my own life. It hurt so deeply. I had to submit blood work for an entire month, and I couldn't be left alone, just in case the pregnancy ruptured my tube. The only person I was able to talk to about it was my grandmother, who shared she had gone through an ectopic pregnancy also.

She always seemed to have the right words at the right time. I was told I would never have any more children after the ectopic pregnancy, but my God had a different plan. Two months later, I became pregnant with my fourth daughter, Aniya. Three years later, I would have my sixth and final child Jace. My doctor couldn't believe it!

My grandfather also died during this time. He had a lot of health issues. My grandmother had been taking care of him for a long time. I remember her calling me the day he died. She told me she was outside gardening, that she didn't want to see him die. My heart broke for her. My grandmother was the strongest woman I had ever known, and I could hear the pain in her voice. I didn't know how to comfort her over the phone, so I just listened. I tried to finish my dissertation, but it just seemed like I couldn't get any momentum. I wasn't in the right headspace. I couldn't focus. I went through a long mourning period with the pregnancy losses.

Over the years, I would try to reconnect with the school and my professors to finish my dissertation. I finally made some momentum with a new faculty member. She was really on top of it. We met regularly and got a rough draft of the first two chapters. We were beginning the third chapter and set an appointment to meet, but she didn't show up. I was very surprised because she always kept our appointments. After a few days had passed, I called the program and was informed that she had left the program. I thought it was odd that she did not contact me, and then I received a message from her to join a Facebook group where she basically announced that she had left the program for a new position. I responded, "Congratulations," because I didn't know what to say. She sent me a message back and said, "Good luck." Really? I couldn't believe it. I was so disappointed and angry. I really don't like to depend on people because 99% of the time, I end up hurt. I have always tried to avoid situations that require a high level of trust on my part. I didn't even know what to do! I only had one semester to finish everything. She was my last hope. I had already lost two committee chairpersons who had previously left the program. This would be my fourth time putting my committee back together.

I couldn't even believe this was happening. I literally was exhausted all the time, but I had to complete the program. I tried to speak to any and everyone I could, all the way to the provost. That meeting was so bizarre. I had gone to the school countless times, and that day I got lost. I drove my car into a muddy swamp. I called a tow truck, he came, and he got stuck. I put the white loafers I had on in a plastic bag, folded my linen blaze neatly on top of them, and tied the bag up. Then I put on a pair of high heel black Mary Jane pumps. It hurt my heart to sacrifice them, but it had to be done! I climbed out of the sunroof of my Honda Pilot and began walking down the muddy path toward the tow truck. As I walked down the muddy path, blood began dripping down my arms, and the mosquitos were eating me alive. Once I got close enough to the road where the tow truck was stuck, I handed him my keys and said, "Call me when you get it out." I continued to walk down the hot (and I mean hot) paved road until I came to a little red house. A woman sat on a screened porch. I took off the muddy shoes and carefully put on my white loafers and slipped my arms through the linen blazer (it was lined, so the blood didn't show through immediately). I tapped lightly on the screen door and said, "Excuse me, ma'am, I'm so sorry to disturb you, I am a doctoral student at UMES, and my car is stuck in the mud down the road. I have an important meeting with the provost, and I really need a ride." She looked at me and smiled. Then she yelled out to a gentleman in the backyard and asked him to take me to the school, but he had been drinking a few beers, and he was in no condition to take me.

She looked at the desperation in my face, and by this time, the blood was soaking through my blazer. She said, "Hold on, baby, let me get my purse." I offered her money for taking me, but she wouldn't accept it. She dropped me off on the campus, but the provost's office was on the other side. I couldn't bring myself to ask her to take me to the other side of the campus. So, I got out quickly and thanked her. I ran as fast as I could (and if you know me, that's not very fast). By the time I got to the provost's office, I was so out of breath I couldn't even speak. I tried extremely hard to compose myself, but I felt like I was having a heart attack! Needless to say, it was not a productive meeting, but I realized, at that moment, it was just too much! I needed to move on. A few of my classmates were having a similar problem and wanted me to join them in suing the school. I met with the lawyer, who said I had a strong case, but I decided that was not a route I wanted to pursue. I wanted to finish what I started, period! I wasn't interested in blaming anyone.

Most programs will not allow you to transfer credits or only accept a small amount. I decided to suck it up and find a school that would let me transfer something. I found an informational session flyer online for Manhattanville College Doctorate in Education Dissertation Completion (ABD) Pathway. "Because of the Lord's great love we are not consumed for his compassion never fails. They are new every morning; great is thy faithfulness." (Lamentations 3:22-23). I was back on track!

I started the program in February 2017, and in March, my sister died. I felt terrible both mentally and physically. I found out that she was my sister when I was 23 years old. She was a few months younger than me. I was so disappointed in myself that I let the politics of my family and my disappointment in my dad for not telling me sooner that she was my sister keep me from developing a relationship with her. I still carry that guilt, and it can be emotionally draining. The entire time I was at the funeral, I was physically exhausted. I wasn't feeling well at all. I thought it was the fibromyalgia flaring up again. Two weeks later, I was diagnosed with breast cancer. I could not believe it! It began to feel like I was carrying the weight of the world on my shoulders. I was taking care of my grandmother during this time, who was suffering from mild dementia. I had four children under the age of 12 (my youngest was two years old), my two older children had already lost their father to cancer, and my husband was trying to be strong for me, but I could see the worry in his eyes. I almost never feel sorry for myself, but this time I didn't know what to say or do! I was so worried about who would take care of my family. I made the mistake of Googling triple-negative breast cancer, and it made me feel worse. I had just gotten back on track. I hadn't even completed the first class, and here again, I was battling a health issue. I decided not to think about the journey, but I literally took one day at a time. I dealt with what I could deal with. I had some good days and some bad days, but I tried to be thankful for every day!

The faculty at Manhattanville is AMAZING! I took a leave of absence from work and thought it would be best if I put my dissertation on hold, but my professors encouraged me to continue. They encouraged me to stay in school, so I did! It was hard. When I had my first breast removed, I was more afraid of dying in surgery than I was of cancer. I remember waking up and not feeling as bad as I thought I would when I saw that my breast was gone. I was so happy to be alive. I got out of the bed and put on a pink nightgown, did my hair, and put on a pink robe. If you haven't guessed already, PINK is my superpower!! I remember the nurse coming into my room and saying, "Who got you dressed?" I said, "I got myself dressed." I needed to feel like myself. I didn't want to be sick or look sick.

I had seven surgeries (I decided to remove my other breast), and I only took off one semester for chemotherapy. Chemotherapy was hard! I managed to smile and be in good spirits through all the surgeries. However, when I started chemotherapy, they told me I would not lose my hair, but I would go into menopause. I didn't care about going into menopause; I was already on track for that at 45, and I already had six children. I didn't go through menopause, but my hair did fall out! When I looked in the mirror and saw all the bald patches, I just stood there and cried! I didn't realize how much of my identity was wrapped up in my hair. I picked up my husband's razor and just shaved it all off. It felt good to not just let one more thing happen to me but that I had some control over how it was going to happen.

It's funny what your mind goes back to. After we finished taking all the pictures at my defense, I thanked my committee, and I began planning my party! I didn't finish my dissertation in time to walk for May 2019 commencement, but like most of my journey, I sucked it up and decided as long as I finished, it didn't matter. My grandmother got to see my diploma and celebrated with me; I could wait a year to walk. However, 2020 brought COVID-19 and disrupted everyone's one's plans. I lost three uncles, two aunts, and my beloved grandmother. My graduation was online. Nothing like I planned, no cap and gown, no pictures, but it was better than nothing. In 2021, the college decided to have an in-person graduation ceremony, and I walked across the stage fighting back the tears. I still fight back the tears when I think about it, wishing my grandmother could have been there. My degree belongs to her! A RIGHT she was denied! Thank you, Mama, for giving me what you had. It was more than enough!! Thank you to everyone who believed that "I was enough!" God is Faithful!

"For I know the plans I have for you," declares the LORD, "plans to prosper you and not to harm you, plans to give you hope and a future." (Jeremiah 29:11).

CHAPTER 18

Kristin Robair's Story

KRISTIN A. ROBAIR knows first-hand about trials, sacrifice, and hard work. She believes in the scripture, "Blessed is the one who perseveres under trial because, having stood the test, that person will receive the crown of life that the Lord has promised to those who love him." (James 1:12)". She is a doctoral candidate at Louisiana State University in the Educational Leadership and Research program specializing in Higher Education Administration. As a first-generation college graduate, Kristin believes that educational access & sharing personal experiences can contribute to more African Americans, especially women, obtaining an advanced degree. She believes that every person's individual life experiences help to craft society through community and career involvement. Her research interests involve critical issues in urban education, student development, career readiness, interdisciplinary writing, culturally relevant pedagogy, and pop culture & multicultural literacy. Currently, Kristin works as a Literacy Coordinator in the EBR Parish School System, located in Baton Rouge, Louisiana. She is responsible for providing teachers with professional development around effective literacy practices and the foundations of reading while also coaching & engaging teachers on best practices, literacy intervention activities, and model lessons.

The Making of a Black Pearl

"A pearl is a beautiful thing that is produced by an injured life. It is the tear [that results] from the injury of the oyster. The treasure of our being in this world is also produced by an injured life. If we had not been wounded, if we had not been injured, then we will not produce the pearl.'" —Stephan Hoeller

QUIT! That single four-letter word has so much power depending on how it is used, and yet, it tried to take over my journey. When I was four years old, I always wanted to be a doctor at a university. I don't really remember who I knew that had that role, but I always wanted to be a doctor, LOL. The irony as I grew up was that I was interested in the medical field but always had a passion for helping others. As I matriculated from elementary to high school, I realized certain terms about being a first-generation college student, FAFSA, and student loans were frightening. Coming from a single-parent household, I, along with others, stressed out about how my mom was going to pay for college. Moreover, I did receive my B.A. from Southeastern Louisiana University, followed by my MPA from Southern University A&M College; however, when it was time to prepare for the next step of my educational journey, I yearned for out-of-state. Of course, that was not in God's plan for me.

I started my doctoral journey in the summer of 2016 at Louisiana State University. The set of instructors that I had always gave me hope to "change the world" and highlighted the differences in people that called for positive and equal change in systems. From there, I learned four key lessons that helped me during my doctoral journey.

Here are some quick tips that I would recommend for ANY Black woman to follow, especially to be successful.

1.) **Make sure that you KNOW your topic of interest before applying or by the end of your first semester. This will set the foundation for your journey.**

When I first started at LSU, I had no clue as to what I wanted to research because I was interested in several different topics. I often thought about if I were to graduate today, what type of job would I want. I thought I wanted to work with athletics, then Greek Life, then Title IX, then Academic Affairs, then Student Affairs, and the list goes on and on. My issue is that I am so interested in so many different topics that I never stopped to really absorb all the information that I gained. My first-year instructors took a great opportunity to explain their backgrounds and what interests them, yet I was still so confused as to what to write about. In each class, I learned about concepts that I had yet to even be introduced to, and yet, it was very insightful. Between learning about theories such as intersectionality, critical race theory, and social and cultural capital theory,

I was mesmerized by all of the intellectual ideas and concepts that had me feeling like, "I'm not crazy. There are people in the world that think and see things differently like me." I was so engaged and enlightened in the class research and dialogue that before you knew it, two years had passed, and BOOM! I needed to schedule and prepare for my proposal defense. That's when I began to talk with my cohort colleagues about what they were writing about, and that's when it hit me—I HAD NO CLUE what the foundation of my dissertation was going to be about.

Through this journey, I realized that I should have selected a topic that I encountered in my everyday life: literacy in urban education; however, I was interested in two main topics related to higher education: student development and career readiness. Through researching these topics, I reflected on how my own undergrad and graduate journey helped to develop me as a successful Black woman within my profession. I realized as a first-generation college student that not only did matriculating through leadership roles in student organizations help, but also in my sorority. Within that self-reflection, it allowed me to FINALLY develop my research topic.

2.) Find a STRONG group of colleagues that will support you.

I will forever be indebted to the following people: Anissa, Kala, Jovan, Aeryel "Sunshine," Runell, Ariana, Danielle, Trey, Adam, Marvin, and a host of others that have been so very supportive and influential in helping me stay on track. As I started my journey, these people had influenced me in many ways to help uplift me when I was down and just didn't think I was worthy of being in this program. As they began to graduate and move on to various career opportunities, I had to figure out how to not lean too much on them but to continue to push myself to finish and complete my goal. It was through each of their journeys that I learned that it's not about how fast you finish but that you just finish. As stated before, I had to continue to remind myself that these people worked in the field that their research was tied to, whereas my initial research topic had nothing to do with the field I worked in. Because they were so immersed in their work, they could see a need for a change, a need to create something new.

Additionally, my "social media family" is my other set of colleagues that I can lean on. I found social media groups to support me in my journey through our connections of motherhood, being Black, females, and being qualitative researchers. These groups helped me with my mental health as well as in areas of improving my research. On Facebook, I leaned heavily on the Qualitative Research in Education group, Literature Review Resources group, and Doctoral Mom Life group. These groups keep me motivated to push through as we are all experiencing similar situations in life and research. Additionally, the PhD Doc Students Group Me is beneficial for me as well. This group not only provides uplifting dialogue but writing group time as well. For me, this is needed in order to be held accountable for my progress and to push through to finish.

3.) **Find a SUPPORTIVE Chair and Co-Chairs who believe in your research.** Initially, the advisor that I had did not align with what I wanted to write about. In hindsight, she was trying to help and gear me toward an area of expertise which was teaching and training higher ed faculty on the teaching and learning preparation of K-12. I was NOT interested in that. Unfortunately, that caused several debates for three semesters. I had to change! When you are going through this doctoral journey, you must be passionate and immersed in your topic because you will spend a LOT of time on the work. For that reason, I changed advisors. My current chair and co-chairs were all professors that I felt enlightened, motivated, and inspired by. They all believed in the human capital of people. The way my brain worked, I was all over the place. I was interested in so many different things that it was hard to narrow down to one specific research question. When I finally did figure out what I wanted to research, they were supportive and helped me to navigate my topic to a more streamlined style. They were interested in the topic, which is the opposite of what other doctoral students encounter. Even through the obstacles that I encountered, they occasionally called and checked on me to push me to the finish line, knowing my struggles. For that, I am always grateful and will pay it forward. A supportive committee does make a HUGE difference in your outcome of success.

4.) **Don't be so HARD on yourself because self-care is a KEY ESSENTIAL!**
I attended as a full-time student while working full-time as a teacher and as a single parent. You know the saying, "This is too good to be true?" Well, that's exactly how I felt when I began attending. That's when my obstacles for each semester began to start.

First, the Great Flood of 2016 in Baton Rouge happened. This was when a horrible thunderstorm occurred, and it seemed to consistently rain on top of Baton Rouge for almost seven full days. My house was 100% flooded with 12 ft of water. I lost everything, yet again. I think that is when the beginning of my anxiety started. My family and I are originally from New Orleans and relocated to Baton Rouge following Hurricane Katrina. We lost everything in that catastrophic storm as well. This time was different as I was a single parent and a caregiver. My family had to split up yet again because there was not enough room for us to stay together. My son & I lived between co-workers and family from out-of-town in order to have some stability, while my mom, stepdad, and younger sister stayed with her in-laws and my stepbrother. School was my outlet as I was able to always provide various insights coming from my perspective and those narratives were respected; moreover, they provided my colleagues with different perspectives as we all came from various backgrounds, ethnicities, and cultures. In that semester, I had a classmate that repurchased books for me and was constantly motivated to keep pushing forward, as I felt like maybe I should quit. I had friends donate enough money for me to purchase a laptop.

In 2017, it was no different. I had someone break into my car and steal, if not all, but the majority of my belongings. Guess the primary thing they stole; my pride and joy at the time: my book sack (with all my articles from class), my notebooks from statistics (Lord knows I NEEDED that), my books from my classes, and most importantly, my flash drive with all of my class assignments on them. I thought about quitting, but I was encouraged by a classmate who gave me methods to succeed. She created an email address just related to her doctoral journey. She emails everything to herself on that email address while adding and saving her writing progress in Google Docs and Google Drive. (Little did I know, this was a game-changer for me!)

In 2018, I was in a horrible car accident that caused a major concussion on the left side of my head. This concussion affected my language processing skills, memory, and the way that I process information to the point that I have brain fog, memory lapse, and struggle to process information in a swift and efficient way. Talk about a train wreck for someone in a doctoral program. This had a major impact on my matriculation in my program as I struggled to balance deadlines, put together information, and bridge the gaps for my own research to develop a proposal.

In 2019, someone stole my car. Of course, I had just come back from the library after researching & writing 80 pages of my already completed proposal. I had to pretty much start from scratch at this point while figuring out a new method of transportation. Additionally, I was named Middle School Teacher of the Year for my school district, which opened many other doors of opportunities for advancement. This distinguished honor caused my focus to shift from school to work, at which [point, I struggled with time management balance between the two. I start thinking there are signs telling me that this isn't for me. *You need to quit now!*

COVID-19 Pandemic, Program Time Out, and Family Matters.

At this point, I had figured out my topic, yet nobody was in the mood to conduct interviews for me. People were quarantined and concerned about the pandemic, which I could do nothing about at all. It was stressful and depressing. Social media was the primary way to learn how several family members and close friends died. It began to take a toll on my mental health big time. The uncertainty about completing school, maintaining a job, and my child's education, was very desolating. It wasn't until the end of the spring and the beginning of the summer that I was able to start conducting my interviews to begin to complete chapter four. Soon after, my mom and stepdad began to experience several health issues that triggered more round-the-clock care at times. On top of that, the most dangerous time for a person that is in a doctoral program is the writing time. That has been a challenge. It has been such a challenge that I'm close to the "time-out" period of the completion period of my dissertation time in my program. Within two years, I became even more stressed out, developed high anxiety levels, and started to experience moodiness, weight gain, and other symptoms of depression.

At times I feel very accomplished, yet I still feel incompetent. I feel like it is not enough. I feel like it doesn't make sense. I feel like this is not for me. I feel like I want to QUIT! I need to QUIT! I need to close this chapter of my goals and dreams because it is never going to happen.

Between going to class full-time, working full-time, and being a full-time caregiver, I felt the burnout immediately. Honestly, I felt and felt like I was a nonstop merry-go-round. If, at any point, I stopped to take a break, then I thought that I would immediately be judged. At some point, I should have taken a semester or two off because I knew that my mental health was causing an issue. At some point, I developed anxiety and bouts of depression. After my own "Series of Unfortunate Events" during this journey, I should have seen what is unspoken in the Black Community, a therapist! YEP! I said it. I should have seen a therapist earlier to help me unpack my trauma to better prepare myself as I go through this journey. Although I had friends and colleagues to motivate me, a trained professional would have found and suggested other ways of healing rather than me assuming and thinking school would be my "coping mechanism" because that is all that I knew. By the time I started seeing a therapist for "drop-in visits," or so I like to call them, I was already too far gone in my doctoral journey; however, it is never too late. This is so very important as you matriculate within your journey. It is important to take a break, have a movie night, dinner date, read a book, visit a museum, and hang out with friends, just to give yourself a brain break from crafting your masterpiece. However, don't get too distracted because it can cause you to delay your journey to finish.

However, I have always had a "ram in the bush" mentality, so people say. Through this journey, God has always sent someone to give me an encouraging message to continue. Through one of my social media groups, I have had the blessing to encounter a sorority sister, Dr. Callie Womble Edwards, who owns a coaching company called "A Life of a Scholar." Through this program, she has helped me restructure and refocus my energy on fixing my dissertation issues and talking things through so that I don't feel insane. She has not only become my coach but a friend & guide when needed. My chairs and former professors have always been encouraging and supportive. Although they hold prominent leadership positions on campus, they have always given me advice and guidance when I needed or asked. The women in this book have been encouraging because it makes me feel supported and not alone in my journey.

In closing, it is okay to have stumbling blocks. It is perfectly fine to feel inept at times because you are proving why your problem is beneficial for the world to recognize, learn, and apply further research into this problem. No one is perfect, and no one perfectly goes through a doctoral program knowing all the answers. These lessons are things that I wish somebody had told me before I applied for a doctoral program as a Black woman. It would have made my journey possibly less stressful than what I made it. My hope is that my experience will help the next Black woman become successful in their doctoral journey. My hope is that I will encourage the next Black woman to stand strong, not give up, and continue to break barriers for others. My hope is one day, someone will speak my name in a room full of people, reference this book, and keep striving. Remember, everybody may run the same race, but their journey is not the same. It's not important how you start, but how you finish. Best wishes and blessings!

CHAPTER 19

Shanel Robinson's Story

DR. SHANEL ROBINSON is an Assistant Professor at the Chicago School of Psychology, where she teaches and engages in research. She earned her PhD in Counselor Education from Auburn University in Auburn, Alabama, in 2020. Dr. Robinson researches the career decision-making of women of color (WOC) in counselor education as well as ways to recruit and retain WOC in counselor education. She is a collaborator at heart and has engaged in numerous projects surrounding multicultural competency, gifted Black males, affirming LGBTQ+ youth, supervising millennials, and more. She has accepted and published articles in the Journal of Professional School Counseling, Journal of Counselor Education and Preparation, the SAGE Encyclopedia of Marriage, Family, & Couples Counseling, and the Alabama Counseling Association Journal. In addition to her scholarship, she owns Mind Your Mind Counseling & Consulting, a private practice treating individuals and couples in Atlanta, Georgia. She is a Licensed Professional Counselor, Certified Professional Counselor Supervisor, National Board-Certified Counselor, and Certified Clinical Mental Health Counselor. Her clinical practice has included counseling in community, psychiatric in-patient and out-patient facilities, college, residential, and private practice settings. In her free time, Dr. Robinson cultivates new recipes, spends time with family and friends, finds new music, or travels.

Let me begin by saying my story is going to be authentically written in my voice, with my mannerisms and my humor. It's a story of accountability and honoring your experiences while getting what you need. Feel free to have an authentic reaction to what you read.

The Warm-Up

I recall my first day at my institution and the excitement that I felt knowing I was going to do something no one in my immediate family had done, work towards my PhD I pulled into the parking deck on the first day blasting "Grateful" by Hezikiah Walker in full-blown worship mode, and by the start of the second semester, I found myself turning up to "God's Plan" by Drake. On my very first day, I knew that earning my PhD would be the most rewarding yet isolating experience I'd ever had. For starters, upon walking on campus, I immediately knew I would be one of few students of color. Oddly enough, I didn't get that familiar pit in my stomach that boasted of fear. I did, however, feel a sense of uncertainty, having experienced both rejection and acceptance in predominantly white spaces. It was no secret that my institution had a long-standing history of failures to attain and retain students of color. In fact, it inspired my dissertation topic (which I will discuss later on). I would literally count the few people of color I'd see in passing on campus from the parking deck. To make matters worse, when I got to my first class and met my cohort, I was the only student of color among five white women. Now don't get me wrong, I got along well with my cohort, but there's no experience that compares to always being the "only one." The only one who can speak to the marginalized Black experience. The only one who's consistent in vocalizing and seeing the need for "racial" social justice and advocacy. The only one everyone looks at when more representation is needed at the table. You catch my drift? Not only did I struggle to feel included in my cohort, but even with students who looked like me. I was having a deep internal battle, yet, wearing a smile and presenting poise in any academic setting. Everyone had agendas they were trying to navigate, and that didn't always mean chit-chatting over a cup of coffee to catch up on the "Black experience at a PWI." We all had tons to do. So, when I went from gospel to rap, I knew it was really a need to quickly connect to my Blackness at the end of a day full of navigating white spaces.

I had an amazing experience with the faculty in my program. I'm naturally a go-getter, so I was meeting with my professors to connect and establish a working rapport. I was committed to not just taking classes but growing my connections and expertise. I wanted the full PhD experience, especially after taking the leap to quit my full-time job to fully invest in my career (thank God it paid off). Like many educational programs, there was a lot of chatter surrounding favoritism, tokenism, racism, and several other isms as complaints. Despite this, I knew my biggest obstacle was myself and the imposter syndrome I constantly felt.

Impostor syndrome was alive and flourished throughout my experience. Doubt plagued my mind. I would sit in classes, present at conferences, and speak on various issues, yet there was a war going on in my mind. I was constantly asking myself questions such as, *"Do you know enough to speak on this? "What if you don't sound smart enough?" "How will people receive my thoughts?"* That thinking crippled and cost me so many moments where I could have shined. It was hard to find the confidence to be unapologetically myself with no fear of consequences. Every moment felt like an interview in which I needed to be the best candidate for the job.

At the time, I didn't realize the impact of being the "first" in my immediate family. I was the "first" to earn a master's, the "first" to pursue a PhD and the "first" to truly pursue my educational dreams. Being the first comes with both celebrations and setbacks. I had no one to give me the blueprint or to go before me and show me how academia works. While I didn't want to appear I didn't belong, I felt like it within. It took me a while to realize these institutions were not created for people who looked like me. They were created for a majority experience, and I was having a minority one. The root cause of my imposter syndrome was that I was existing to belong instead of existing to bring my authentic self as a contribution to the academy. I had to remember that many before and after me would identify and have similar challenges in earning their PhD. What was critical was that I honored my own experiences and recognized that I might navigate the space differently than others on the journey. I realized that on the road to PhD I had to overcome self-doubt, feelings of being unworthy, procrastination, excuses, and most importantly, thinking that the degree would be handed to me and not earned. Earning a PhD is like something I'd experienced before. While it was critical that I had personal support systems, mentors, and departmental collaboration to complete my degree, the weight of my goal was on me.

The Race

Despite my growing up in a family that didn't pursue higher education, I was raised to be a self-starter and a go-getter. Being raised by entrepreneur grandparents had benefits that included instilling motivational self-talk. My grandmother told me early on that the early bird got the worm, and nothing would be handed to me. She taught me that anything in life worth having was worth fighting for and working for. In the midst of earning my degree, which consisted of a full load of courses, I was presenting, working on publications, engaging in leadership, and networking with people who shared my interests. Not to toot my own horn, but I presented 29 times during my studies. I engaged in research with my peers and faculty becoming a published author and scholar. I took on local and regional leadership roles in various organizations and made connections and collaborated with people all over the United States. I did this while working part-time at a psychiatric hospital 45 minutes away from the school because I needed the extra coins! We don't give ourselves the flowers we deserve for the work we put in to win the race and make a career of it. Winning takes perseverance, drive, endurance, and determination. It's not just about making it to the end, but what we do to get there and how we sustain thereafter. So, pat yourself on the back, give yourself a high-five, and celebrate yourself; I sure did. Who better to commend you for a win than you? Those small wins are major to you staying the course and overcoming the trials because in life and, specifically, in getting a terminal degree, trials are inevitable.

Now that I've shared the ups, I want to confirm there were downs. I compare the road to PhD to running track and field, specifically 800 meters (I ran this race in high school). The thing about running a race is those watching only see the challenges that are broadcast; the lack of momentum gained in the beginning, the person who has an advantage over you, the overcoming of obstacles along the way, and an eventual defeat over the competition you face. What I've learned is that race is deeper than what people can easily see. It's the sweat and tears, the lack of sleep, the work you must put into your craft, the aches and pains you endure to push through for the win. I liken my process to this type of race.

There were days I was overwhelmed and cried before heading to campus. During my second lap in the program, which is the point I'd wrapped up on coursework. I woke up to prepare for my first day back on campus after a brief summer break, and as I looked at my reflection in the mirror (literally), I was overcome with emotion. Not only did I have personal issues I was dealing with, but I'd also submitted my comprehensive exams and didn't know if I'd be continuing to propose my dissertation topic or delayed a year because I'd fallen short. I cried as I thought to myself, *"I'll have another year of sleepless nights and never-ending tasks to do."* That feeling of still having to prove myself was alive, well, and killing the first-day vibe I was going for. Instead of excitement, I felt anxious about the possibility of spending another year in the program. As mentioned earlier, I was the "first." No one was prepared for me to pursue a doctoral degree. Friends and family didn't get what I was experiencing. They couldn't relate and provided encouragement that largely consisted of "girl, you got this" and "you'll be okay, you always have." I was thankful they poured into me what they could, but truthfully it wasn't enough. I was concerned about the financial burden of being in the program another year. Even with an assistantship, I had big girl bills to pay. Thank God I had a new group of friends equally going through similar battles pursuing a doctorate, though, in different programs, they understood and were the wind I needed to endure and push forward.

I cannot express enough how important it was for me to have a community. I would not be where I am

The Ceremony

The fears I had never came to pass. I successfully passed my comprehensive exams and proposed my dissertation on the same day. I'd gotten an internship at a university in Atlanta to complete the remaining core areas of my program. Unlike undergrad and even my master's, I spent most weekends at Barnes and Nobles with a coconut milk macchiato and spinach and cheese quiche, drilling through data and analyzing my results. I did a qualitative dissertation on the lived experiences of women of color and believed they deserved my best. There were weeks at a time I was unmotivated and had to take a step back. There is nothing worse than trying to honor someone's experiences when you're not honoring your own needs. For me, that meant defending in July instead of May as originally intended. It meant having a little fun while working to create balance, which COVID-19 tried to rob me of.

Only July 8, 2020, from the comfort of my home office, I became Dr. Shanel Robinson. I cried like a baby. It was the most exhilarating feeling to know that I was PhinisheD! It was like I'd dropped the mic and walked off stage. My committee had zero questions about the work I'd done and spent the remaining question and answer time affirming the study I'd completed. While I appreciated their affirmations, I was also very proud of myself. It takes a tremendous amount of dedication to complete a PhD program. I truly understand what people meant when they said it is not a road for everyone, but it was the road for me.

COVID-19 robbed me of a graduation, yet I was surrounded by friends who loved and supported me on what would've been graduation day. As a Licensed Professional Counselor, I engaged in clinical work. Seeing clients during a pandemic I was also experiencing was a new challenge, but God was using me for something great. I spent a year doing adjunct work everywhere. I worked at three institutions simultaneously to gain more teaching experience for a full-time faculty role. Hiring committees were frozen with so many unknowns surrounding the pandemic. I did all I could to still enjoy the benefits of the biggest accolade under my belt. Less than a year later, faculty roles were opening everywhere, and I was booked and busy with interviews. I soon secured a position, and it's been up and stuck ever since.

I can't lie; the imposter syndrome and race have continued. I still find myself questioning if I belong, if I'm doing enough, and if I deserve to be here. The truth is I know I do; you don't put in the type of work it takes to earn a PhD and not deserve it, yet I'm human. My Black history is rooted in inferiority, struggle, and strife. Then I remember, before that history, I came from kings and queens, people who knew themselves, had their own values and beliefs, and were rooted in rich experience. So when those thoughts creep up that tell me I'm an imposter, I tell the thought it's a lie. I fought for this. I deserve this, and so do you.

CHAPTER 20

Briana Spivey's Story

BRIANA SPIVEY IS currently a third-year doctoral student at the University of Georgia in the clinical psychology program. Briana is a proud alumna of Spelman College and a true Georgia Peach. Briana's research focuses on examining the implications of cultural and environmental factors on the mental health and well-being of African American women across the lifespan. Specifically, Briana focuses on the implications of the Strong Black Woman (SBW) schema on health outcomes among Black women. With this focus, Briana plans to utilize the experiences of Black women to inform the development of culturally relevant and adaptive treatment options for communities of color and, more specifically, Black women. She is a firm believer in me-search being research and thus uses her experiences as a Black woman to inform the trajectory of her research.

Currently, Briana is working on a project highlighting the experiences of Black graduate students attending Predominantly White Institutions (PWIs) and its relationship to the retention and success of students of color. Briana is currently the Graduate Coordinator for the EMPOWER Lab and actively working to ensure that the research we do can be translated into action and change for the Black community and other communities of color.

It Won't Always Be Easy

When I made the choice to attend Spelman College for my undergraduate education, I was breaking down barriers. I was doing something no one in my family ever did. I made a promise to be better than my parents, and this promise was the start of my journey in academia. It was when I arrived at Spelman that I was first introduced to a space where Black women were celebrated for thriving and excelling in style. Spelman was the place that ignited my passion for protecting Black women, their health, and their stories. Throughout my four years at Spelman, I found myself as a Black woman and began to sew together the narrative that would make me who I am today. Now prior to becoming immersed in the field of psychology, I was simply just trying to find my way. I knew I loved the mind and the way the mind works together with our health, but I had no idea where this love could take me. From the moment that I entered the psychology department at Spelman, pursuing a PhD in clinical psychology became more aligned with my purpose and became the main focus of the work that I engaged in throughout my four years. I gained sisters, friends, and forever mentors while at Spelman. I can look back on all the women who poured into me when I decided to pursue a doctoral degree, but one of the things I never knew starting that journey was how much of a transition it would be for me. I also underestimated what people around me meant when they said, "It won't always be easy."

Application season was the first introduction to my graduate career. This was the first time that I noticed and faced my anxiety. It was the first time that I noticed myself beginning to worry, and it was the physical worry (i.e., tightness in my chest and muscle tension) about whether I was going to get into graduate school, who I was letting down if I didn't, and what does that means about me if I don't get in. I didn't have a Plan B, C, or D. My only plan was to get this doctoral degree in clinical psychology. Applying to graduate school was the first time I had a panic attack. If I knew then what I know now, I would have known that it was a sign of how difficult, stressful, and overwhelming graduate school could be. After applying to 17 schools, receiving eight interviews, and being accepted into 4, I found my person and the place that was best for me. Following various conversations with my parents and my friends, I knew what I had to do. The Monday after spring break during my senior year, I sent the email committing to the University of Georgia. This commitment was so big because it highlighted that not only was I on the right path, but this path felt perfectly created for me. I celebrated beginning graduate school in the summer and graduating from the #1 HBCU! This celebration felt short-lived and truly not long enough. Two weeks after graduating, I packed all my stuff, said goodbye to some people, and see you later to others, and moved to Athens with the help of my family.

When I made the move, it was probably the hardest thing I had to do. I didn't have my support system readily available. It was just me here trying to figure it out with my new mentor, Dr. Isha Metzger. I didn't know anybody but my new mentor. What I will say is that this summer was the time I needed to get myself acclimated and build an amazing bond with my mentor. She poured into me, encouraged me, and reaffirmed what I already knew. I was where I needed to be.

Now it wasn't until the semester started and I walked onto my first predominantly white (PWI) campus that the loneliness of graduate school kicked in. That first moment was when I started to see what people meant when they said, "It won't be easy." I felt so out of place and lonely. Coming from a predominantly Black city and upbringing to now being in a predominantly white environment was jarring and depressing. It was a struggle to see people who looked like me and even just to find the food I love (e.g., I'm from Atlanta, so I love my hot wings). I knew very few people, and it was disheartening being in a space where I was an anomaly and not the norm. I grew up in Atlanta, so my background from elementary school to undergrad placed me in spaces with people who looked like me, understood me, and SAW me. Now I felt like I was in the shadow and really realized I was going to have to prove myself. I had to show that I worked hard to be here and I deserved to be here just like my white counterparts.

Between being alone, being in a new place, being one of 3 Black women in my cohort, and coming straight from undergrad, I felt lost. I will be honest with you and say that graduate school is difficult. It truly isn't easy because not only do you have to balance academics, but you have to balance being a human with a social life, which is a different beast. For me, in a clinical psychology program, I also had to learn how to balance academics and clinical work and everything under the sun. While I learned a lot from my experiences at Spelman, one of the main things I didn't learn was how to make the transition to a PWI. I struggled with how to navigate microaggressions in this space, feeling like this journey isn't just about me but for every Black woman after me, and then having to fight to dismantle a system that was never created for us. I will tell you now it will take our whole lives to dismantle this oppressive system that is deeply rooted in academia. However, don't let academia make you feel inadequate or feel that you don't deserve to be here.

It was during the second semester of my first year (March 2020) that the pandemic started! I will never forget going home for Spring Break and not returning back to Athens until August of 2021. The pandemic, coupled with racial injustice, was hard. I began to question whether what I was doing was making an impact; am I helping my people? I battled a lot with the peace I was feeling of being at home with my parents, but also the stress of being in graduate school online. I constantly worked hard to find ways to keep my motivation up (e.g., having Zoom parties with my friends, connecting with my friends in PhD programs, and just relaxing the best I could amidst the constant unrest) but let me tell you, *it wasn't easy*. I'm gonna fast forward to post-pandemic (kinda because we are still navigating it) and talk about a change that happened that can be your biggest nightmare as a graduate student- my mentor left! She left the summer of my second year, going into my third year. Let me clarify, she left my current institution and became faculty at another one. Now, this was something I never wanted (I wanted her to stay with meeeeee) and something I still grapple with from time to time.

This decision was one that I didn't know how to navigate, the option was there to follow her, but I felt I was in too deep. I was going into my third year, working on my thesis, and it just didn't seem possible. As much as I would have liked to follow her, my heart couldn't let me do it! I felt firmly planted and, in some ways, had adapted to an already abrupt and jarring transition, and to navigate another big transition like this in the middle of my program was too much for me. I bet you are wondering so what happened, or rather, what happens now. Well, my mentor was able to become an adjunct faculty member and is still able to oversee my progress, stay on my committees, and be there for me the way she was my first year. This is also to say that things are different, she is adjusting to her new position, and I am adjusting to her leaving, so we are making the best out of what can be seen as a series of unfortunate events. I wanted to highlight this piece of my doctoral journey to say your mentor may leave. Unfortunately, it was a reality that I didn't think would be mine, but it was. It was a moment when I started to think about myself and what I wanted for myself. It was a moment where I had to make a choice and be prepared for the consequences. It was also the moment in time when I had to trust in the process more than any other time in life.

Finding myself an academic

As I made my way into graduate school, I realized that while I have the goal of becoming a tenure-track professor, there is nothing in the handbook that says I have to sell my soul to accomplish that. It was through my time conducting research at Spelman and beginning new research projects while at UGA that I realized my research is ME. It is representative of the social and identity groups I am a part of, the narratives I want to rewrite, and the people I want to ensure access to and receive better mental health services. My research became *me-search*, and I knew that while there were all these hoops to jump through, I could make this journey what I wanted to make it. You can come into graduate school wanting to research one thing, and I want to be the one to tell you that your research interests can change, and that is okay! Graduate school is where you learn and find what you like, so don't be afraid to lean into that new line of research or jump on that project! Finding myself as an academic also consisted of me being able to let go of some of the socialization messages we receive as Black women in higher education. We are always reminded that we have to work harder than the next, we are expected to go above and beyond, and that we are always going to have to fight for our place in the world. While I see this time and time again, looking at all the women who have paved the way for me, I realized that these messages don't have to define the process of getting my PhD and my future of having that tenured position at an R1 (Research One) institution. These messages serve as warnings about what society expects of me and reminders that I want this, I can do this, and NOBODY will stop me from reaching my goals. The messages we receive are also subtle forms of advice that, now in my third year, emphasize taking care of yourself in whatever way that looks regardless of the toxic work culture expected of us in academia.

I study the Strong Black Woman (SBW) schema, and one of the things I had to learn is that we can be strong and not have to break ourselves in the process. Whether it is physical, emotional, or mental damage, we don't have to do it to show strength. Being strong is being able to ask for help, being able to say NO! Now that last one is big!! Once you learn the power of no, you will have the grace you need to do what you want! Being strong is taking a nap, responding to that email tomorrow, and being okay with creating boundaries for yourself. I wanted to also emphasize this because I see myself always trying to be strong, but I realized it was becoming more harmful to me. It was leading to burnout, exhaustion, agitation, and even more anxiety. Some things we do are because they have been helpful and provided us protection, but sometimes we have to look at where we are in life and question whether we need to do things as usual at this moment in time or can we rewrite the narrative? Write your story in graduate school, and don't be afraid of how the story looks!

Now I started this chapter by discussing how difficult it was to find myself in this white space. I don't want you to think that you will go into academia and go through an identity crisis and be depressed. That is also to say that it may happen, and that is okay! I want to assure you that you can make it through regardless of the trials and tribulations that you experience! One of the biggest things that were important to me but have also helped me tremendously was finding my community. My community became my friends (from home and school), my family, my mentors, and my partner! It is because of them that I continue to push and remember my why. Graduate school is lonely, and the PhD is lonely! I want to reiterate that because that was something I didn't find out until I was in this space. So ask for help. For now, ask those difficult questions now about what it is like being Black in a PhD program? What does that look like for other intersecting identities? And make sure you are talking to graduate students who have nothing but the desire to protect you and keep it real! Another thing I recognize will be important as you read through my chapter is knowing that life will happen! Too often in graduate school, you will feel like that is all that is going on! Remember that graduate school is not YOUR life. It is a piece of your path, but it is not the path. There will be so many things that happen in your life and the lives of the people you care about, so make time for those weddings, birthdays, and solo trips because when you leave graduate school, you will see how many people have changed over the course of 4+ year program.

I give you a sneak peek into my journey to highlight that *it won't always be easy*, but remember you made it here, and you can do it. This PhD is for you and everyone who came before you and will come after you. Below I have provided some of the gems I never knew I needed that have helped me manage the chaos that is graduate school. Keep in touch and remember that you are loved, you are important, you are kind, and you have made it! <3

Gems to Hold on To Along the Way

1. *Extend yourself grace:* Be kind to yourself throughout graduate school and beyond. It is okay if you cry. It is okay if you are struggling right now. These things are okay because you (See #2).
2. *Know your worth:* You have beaten the odds and entered spaces that some people don't even know they can be in! You are worthy of being here and thriving here. They (we all know who they are) are paying YOU to come here and learn and grow and become the next generation of PhDs. They wanted YOU, so remember that it was a choice, and they chose you. You deserve to be here, and don't let anyone tell you differently!
3. *REST:* Remember that rest is a form of resistance. Don't feel bad for sleeping, taking an extended break, or napping in the middle of the day. Too many times in academia, we feel like we have to keep going or we have to work for hours on end. IT IS OKAY TO REST! Rest is you taking back your time, and it is you acknowledging that the toxicity of academia ends with you. You need rest in order to show up as your best self, so don't neglect that just to get that paper done or to finish reading that article.
4. *Find your people:* As I've mentioned, community is integral to being able to make it through. Sometimes we think we can do it on our own, and rightfully so! But now you lean on your people, find your people, and ask for help! People are rooting for you, and they will do anything to support you! If your community is small, reach out to me! I got you. Just remember that you find your people and let them pour into you so you can get that degree walking across the stage and not crawling!

5. ***Do today's best:*** I can't remember exactly where I heard this, but it has become my mantra for all things in life and school. Do your best today, whatever that looks like. If you only read one article today, that is okay! If you went hard in the gym, ate a great breakfast, and cut your to-do list in half, that is okay too! Every day our motivation shifts, so lean into it and remind yourself that through it all, you did today's best! Also know there is tomorrow, so don't forget that!

CHAPTER 21

Emmanuela Stanislaus's Story

DR. EMMANUELA STANISLAUS is a multi-passionate higher education administrator and entrepreneur who earned her doctorate in Higher Education Administration. She founded her company, Dr. Emmanuela Consulting, where she serves as a diversity consultant and doctorate coach. As a doctorate coach, Dr. Stanislaus supports women of color doctoral students through her speaking and coaching services as well as her podcast, Writing on My Mind, where she discusses the ups and downs of pursuing a doctoral degree through personal stories and revealing conversations with other women of color. Her combined experiences have helped her clients to reclaim the power they have over their careers and doctoral journey. She continues to produce scholarship that focuses on first-generation college students, experiences of Black women college students, and minority-serving higher education institutions.

Go Where You're Accepted

I didn't always know that I wanted to pursue a doctorate. In fact, I vividly remember telling folks that I had no desire to get a doctorate. I spent ten years after completing my master's program trying to work my way up the higher education administration ladder, and I made it up to associate director, something that I was pretty proud of, but then when I looked around, I saw that there were others who didn't look like me who were further up the ladder with similar credentials. So, I decided that it was time to pursue my doctorate as I didn't want to be excluded from an opportunity for advancement because I didn't have a terminal degree.

Entering my doctoral program, I didn't anticipate some of the challenges that I experienced. I wasn't the oldest person in my program, but I also wasn't a spring chicken right out of a master's program. I wasn't a spring chicken. And it seemed like I was on the receiving end of punishment because of that. Others had opportunities to co-author manuscripts with faculty. Men in my program were invited to chat with faculty over coffee and wine. For one reason or another, I was not invited to coveted outside the classroom social events which could lead to potential collaboration opportunities, so I took matters into my own hands. I'm so embarrassed to admit that I was so desperate to cultivate a relationship with a faculty that I admired that I offered to treat him to wine. I offered because that's what I had noticed was happening with others in the program. Faculty were meeting with students over coffee to help them sort out their research topics. Faculty were meeting over wine to discuss collaboration opportunities. I often felt like I was the only one not having these meetings that could help faculty get to know me and provide clarity around my future endeavors. I was crushed when my efforts were not fruitful. I was in search of mentorship while attempting to understand the politics of higher education that were much different from my experience as an administrator. I also felt like there were unwritten ways of being a doctoral student that I had not known about.

There were rewards if you were a full-time doctoral student.

Rewards for being straight out of your master's program.

Rewards for identifying as a man or male-identifying.

Rewards for not having children or being in a committed relationship.

Rewards for wanting to pursue the faculty route instead of something more obscure.

As a Black woman who was (and still is) married and working a full-time job while pursuing my PhD, I was often made to feel like I didn't belong. These feelings weren't all in my head. I literally had my advisor tell me he and faculty, in general, don't care about doctoral students until they're in the dissertation process. Ironically, my feelings of alienation didn't dissipate once I reached the dissertation phase. The care that I received from my advisor was related to receiving quick feedback and revisions to my document. I didn't have any care ethic in terms of how I was doing as a human being, exploring my career goals, etc. My experience was heartbreaking, given my hopes when applying to the doctoral program. I envisioned a built-in mentorship relationship with my advisor. I also expected a structured community, one that would support one another and where collaboration was a given. I didn't conjure up these thoughts in a vacuum. These expectations were based on what I saw with other doctoral students who had become good friends with their advisors and, in some cases, became like family. Sadly, I was reminded that reality often does not mimic fantasy.

I didn't know what I didn't know, and there were times when I wondered if I should know more. These thoughts were exacerbated, especially as someone with over a decade of experience as a higher education administrator. I remember telling a faculty member that I was interested in pursuing the faculty route, and his response was, "It's too late." That was the full response. No other explanation was offered to help me understand his rationale. As a Black woman, I'm often battling the desire to be seen, heard, and understood. And I truly felt unseen and unheard in my interaction with this faculty member. I was open and vulnerable by sharing my interest in learning more about the tenure-track role as a potential career path for myself. I was open but wasn't sure what he saw. I'm guessing he saw a full-time administrator who was destined to be a lifer. Maybe he thought I didn't have the chops to be a faculty member. I'll never know because he never explained. I was left to extrapolate and assume, which ultimately led me to doubt myself. It's ironic because all I really wanted was a mentor, a guide to show me the way and potentially make my journey toward the PhD easier.

I was so surprised by his crass and matter-of-fact response that it left me frozen without a clever response or follow-up question. I thought to myself, "Had I missed something? Was I supposed to already know that it was too late? Was I being treated differently because of my gender? Was it because of views related to my race? Was it because I am a child of immigrants? Was this tied to being a first-generation college student?" I often felt this way throughout my doctoral journey....like I was five steps behind. How could I make up the ground that I had lost?

I recall mentioning the "too late" comment to two other faculty members, and they had puzzled looks and offered words of encouragement.

I remember sitting in the car in my work parking lot, feeling lost and confused. I was shaking and felt like I was having a panic attack. I knew that I needed to speak to someone. I picked up the phone and called my husband and began unloading on him. He then shared that I may be suffering from anxiety. For some reason, his words resonated with me and started me on a path of reclaiming my power. My therapist helped me to unpack some of my feelings and come up with strategies to communicate with the faculty who were making me feel so inadequate. I eventually realized that I needed to focus my energy on those who were there for me and not waste my time on others. I deserved to be in my program, and I brought a tremendous amount of value to the table. I couldn't allow others, including faculty, to make me feel as if I did not belong there. Their hang-ups were not a reflection of my capabilities or something for me to internalize. I'm glad that I sought the help of my therapist to come up with a plan and eventually get to a point where I didn't let their actions, hurtful comments, or inactions get to me personally. However, I am still disappointed that I wasn't able to foster the connections and collaborations that I desired with a few of the faculty within my program.

...

The room was dark, with Neo-soul playing from a speaker in the front of the room. I could have sworn there were candles and incense burning. So many Black women in different shades and hair expressions filled the room, a camaraderie that I would come to discover in different parts of the doctoral journey I had been lacking. I immediately had a wave of emotions flow over me. There was something familiar here. Something that I didn't know that I was missing. I felt at home. The conference session was called #Sister PhD Lessons from Year Two and it was presented at the NASPA 2017 annual conference. I attended the session in search of community. I was in my second year of my doctoral and was feeling a little isolated and lost, not only in my program but as an attendee of this conference which I hadn't attended since my final semester of my master's program, 12 years prior.

The presenters were four Black women who detailed their experiences building community and supporting one another through the ups and downs of pursuing their doctoral degrees and the added challenges when doing so as Black women. They called themselves Sister PhD. I was so moved by the stories they shared of experiencing the loss of a parent, breakups, isolation, and so much more. I wasn't the only one drawn into their stories and inspired by their support of one another. There were others who were emotional from the beautiful display of sisterhood. At the end of the session, I stood up and declared that I wanted to create a support group of my own and invited anyone who was interested to let me know. I was blown away that eight women found me after the presentation to express their interest in starting a group. I had no idea what I was doing, but we allowed each other to play different roles in constructing our community. It was a community that suited us and our needs where we could be our whole beautiful, complicated, diverse, and intelligent selves. Sister PhD provided a blueprint for how we could thrive, and we took it and ran with it.

My group was made up of women in various stages of the doctoral journey. A few of us were still thinking about pursuing a doctorate; a couple were navigating the doctoral journey with children, some were full-time while others were part-time doctoral students with full-time jobs, and mostly first- and second-year doctoral students. We created a GroupMe group chat to help us communicate. We set up monthly video calls to share our experiences and offer support to one another. Discussions were well beyond the doctoral process and expanded to family obligations, health issues, work challenges, demands, and our love lives. Some of us collaborated on book chapters, reconnected at conferences, and attended each other's defenses.

This group of ladies meant so much to me and still does. They motivated me to keep pushing through my program during times when I felt lost and as if no one cared. They encouraged me. They inspired me. They helped me to refine my dissertation topic and find the courage that I needed to change my topic after my third year in the program and not feel like a complete failure.

Additionally, I found some other faculty members that I was able to befriend in other programs at my institution and even faculty at other institutions who provided some of the support that I yearned for. A faculty member in another program held monthly group meetings with students that she chaired, and I asked if I could join. I admired the care that she provided to her students and wanted to be in the environment. I wasn't yet in the dissertation phase of my program, but I gained so much just by being in the room with others who were further along than I was. I reached out to a faculty member whose work I admired and ended up citing in my dissertation. I expressed my admiration and interest in collaborating. We eventually met virtually for an informational interview then she invited me into her research group. There were other similar stories that helped me to build out my personal board of directors that filled the void of my program's faculty. I was often surprised by how open, and welcoming strangers were to me. Perhaps they saw themselves in me. They probably saw how I was wounded by the rejection I felt from my program's faculty and how desperate I was for a connection and a safe space. It was refreshing to have other faculty members who were inviting and encouraging. These were also folks who affirmed me when I shared my interest in learning more about the faculty career path. They told me how important my research was to the field. I am forever grateful to them.

...

The rejection that I felt from my program's faculty fostered feelings of self-doubt and negative self-talk. People would probably say that I experienced imposter syndrome, but I have a different take on imposter syndrome. Imposter syndrome is something that I refuse to adopt as I think that there are players in higher education institutions who take on an active role in making folks feel like there's no place for them in these settings. There was nothing imposter-ish or fake about me. These spaces and actors just didn't like what I embodied or represented.

These places and actors often want doctoral students to look and act one way, and because I did not fit into that mold, I was left in the cold and left on my own. I made it to the other side in spite of their treatment.

In their book *Burnout: The Secret to Unlocking the Stress Cycle*, Emily and Amelia Nagoski stated that "meaning is not made by the terrible thing you experienced; it is made by the ways you survive." There was a constant renegotiation of life for me. I learned, and I'm still relearning the value of speaking my truth and knowing that what I want and need are important. I shouldn't shrink because of a desire to not make others uncomfortable but take up space. Taking up space means acknowledging who I am and what I need and asking for what I need. I did this in my home by negotiating my responsibilities, reframing my ideas of what a wife is (or letting go of myths of what makes a good wife, daughter, sister, and employee), and not apologizing for what I need. In some cases, I wished that I had found the courage to speak up sooner instead of allowing things to eat at me further, causing additional stress. I didn't get to this place alone. I worked through ideas of advocating for myself through therapy.

I didn't have the support that I wanted, so I built my own. I went where I was accepted. I created spaces where other doctoral students felt accepted. I'm forever grateful to the women of the original SisterPhD who inspired my group and others. They helped me to envision what support can look like for me and provided the motivation that I needed to create my own and not wait for my program to create it for me.

CHAPTER 22

Deja Trammell's Story

D EJA TRAMMELL IS pursuing her Doctor of Philosophy in Educational Psychology with a specialization in Higher Education Administration at Auburn University. Her research interests involve the use of culturally sustaining frameworks that provide anti-deficit orientations to research, teaching, and practice. She received her Bachelor of Science in Psychology from Alabama State University, her Master of Social Work from Clark Atlanta University, and is pursuing her Master of Science in Education Research, Measurement, and Evaluation in addition to her doctorate. She currently serves as a Career Development Counselor in the University Career Center, prioritizing the needs of graduate and undergraduate students, and serves as the Career Lead Mentor for the Young Professionals in Training Organization. She is also a member of Sigma Gamma Rho Sorority, Incorporated, where she continues to provide educational resources and access to individuals in her community. Deja has dedicated her career to the advancement of students of color in higher education through academic and professional support services. She is committed to enhancing the professional identity development and professional growth of students of color in higher education by providing diverse, equitable access to institutional resources and programming. Deja is the founder of the Trammell Mentoring Scholarship, which provides undergraduate students at her alma mater, Alabama State University, with resources and guidance to achieve their professional goals. As an advocate for education and opportunity, Deja believes that real experiences and stories from African American women in higher education can impact the lives of individuals who are interested in pursuing an advanced degree. One thing that she has realized is that with some experiences, we learn it so that others can live it.

The Unspoken Realities within Academia: Debunking the Myths

When I was first notified that I got accepted into my top two choices for a doctoral program, I was both elated and nervous because obtaining my doctorate has always been a personal goal, and it was becoming a reality. Some of the anxiety from the application process had eased, but there was still this unknown reality I could not have anticipated being a first-generation student with an advanced degree in my family. Now that I am well into my second year, I recognize that there are some implied expectations that we, as African American women, aren't always privy to that could help us feel more prepared to navigate the academy. Often, we don't know what we don't know, so how can we ask the right questions to see what program is the best fit for us? I want to take some time to try and demystify some of the doctoral process based on my experiences and hopefully provide you with some things to consider when trying to grow and thrive in your respective program. My experience may not speak to all your questions and concerns, but I do hope it provides you the space to make decisions based on your needs and desires for professional growth.

Discipline to Career

One of the most vivid (and shocking) memories I have when I arrived on campus for my second class of the semester, was hearing that the field was saturated with PhD's and the job market was not as promising as it once was. I was under the impression that obtaining a terminal degree would guarantee endless job possibilities and provide me with the ability to negotiate my salary and find a satisfying career in higher education. To be the only Black woman in the class and the only individual who did not have the inside knowledge about the reality of the doctorate made me feel as if I was unprepared for my program and at a disadvantage from the start. The doubts and feelings that I had worked so hard to be in a position to be successful and it wasn't enough started to set in. Finding out that I would have to continue to diversify my experiences to stand out and find a position that uniquely fit my needs did not deter me from obtaining a degree but helped me start to really focus on what I wanted the next four years to look like. I took some time to explore the realities within my discipline area. What kind of jobs could I expect upon degree completion? Does my program of study truly prepare me for the career I want? How do I find opportunities and ways to increase my marketability so I can obtain a career that meets my financial expectations? What is a realistic salary coming out of my field? These are some questions I had to consider when thinking about the benefits of a doctoral degree and what I wanted from my program.

Coming into the Educational Psychology program, I did some research on the application process and what careers in educational psychology would look like, and I was interested. I envisioned my program leading me to a career as a Chief Diversity Office for Diversity, Equity, and Inclusion or an Executive Director within the government/higher education institution focused on education policy and programming for all students. However, during my first year in the program, I realized a few things that made me feel like the research I had done on the program wasn't enough. For my program, Educational Psychology was housed in the College of Education and had a P through12 focus. As I have a passion for working with college and professional students, I must work hard to find areas of interest that can help me achieve my career goals while still completing the requirements of my program. This distinction may have been minor if not for the fact that searching for positions as a tenure-track professor or in other areas of higher education had requirements that did not closely align with my background and experiences. We'll get to career thoughts and aspirations later. For me, understanding institutional structure and what college or department my program aligns with helped me prioritize my academic and professional needs and the work I would have to put in to be intentional with my experiences. I wanted this process to be connected to my purpose and who I wanted to be for myself and my community. Knowing the mission, vision, and course offerings of the program helped me to develop my research and professional interests. There were many things I did not know to ask, but I learned with time that the process was to identify growth areas and learn how to learn in a way that helped me occupy space as a Black woman.

Responsibilities of the Doctoral Student

When I was interested in becoming a tenure-track professor, I had to find ways to develop skills in four areas that were necessary to become a professor: research, teaching, service, and outreach. I chose an institution that had a heavy research agenda and a strategic plan that spoke to their focus which was research and economic development of departments on campus. I was responsible for working on research projects such as conferences, symposiums, grant writing, etc., producing publications, and enhancing my CV (curriculum vitae – an academic resume of sorts). Along with these responsibilities, there were financial obligations that were not included in my tuition and fees (such as conference registration, hotel, flights/mileage, professional association fees, professional development fees, etc.). There was even an expectation of completing outreach and service activities to develop a well-rounded portfolio for myself after my degree. Because of these multiple hats I had to wear, my top concern was how I could find balance within the Academy as a Black woman, and did I even want that responsibility, or was I feeling obligated to be a representative for students of color so they could succeed?

In full transparency, I have been deliberating between joining the professoriate as a tenure-track professor and working in higher education in a leadership position for some time now. As the service-oriented individual I am, I enjoy creating programs and increasing program efficacy to serve and support students, especially students of color, in all endeavors. Yet, I also want to be versatile and marketable for any position that interests me, so I accepted some responsibilities that allow me to develop a variety of skill sets that still align with my passion. From working as a graduate assistant to participating in service organizations, it has not been easy wearing these hats and wanting to give 110% in every area, but I have learned that I get to choose how much I invest in each experience to maintain my sanity and boundaries. Now that I have experience in multiple areas of higher education, I will focus more closely on positions of service that allow me to be a practitioner but give me the flexibility to leave work at work and still support the students through access to resources and opportunities to grow. Is this a good opportunity for me, and how significant is it to where I want to be? How does this put me in a position to continue to grow? I always think about the demands of my program and future career and think about the reality of how I want to spend my time.

Being the Initiator and the Initiated

The adage, "It's not what you know, but who you know," is one of the most powerful statements for me when it comes to graduating and finding gainful employment. As one of the few Black women in my program and one who started her doctoral journey during a pandemic, I struggled to connect with colleagues and faculty in my department and college, unable to fully immerse myself in the academic environment. Even with being resourceful, there were time conflicts and extenuating circumstances that did not provide me the opportunity to meet with all professors and research faculty. Being an HBCU graduate of Alabama State University and Clark Atlanta University, I knew that I would have to create my own support systems and initiate contact with outside professionals to thrive in my program. By having this tenacity, the initiator ultimately became the initiated.

I initiated connections that I felt would help me to grow and keep me accountable throughout my academic journey. I built networks within all departments, from the Graduate Dean to the President of the University, to help continue my progress. Even with all these powerful resources and allies, I still actively search for communities of color who can help me understand this process and reach out to individuals from social media who are completing their doctorate or have already finished. I even found community within social media outlets like a Blk Doc Student GroupMe, which was a pivotal part of my doctoral journey.

During my first year in the program, I had a class that explored research identity using concepts I had never heard of before. Because these concepts were new, I was struggling to understand the assignment and began to doubt that I was prepared to succeed in the program. I decided to reach out to my networks for help. Someone from the GroupMe answered my request and helped me work through the assignment by getting clarity with my professor instead of pathologizing my experience. This one moment cemented the value of having healthy support systems and resources and helped me develop a professional identity that would not be reduced by imposter syndrome. When moments in my program become overwhelming, and the self-doubt creeps in, I rely heavily on the individuals in my life to keep me centered and remind me of my goals for completing this program.

Advice from the Advocates

Some of my most important lessons came from the most uncomfortable growth experiences learning throughout my program. A few pieces of advice that have remained with me to this day are:

"Remember that this journey is a process. You can't eat a whole cake in one bite, let alone the whole slice." - Dr. David Marshall

A huge part of the doctoral process is picking a dissertation topic and structuring time to work on this project that will take up most of the time in the program. As I was thinking about my purpose in the program, I remembered that I did not have to have my entire career figured out in the beginning. I take a deep breath, find my rhythm, and take it one bit at a time.
"Don't be good at everything, be the best at something that you love" - Dr. Andrew Pendola

In this program, I started off wanting to make sure I was well-rounded and that I had all the skills necessary to develop a versatile portfolio for a career, so I tried to be a part of everything. As I progressed in the program, I realized there were more opportunities than I could complete, and some of them were unfulfilling and uninteresting, to say the least. I really struggled with saying no, fearing it would impair the relationships I had created with career professionals and faculty, yet I feared being overwhelmed and experiencing burnout as I experienced in my master's program even more. Dr. Pendola reminded me that employers and institutions are not looking for perfection in everything but individuals who have expertise in a specialty area. I make sure to consider every opportunity as a position of leverage – will participating in this opportunity bring me closer to my professional goals and help me obtain the position I am most interested in?

"Would you rather work to serve the population you're passionate about or be able to allocate the resources for that population to have greater opportunities to succeed?" -Dr. Tierney Bates

Thinking about careers and opportunities of interest, I have always wanted to do work that provides access and resources to communities of color, especially when it comes to education and career aspirations. Dr. Bates posed a question that continues to marinate in the back of my mind as I had never thought about the type of resource I wanted to be. He asked how many people do you know that can create programs for Black and brown students? On the other hand, how many Black people do you know that can handle multi-million-dollar investments and allocate those resources to individuals who create those programs? His question really gave me pause as I debated the impact I wanted to have on my community and if I wanted to just work with students or provide opportunities of leverage for all students by having direct access to these resources.

"You've had enough experience and exposure. Now is the time to advocate for your needs and to ensure your time and hard work are valued and respected." - Dr. Dee Lisa Cothran I came into my program knowing that I had certain skills and abilities that would help me continue to grow as a professional, but I did not always feel like they were proficient or adequate for a doctoral program. I soon discovered that I was more than prepared and equipped to be in a doctoral program, and I did not have to overwhelm myself trying to prove my work was sufficient. My passion and work spoke for themselves, and I had to walk in that. I shared my thoughts with my advisor, and she said, "It's good that people are recommending you for positions and asking for your help but are they writing you into the grant, giving you credit for the program you created, paying you for your services, putting you as an author on the research you contributed to?" She helped me to understand and reflect on my experiences to determine the value I placed on myself and my work. What kind of boundaries did I set for myself as a professional scholar with experience? I make sure that I am compensated for my time and efforts. Whether that is a promotion, paycheck, credit/authorship, or networking leverage, everything I do has significance and value.

Give Yourself Some Grace

The last and most important part of my story is my true understanding of giving myself some grace! There are many expectations placed on me by family members, my community, and mainly myself, but I am right where I need to be. Whether you are about to apply for a graduate program, in the middle of your program, still figuring out what you want to be in this life, or in the midst of transitioning from one line of work to another, you are enough. The one thing I have learned is that completing a checklist is only good for the list and those who benefit from the items on that list. I want to continue to celebrate my successes, acknowledge my lessons, balance my failures, and enjoy every moment, and I want that for you too. You get to engineer how your story will look and unfold as you walk in your purpose. I have allowed God to orchestrate my steps and have faith in what talents he has bestowed on me, and I fully believe that we are put here to do great things. If you need a friend or feel alone, remember you are not alone, and we are all rooting for you no matter where you are. From one sister to another, whatever you choose, you got this!

CHAPTER 23

Charity Watkins's Story

CHARITY S. WATKINS, PhD, MSW, LCSW-A, is an Assistant Professor in the Department of Social Work at North Carolina Central University after completing her PhD in Social Work at the University of North Carolina at Chapel Hill. Dr. Watkins's dissertation research focused on differentiating the effects of racial bias and socioeconomic inequities on parenting factors and the academic achievement of Black children in elementary school to identify factors that mediate and moderate academic resilience. Dr. Watkins has expanded her research to include Black maternal health, social determinants of health, and the mental health of Black helping professionals.

Once the Book is Written, My Story will be Told

That was my mantra for the last five years of my doctoral journey as I reflected on all I had been through and all I was still trying to accomplish. The mantra can be understood from both a literal and metaphorical sense. Literally, my dissertation—a 119-page book composed of five chapters that were crafted to demonstrate my expertise in advanced secondary quantitative data analyses—told the story of my research on parenting factors that promoted academic resilience among elementary school children experiencing socioeconomic marginalization. It thoroughly examined existing literature on the topic, systematically reviewed the significance of the problem, and objectively identified gaps in the research. It met the formatting requirements of the Graduate School and the measures of rigor among my dissertation committee. Overall, it was a standard three-paper dissertation in the field of social work. Metaphorically, my dissertation was far from standard. Beyond the literal meaning of those ten words, the mantra meant that once my dissertation was written, I would be able to share the story behind it. I would be able to talk about the immense challenges I faced while writing those five chapters. I would have the chance to discuss the feelings of marginalization, self-doubt, and imposter syndrome I experienced as I double-checked my margins, spacing, and in-text citations. I could finally expose the white supremacist structures I had to navigate while mastering structural equation modeling. I could finally rededicate my time, mental space, and energy back to myself and the people I dedicated my dissertation to. I would finally have an outlet to emotionally process what had, at many points of the journey, felt like academic hazing within the ivory tower of higher education. Unlike the chapters of my dissertation, this chapter is for healing, for recovery, and for growth beyond the confines of a doctoral program.

Charity Starts at Home

To know me is to know where I come from: the metropolitan area of Rochester in Upstate New York. With a population of 211,000 people, Rochester has an overall poverty rate of 31.3% and a child poverty rate of 47%; rates of economic disenfranchisement that are more than triple the national rates of child and overall poverty. These economic disparities carry over to negatively affect social outcomes faced by Rochesterians, including staggering rates of violent crimes, declines in academic proficiency, and rising rates of high school dropouts. I was aware of where I lived and had some sense of how much my mother worried about my safety there, but it was home. Yet, despite it being home, I had begun to feel somewhat distant from what was happening right outside of my window. The precautions my Southern-raised, military-trained mother of two took to shelter me from the harsh realities of "ROC City" through enrollment in gifted and talented programs, Advanced Placement classes, and college-level International Baccalaureate coursework provided me with new tools to navigate the world. A world beyond Rochester.

North Carolina, Come on and Raise Up

Although I was born and raised in Rochester, I did not grow up until I came to North Carolina. My undergraduate years at the University of North Carolina Chapel Hill provided the context for much of the growth I endured to become the person I am today. My first month living on campus was the first time I was called the n-word (with an extra hard 'r'). My friends, who were also the subjects of the slur, were mostly from the South and were more familiar with the use of this derogatory term. But I, feeling the sting of this word from a white person for the very first time, was ready to chase down the coward who ran as soon as that extra hard 'r' left his lips.

Those not experiencing the novelty of the n-word stopped me as my body inherently lurched towards the exit. "We don't do that down here," they told me, warning me of the consequences that could follow and far outweigh the emotional pain of that word. Was I just supposed to let it go and not release the burden of this demeaning experience by bum-rushing that fool? Withhold evidence of the harm inflicted on me in order to protect white folks from the consequences of their actions; was that the only way I could stay safe? In that moment, racist violence in this overwhelmingly white environment felt so much more dangerous than the neighborhood violence of my beloved hometown. I knew how to avoid that violence, but how was I supposed to avoid racism when I chose to surround myself with it for the next four years? There had to be a better way.

Came Here for School, Graduated to the High Life

So, let's fast forward four years through my "gap year" to the real growing pains: graduate school. After working various jobs in the mental health field, I was excited to go back to school. Adulting with a 9-5 job (and 3rd shift campus security gig) was boring and predictable. I wanted to return to the classroom and to learning with and from others. And for those two short years, I wanted to take full advantage of the graduate school experience. I was everywhere doing everything with my Black womanness present in all my roles. My Black womanness was evident during class discussions, in which I had to balance the urge to ensure racism was not left out of the conversation with the need to not be viewed as the representative of the Black delegation; in me developing opportunities for students to directly communicate their concerns about the school's racial climate with administration; and in me assisting in the recruitment of Black students into the master's and PhD programs by speaking on student panels, writing pieces for the school blog, and, of course, being pictured on the school's website, brochures, and other recruitment materials. At one point, there was a wall near the student lounge on the fifth floor that had nine random pictures from events that were hosted by the school over the last two years; my face was in 5 of them. I maintained my prominent role in the MSW program even after being accepted into the MSW/PhD Continuum Program. I facilitated orientation discussions, attended trustee luncheons, and delivered a speech at graduation. I was a model student, a model Black student. But then Ferguson, Missouri, gained our attention, and my role as a doctoral student effectively changed forever.

Same House, New Tools

On August 9, 2014, unarmed 18-year-old Michael Brown Jr. was shot six times by Ferguson police officer, Darren Wilson. Brown was left in the street under the hot summer sun for four hours as neighbors, and other residents pleaded for the police to treat him humanely in death if not in life. As injustice was served for yet another murder of a young Black person, national outcries to value and protect Black lives resonated throughout the United States, including within the walls of the Tate-Turner-Kuralt building. The outcries only became louder after the following words were received by social work students, staff, faculty, and some alumni ten days after Michael Brown's murder:

> As I watch the news and see what is unfolding in Missouri, I am struck by the anger, fear, and terror, as well as the complicated nature of the situation. The shooting death of Michael Brown is the spark that ignited the latent undercurrent of rage likely caused by poverty, racial disparity, and lack of opportunity for minority populations. Our reaction to this event has to be tempered with the need to provide legal, due process, and appropriate investigation for the police department and officer involved. I am reminded of the Duke University Lacrosse team event several years ago, in which friends, colleagues, and community members protested and signed petitions to express their outrage at predominately White team members who had apparently sexually assaulted a Black female. As you may know, these "facts" turned out not to be "facts." Due process is a necessity, not a luxury...."

How can I describe the range of emotions I experienced as I read that email and then read it again for confirmation? First, anger. Then, betrayal. Next, sadness. And last, disappointment. How could such a dismissive, demeaning demand for calm when the country is literally on fire come out of a school of social work—a profession guided by the principles of social justice, advocacy, and equity? This was the moment when I realized that my role in the school was about to shift. I would need to move from the inside to the outside track. As a student leader, I had the position and platform to address various issues in the school *with* the support of the school administration. I had gained some insider access; a seat at the table, although it was the kids' table. But this right here, this blatant disregard for Black humanity in Ferguson and Black hurt in Chapel Hill, required me to step outside of my model student status and, in many ways, to step outside of who I thought I was in order to require more from my institution. I started off with just one foot out of the door: an individual meeting with the dean, in which I read a typed letter that outlined the harm I experienced from the email and proposed steps that can be taken to acknowledge and address that harm with fellow Black members of the school community and me. Next, I joined forces with other outraged students to coordinate meetings between my school's leadership and the leaders in diversity, equity, and inclusion on our campus. At first, these were conversations presented in the spirit of collaboration, but once leadership began skipping meetings, ignoring emails, and halting communication altogether, my spirit was moved in a different direction: agitation. We continued the meetings without leadership, reaching out to the Ombuds office, the Graduate School, the provost, and the chancellor. We held two town hall meetings to focus squarely on the harm experienced as a result of that email and the "latent undercurrent" of white supremacy and anti-Black racism it represented. We organized a student advocacy group and presented a call to action to tenured faculty and administration. The amount of DEI work we did for free was ridiculous, but it was worth it when the school's leader stepped down. That was a win, a big win. But then what? Well, the struggle continues.

It All Falls Down

In the fall of 2015, as I entered my third year in the PhD program, my focus and role began to shift again; I was pregnant and preparing to become someone's mama. This was going to be my first child, and I was beyond excited. In between drafting papers and running statistical models, I was nesting, reading *What to Expect When You're Expecting*, and thinking about baby names. Although I wished I could put all of my time and energy into this life-changing experience of pregnancy, my role and responsibilities as a doctoral student were ever-present. Also ever-present, was the feeling of contempt among some faculty and administrators following my student activism the semester before. I really felt like people hated me. Folks who used to smile and say hello to me before now would look the other way. All of those pictures with me in them on the fifth floor were taken down and replaced with generic photos of campus. I began to question myself and my decision to speak up. The regret exponentially increased when I, after a summer of intense studying with my doctoral cohort, was the only student to fail my comprehensive methods exam. On the one hand, I blamed myself for being distracted and not being focused enough on this major step towards earning my PhD. I thought over and over again that what that senior professor told me a couple of years ago was right: I was in the wrong program. I didn't belong here. How dare I believe I can be successful in this rigorous, high-ranking doctoral program? On the other hand, I questioned why I was the only one to fail despite everyone sharing the same difficulties? Why didn't I receive feedback on my exam to know what I failed to do correctly? Was this retribution for blowing up the school's spot less than a year ago? Why wouldn't it be? I had already been denied the ability to keep my dissertation chair after she left the institution, although several prior students were approved to do so just a year or two before me. I felt it deep in my soul that this had more to do with my advocacy than my ability to explain various forms of validity, but there was no way to prove it. That's a battle I had to lose.

The hits kept coming that year as my pregnancy progressed. After waiting the mandatory three months to retake my comprehensive methods exam, I passed it. I then began working on my substantive exam when my mother-in-law's stage four intestinal cancer returned and spread to her lungs, liver, and bone marrow. Between visits to the hospital for my mother-in-law and for myself, I knew I had not turned in my best work. I was embarrassed, exhausted, and simply down and out. A couple of weeks later, now eight months pregnant, I received an email stating that I had failed another section of my comprehensive exam. Here I go again, proving them right and that I did not belong here. How did I fall so far from grace? After sobbing for an hour, I got up, washed my face, and took my mother-in-law to her doctor's appointment. After she was examined and her test results were reviewed, I learned that this would be her last trip to the hospital. Within two hours of finding out that I was one step away from being dismissed from my PhD program, I had to make the difficult phone call to my husband and sister-in-law, informing them that all care options had been provided and their mother would soon be moved to hospice care. I cried with my mother-in-law as we realized that she might not get the chance to meet her first grandchild. On January 29th, 2016, just a week before my due date, my mother-in-law lost her battle with cancer.

After losing my mother-in-law, everything felt very heavy. The heaviness of school was something I couldn't bear at that time, so I began my eight-week maternity leave early. I think my baby even felt the heaviness of that time in our lives as she decided to delay her debut by ten days. After a failed induction, brief natural labor, and an unplanned cesarean delivery, my baby girl had finally arrived; hopefully, after crossing spiritual paths with my mother-in-law. She was beautiful, perfect, and just amazing. I can still hear the awkward yelp my husband let out when he first saw her. For that day, the heaviness was lifted. She was our light at the end of a dark tunnel. She was life following death, love after loss. Until I almost lost myself.

Eight weeks had quickly passed by, and it was now time for me to return to my job as a research assistant. For my first day back on campus, I brought my baby girl with me to meet my colleagues and supervisor. Before pregnancy, I could conquer the hills of Chapel Hill with minor perspiration; however, after adding 30 extra pounds of weight, hormones going haywire, an overpacked diaper bag, and a clunky stroller carrying the most precious cargo, these hills felt like Mount Everest. Your girl was hurt after a ten-minute walk from the parking deck to the building. Instead of getting better with time, the hurt continued. I would feel exhausted going up just a few stairs in my house. I was nauseous and even got sick while changing one of my baby's diapers.

At my six-week postpartum appointment, I explained my symptoms to my doctor. At first, I was told that it was most likely postpartum depression. I was referred to a psychologist for counseling, but my symptoms persisted and worsened. I developed a cough that wouldn't go away, and I couldn't lay flat in bed anymore. I went to my doctor again, and this time was told that maybe I had caught a strain of the flu even though I had received the vaccine while pregnant. How could symptoms of the flu last this long? It didn't make sense. Then, one Wednesday night in mid-April, while pumping and watching Empire, I felt a tightness in my left arm and shoulder. It lasted for about 10 minutes, with only a minor soreness sticking around for the next couple of hours. I dismissed it as a muscle spasm and took some sips of water in an effort to prevent it from happening again. I thought I was okay, but then it happened again just three days later. This time, the pain was more severe and lasted for over an hour. I remember walking downstairs and reluctantly telling my husband that I think I need to go to the hospital. He drove me to the emergency room 20 minutes away as my left arm, shoulder, and jaw throbbed with pain. We arrived at the ER with images of me being rushed to the back like we saw on television shows like Strong Medicine, Chicago Hope, Grey's Anatomy, and, yes, ER. But instead, I was directed to go to registration, provide my insurance information, go through triage, and then wait to be seen. Despite arriving with symptoms of a heart attack, I waited, and waited, and waited to be called back. I waited almost six hours before having to leave, concerned that my baby was crying with hunger under the care of my sister-in-law as my breasts became engorged and began to leak. I had to get home to my baby.

Four days later, I was able to make an appointment with Campus Health.

Although the sharp pain in my arm had finally gone away, the other symptoms had never let up. After hearing my description of my symptoms, the doctor examined me. He asked, "Did you notice that your legs were swollen?" "No, I didn't," I answered while looking down at my feet, slightly swelling over the opening of my shoes. He then examined my abdomen and pointed out that I had swelling there too. He then sent me to get an x-ray of my stomach and chest. After scrolling through my phone for a while in the waiting room, I was called back, but not back to the examination room; I was called to the doctor's office. It was there that he told me that I wouldn't be going home today. My x-ray had revealed that fluid had collected in my lungs, my abdomen, and my heart, which was now enlarged. Within 20 minutes, I was being rolled in a wheelchair down the hill to the hospital emergency room—the same emergency room I waited in for six hours just a few days earlier. During my 3-hour wait in the waiting area, I called my husband to tell him the news and my understanding of what was going to happen next. We also had to come up with another plan for picking up my daughter from what was only her second week in daycare. A classmate was kind enough to wait with me as I tried to make sense of what I was told. I'm a 30-year-old first-time mom in overall good health; what do you mean something is wrong with my heart?

After finally making it to the highly anticipated 'back' of the ER, I received the news that I would be admitted into the hospital. And not just in the regular unit but in the cardiac intensive care unit. After a day, I was downgraded to the normal cardiac care unit as they began administering the medication treatment. After receiving a small dose of medication central to my recovery, my blood pressure dropped so low that I coded. It just so happened that, at that very time, my husband was in the basement of the hospital for my baby girl's appointment. A friend of my aunt who worked in the cardiac unit found him and told him what happened, instilling an even more intense fear of losing me in my husband. I was stabilized, but I would have to start my medication treatment from scratch, extending my stay in the hospital and my time away from my newly expanded family.

I stayed in the hospital for two weeks after being diagnosed with peripartum cardiomyopathy or heart failure due to pregnancy. I found out that my heart was functioning at only 5-10% when I was admitted to the hospital. If I hadn't been able to make an appointment with Campus Health as soon as I did, I may not have made it and would have left behind a husband and newborn infant. For the last four months, my family and I had become too well acquainted with hospitals as we faced the imminent death of my mother-in-law, the birth of my daughter, and now my own near-death experience. Life had changed for me forever. Because of the medications I would now have to take for the rest of my life, I could no longer breastfeed my baby. I was enrolled in a cardiac rehab program where other participants were more than double my age, leaving us all confused as they and I both questioned why I was there. I would now have to see a cardiologist at least every six months to monitor my heart functioning. I now had a serious pre-existing condition. But there was one other 'pre-existing condition' from my pre-heart failure life that had endured—the condition of being a Black doctoral student at a historically white institution.

Get Up, Stand Up

My heart failure diagnosis had knocked me out for a minute, but I wasn't down for the count. After taking some time to recover, I returned to my doctoral studies. By the end of the year, I had completed my comprehensive exam re-do and wrote and orally defended my dissertation proposal, becoming a doctoral candidate just months after becoming a heart survivor. Reflecting on the numerous factors that may have contributed to my heart failure, including the stressors of being a student activist, I pulled back my involvement in my program. I tried concentrating my attention unilaterally on writing my dissertation and entering the job market, but I always had my ear to the ground. In the case of the 2017 doctoral program cohort, I had my eye on the school's Facebook page. That's when, for the fifth year in a row, I didn't see a Black student admitted into the PhD program. The last time a Black student was enrolled in the doctoral program was in 2012 when two other Black women and I entered the program representing half of the cohort. But not one since then; the two of us still in the program were it. I had brought up this issue as well as the lack of racial equity within our faculty and curriculum to the new school leadership in carefully written emails, well-planned meetings over breakfast, and in collaboration with our university's Chief Diversity Officer. I had exhausted the inner track, and nothing had changed; it was time to position myself as an outsider yet again.

Without consulting my mentors or faculty in the program, I took a risk and penned a letter to the editor of the university newspaper calling out evidence of racism within my doctoral program. I pointed to the lack of Black representation among our students and faculty. I discussed the dearth of courses and class material dedicated to the advancement of social justice. The responsibility of realizing the school's mission statement was above me now. I was tired, burnt out, and still in recovery. This racial equity work was no longer my burden to carry alone. It was time for the school's leadership to answer to someone else.

I found out that the op-ed was published from an email sent over the school listserv, in which the school administration attempted to get in front of my claims before faculty, staff, and students read the piece for themselves. To see my reality not only downplayed but denied over this public forum was infuriating but mostly hurtful. After that, I felt an intense need to distance myself from the school.

Despite knowing that there was going to be blowback from the op-ed, seeing it in text online and in the avoidance of eye contact in person was so difficult. I began to have a physical reaction while entering the building. My stomach would turn, my hands would sweat, and my still recovering heart would beat faster as I approached the doors of Tate-Turner-Kuralt. I was now the one practicing avoidance, taking the stairs, working after hours, and spending as least amount of time as possible there to reduce the number of awkward encounters I would have to endure. That went on for two years until I finally defended my dissertation. I felt that I was finally able to raise my head after beating the system that almost beat me. I had achieved what I believed many folks wanted to take away from me. In the face of their denials of my truth, there was one they could never deny: I was now Dr. Charity Watkins. And there was nothing they could do about that.

Through the Fire

Gaining my PhD after losing so much has shown me how important it is to know who you are before entering these spaces. I knew I was a strong Black woman with the power to create change. I at least knew that's who I wanted to be and had the capacity to become with the right tools. I knew I had strong opinions with clear perspectives of what was right and wrong. I knew that the risk of speaking out against injustice would compel me more than the comfort of complacency. I mean, my name is Charity—shouldn't I embody that very value? Self-doubt was always present; from the time I submitted my application to the day I submitted the final version of my dissertation, I quietly questioned if I was smart enough to earn this degree. However, what I realized is that my intelligence, my competence in the field, and my ability to be successful were proven outside of the explicit curriculum. I demonstrated it with my willingness to advocate for changes I myself would not directly benefit from. I modeled it in the unquestionable resilience I exhibited as I navigated the ebbs and flow of life and death while on my doctoral journey. Not only did I provide proof, but it is also now evident in the program itself. It is evident in the Black students who have been admitted into the program every year since my op-ed. It is evident in the Black faculty who now guide the admissions process for the doctoral program. It is evident in critical race theory being added as a central tenet of the master's and doctoral programs. It is evident in the school hiring its first Black female dean in the school's 100-year history. And most of all, it's evident in this book being written and my story being told.

CHAPTER 24

Johniqua Williams's Story

DR. JOHNIQUA WILLIAMS is currently serving as the director of diversity curriculum development for Kennesaw State University and a part-time professor at the College of Education. Dr. Williams earned her Doctor of Education from Columbus State University, her Master of Higher Education from Central Michigan University, and her undergraduate degree from Johnson C. Smith University, an HBCU in Charlotte, North Carolina. With over 15 years of experience within diversity, she has a collaborative and intentional approach to creating an inclusive synergy and development between practice and partnership as a diversity professional. For the past eight years, Johniqua has been a part-time professor at the College of Letters and Science, teaching social justice and equity courses. Diversity and inclusion have always been the driving forces behind Dr. Williams's career. She is responsible for identifying institutional priorities, programs, and initiatives that advance KSU's inclusive excellence agendas for faculty, staff, and student populations. In 2020 Johniqua launched her diversity consulting company, Divine Inclusion. The mission of Divine Inclusion is to formulate the case for diversity and inclusion and develop a strategy for inclusive practices. Additionally, the goals include cultivating training to promote inclusiveness in the workplace. Lastly, through Divine Inclusion, Dr. Williams provides education to edify and activate leaders with her proprietary knowledge and best practices. When Dr. Williams is not working to eradicate systemic oppression, she enjoys leisure time with friends and family.

Who What When Why?

Who the Heck Am I?

Who is Dr. Johniqua Williams? Who I am is a question I find myself asking post-doctoral graduation. I can tell you who Johniqua is. She is a woman from Parkhill, Colorado. Growing up, my life was colored by the impacts of diverse cultures, food, and experiences. I am the daughter of an evangelist and self-proclaimed Black Panther. Activism is the foundation from which I stand. Whether it's advocating for souls to know Jesus Christ or fighting the "MAN" to support the rights of people of color and difference, I am a person who stands in the gap as a believer that a better day is coming.

While I know who Johniqua is, getting to know Dr. Williams has been a journey. Often, when you're on a doctoral journey, all that you can think of is when you're going to be finished. However, there are lessons that you learn along the way, making you stronger. For example, attention to detail was one of the first lessons I learned. I realized that if I took care of the details up front, I wouldn't have to make significant edits on the back end. Additionally, don't take edits personally. I constantly reminded myself that this was the first time I was working on a doctorate and that it was okay not to know something. Finally, I'm learning to walk in the power of the title while maintaining humility.

Less than 3% of women of color have a doctorate, which means that the title comes with much acclaim. While you are celebrated, you also feel like you don't fit in. There are times I have sat at tables that I fought and worked hard to sit at, to only feel like I wasn't an expert or wasn't smart enough. There have been a few instances with family or friends when I felt envy or as if they were trying to compete with me or prove their intelligence in a conversation. I wanted and still want people to know that I'm the same. I am the same woman who can sit at the table with fine china or sit on the floor with plastic cutlery. The truth of the matter is, I was different. I spoke properly because the balance of code-switching impacted my scholarly writing and presentation skills. I was different because now, instead of spending my time on trendy things in the culture, I had to really structure my time to be effective in my field.

Being a woman of color who is a first-generation doctoral student, it's imperative that I surround myself with great intellectual minds that seek to stay current and impactful in research. My work has empowered courageous conversations by embracing the awkwardness in the university setting. I monitor university efforts to ensure that students, faculty, and staff have an equitable place to work and learn, regardless of their race, gender, age, ethnicity, socioeconomic status, sexual orientation, or disability. The fear of being open in front of my peers and administration is often complex. Still, expressing my authentic self is vital to the overall dialogue and the understanding of each other's differences on campus. I show my campus that it's important to share for optimal results of open, courageous conversations, even in my leadership role.

What Am I Really Trying to Do?

Have you ever been called to do greater? You knew it would be a great challenge, yet you feel a sense of responsibility to the generations to come to make the sacrifice. That was what I felt before I started the journey of the doctoral program. I must be honest. There were a few years that I danced around the thought of starting the program. Was I smart enough? Could I manage school while I worked? Would I be accepted? The idea of starting the program triggered feelings of insecurity that stemmed back to my childhood. I was never the kid that made the best grades, nor was I always confident in my work ethic. Nevertheless, I knew that there was a push for me to sit at the table for women and people of color.

While working in higher education, I knew in order to have an authentic voice, I needed a seat at the table making the decision. When I looked at those tables, I realized a few things on average. The majority of upper administrators were white, and they were male. Gender intersects with race in higher education: 86% of administrators are white, while only 7% are Black, 2% Asian, and 3% Latinx. Less than a third of college or university presidents have been women, and the majority of them have been white women. Not surprisingly, white men make up the largest number of people in senior positions among faculty members. In recent years, white women have made significantly more gains than women of color. The American Council on Education (2016) stated women administrators were more likely than their male associates to have made sacrifices in their occupations to fulfill family responsibilities.

As I currently have a seat at the table, I am starting to realize that in my field of diversity and equity work, while I have the power in the title, there are still systemic oppressions that impact the very work that I do day-to-day. I've had to push past my wants to fight and advocate for the needs of those that look like me and those of difference. There have been times that I had to go along to get along when I wanted to go against the grain. I knew that if I spoke up, there was a chance that I would be removed from the table and having access to the table and playing the game was more important than a momentary win to get my point across. Once you have the doctorate, you occupy a space of leverage, be mindful that your authentic self will grow. There will be times when you are tried, and you have to advocate for yourself. There will be times when you are challenged, and you have to play it cool. Either way, you are a winner because the goal is much greater than the obstacle in front of you. Keep pushing.

When They Say Anything could Happen during Your Doctorate, Believe Them!

Anyone who knows me knows that my parents are my world, support system, and hype men to my dreams. I'm an only child, and we are three in company. During one fall semester, as I finished my coursework, my father became very ill. While I lived in the same state as my parents, I was an hour and a half away. Often, I would work eight to ten hours on campus then head to the hospital to swap out with my mom so she could get rest, and I would sit with him in the evening from Monday thru Friday and during the day on the weekend. The season tested my faith in God and myself. I completed homework assignments in the hospital rooms and read articles in preparation for my dissertation. I was running on fumes, but my why was more significant than my current circumstance, and I found levels of strength and tenacity in me that I never thought I had.

Little did I know that there would be greater storms ahead post the storm of my father being in the hospital. After each semester, I would treat myself for all the hard work. One semester's treat was a trip to Jerusalem. I just knew this trip would revive me and bring greater clarity to me as I was about to start the dissertation process. Three days later, after returning home from Jerusalem, my uncle passed away. I was devastated. We are a close-knit family, and I was so excited to come home and talk to him about my trip.

Nevertheless, I had to keep pushing forward. That just happened to be when I was starting my dissertation. My focus was all over the place. My suggestion to women in this space is if you find yourself overwhelmed emotionally, take a break, make A to-do list, and write goals of when you want to complete things. If you're not able to finish them, don't beat yourself up but know that you will get through it. Give yourself grace.

"If it ain't one thing, it's another," felt like the model of my life during that period of loss and sickness. I lost my dog, COVID-19 hit, and we were forced to be at home for protection. Talk about being overwhelmed, unsure of timing and my purpose. While I knew what I wanted for my life, I was conflicted with time, the time I had set for job searching, and the time I wanted to be done with my program because It was so life-consuming. Finally, when I was able to sit down with myself and have a pep talk on completing the program, we ran into civil unrest, and my job was escalated to the max. At that time in our society, there was a lack of open and peaceful communication between different cultures and people of different economic statuses. The Trump administration had escalated this issue, and his social media rants exacerbated the problem.

The moral of the story behind "When they say anything could happen during your doctorate, believe them!" is, come what may, keep pushing. My dreams and my purpose are more prominent than any storm I could face. *To whom much is given, much is required.* Without perseverance, your growth and development as a person are severely limited, and this will reflect the amount of success you can achieve.

My WHY is the Fuel to my Dreams

All skin folk ain't your kinfolk! A powerful lesson that I learned along the way. This particular saying is honestly one of the driving forces of my WHY. It's sad to say, but I have had very little experience with having a mentor who is a woman of color. I hesitated to put this narrative in my chapter, but I would be unauthentic to my story if I didn't share it. Post my undergraduate experience at an HBCU, I found that as I navigated in majority spaces, I had to not only contend with the oppression of systemic racism, sexism, and ageism, but I would also have to navigate the waters of women of color not being as supportive as I thought they should be. Growing up, I was surrounded by women of color who were powerful, who were supportive, who were mindful of your gifts, and helped you to elevate. But once I got to the graduate level, I found that experience to be the complete opposite. I found some women of color to be manipulative, vindictive, and lack a sense of empathy. It was those driving forces that caused me to say I will not be what I see. I wanted to be a woman of purpose that was able to still share the secrets of my success. I wanted to be able to support those along the way, even if they take my place in the midst of it. The goal is for me to leave a mark and a path for those behind me, so they know what's possible. Not to stay and haze you why you try to climb.

Earlier in my career and doctoral journey, I did not always feel comfortable claiming my space. Standing my ground was usually met with destructive responses. Some of my favorites include, "Oh, Jay is feeling particularly sassy today," or, "That's presumptuous of you to think you can get all that done at one time," and "Okay, girl. Why you mad?" Those reactions became my kryptonite. I ultimately became so consumed with not fulfilling the angry or sassy Black woman stereotype in my predominately white workplaces that I lost parts of myself in the process. I stopped speaking up in meetings or classes to avoid those negative perceptions. I sought absolute perfection in the most debilitating manner to ensure that my mistakes were not blamed on my race, my appearance, education, or anything else that made me feel othered.

As I overcame this weight and redeemed my Black woman superpowers, I got to a point where I realized that I needed to focus on myself, my growth, and my well-being more than anything. I am. It's the mantra I carried with me as I continued to discover myself again. I am smart. I am capable. I am deserving of every opportunity I am given. I am here. I am powerful. Though I still falter, shrink, and code-switch at times, I strive to bring my full self to work every day.

The more I found my WHY, the more I realized that my experiences were not just for me. My actual WHY is to help others find their purpose and show them the steps to succeed from what I learned. As I close this chapter, I want to leave you with what I learned to help you along your journey.

Find your people

Every space won't feel like a safe space. As a Black woman in higher education, I am often the only woman of color on my team or in a meeting. Most importantly, if you are in a space where you don't feel welcomed or accepted, make a plan to change that space rather than change yourself. Join organizations with like-minded people. Find a mentor that has the job you want one day. Make sure that all relationships are give and take.

Get Moving, But Don't Forget to Breathe

I have turned to fitness to release some of that tension. I make sure I move my body in some capacity every day. I enjoy group fitness classes and taking long walks with an amazing playlist. In addition to that, praise and worship has helped me to realize and challenge my strength. Lastly, I also meditate and do breathwork. Those daily reminders force me to take a few minutes to exhale whatever I don't want to bring with me through the rest of my workday.

Flexing The Muscle

It's important to build up those muscles with practice. Practice your salary negotiation skills with your peers or friends before meeting with your manager. Practice using phrases like, "I was speaking," "I just said that" or "I'm leading this project." Similarly, practice removing certain words and disclaimers from your vocabulary in everyday conversations. Starting questions with "Sorry, but" justifying your questions or beginning factual statements with "I think" or "I feel" are not the way to go. If you don't do it with your friends, don't do it at work. The first time I had a difficult conversation with my manager, my voice was shaking, and I felt like I wanted to run out of the room. But I got the words out, even if I had to read them word for word from my notebook. And each time after that, my voice grew steadier and stronger. Work that muscle until you can flex it like a boss.

I Am

I'm a firm believer in mantras. Imposter syndrome, minority stress, and stereotype threats can sometimes impact our confidence. I have mantras written on post-its around my desk to remember who I am and who I am becoming. Sometimes, all it takes is a glance to the left of my monitor to breathe in that truth. It is easier said than done, but you owe it to your current and future self. Some of my favorites include I am.

I am able to do hard things.

I am more than enough.

I am capable of doing whatever I set my mind to.

References

Johnson, H. L. (2016). *Pipelines, pathways, and institutional leadership: An update on the status of women in higher education* [Infographic brief]. American Council on Education. http://www.acenet.edu/news-room/Documents/Higher-Ed-Spotlight-Pipelines-Pathways-and-Institutional-Leadership-Status-of-Women.pdf

FOR BLACK WOMEN, FOREVER AND ALWAYS

Written by Nicole A. Telfer

BLACK SISTERHOOD IS essential. I wish for a healthy and authentic sisterhood for every Black woman on the face of this earth. I first learned about the importance of sisterhood at 11 years old when my mom, siblings, and I moved for the third time in one year. My mother is often depicted as a reserved woman of little words, especially when around unfamiliar faces, which surprises most people who might describe Jamaican women as blunt and outspoken. Despite mom's reservations, she was always great at quickly befriending folks on the block. In just one week after our move, mom introduced me to a woman named Claudette (may her soul rest in peace), who then introduced me to her children. I eventually began calling Claudette "auntie," and her children and my siblings and I would always spend time together. I became very close with auntie Claudette's youngest daughter, Cloricea, and would often refer to her as my play mom. Cloricea and I would spend the night at each other's house, watching scary and funny movies, and we also played with other kids on the block together. Of course, I was completely devastated and shattered when mom announced that we would be moving *again*. On the night when we were getting ready to drive away from the memories on Quincy Street in Brooklyn, NY, Cloricea gave me a gentle kiss on the forehead. Lord, I can still feel that kiss until this day, and it gives me chills every time I reminisce about it. It was a warm, and *I'll always have your back* kind of kiss that, I believe, only Black girls and women can give. Cloricea and I are still friends to this day, and she is the reason why I have learned to cherish Black sisterhood— through her loving and gentle forehead kiss.

I asked some of the co-authors when they first came across Black sisterhood— in general, and in academia—and they said:

When I started my program, I began to pathologize my experience and how prepared I was for my doctoral program until I met with Dr. Nicholson from my doctoral network, and she helped me to seek clarity in the assignment, not my abilities! I will forever be grateful for communities that support our needs and desires! – Deja Trammell

I first encountered Black sisterhood at birth, as my older sister is pictured lovingly

holding me with such joyful fierceness that is unique to Black girls and women. – Dr. Keila Miles

I first encountered Black sisterhood at a conference I'd convinced my professor to attend. I'd gotten a sew-in and hated my hair. She had no clue what she was doing but took it out as we laughed about the experience. – Dr. Shanel Robinson

I met some dynamic women of color in grad school when I desperately needed to be recognized as a person, not a free space on someone's racially diverse bingo card. – Dr. Johniqua Williams

My first encounter with sisterhood began around the 9th grade through lunchtime chats and sleepovers. Ten years later, those same women and I are celebrating graduations, homeownership, marriages, and babies. Sisterhood transcends time and space. It's an ever-present love. – Angel Boulware

I first encountered Black sisterhood when I met my best friend in 2nd grade. It was the laughter for me. We had unspoken understandings that would burst into a belly-raging, soul-freeing laughter from every range of our voices. We bonded on our own unique frequency. That understanding and laughter were instrumental to our sisterhood as we processed experiences we shared and independent experiences we listened to and supported each other through. – Munazza Abraham

I must say this again—Black women are fighting several wars, both seen and unseen. These stories are evidence of those wars along with the harmful impacts. Our doctoral journeys consisted of tears, growing pains, laughter, more tears, losses, wins, but most importantly— community. Our journeys consisted of sisterhood and strong bonds. It is our hope that our stories give you faith, tranquility, and purpose. We hope these stories bring you contentment and inspiration. Because the co-authors and I were collectively raised in a culture that emphasized relying on our village, we were able to find each other and write this book. We wrote this book for you, and we thank you for reading it.

ACKNOWLEDGMENTS

THERE ARE MANY people to give thanks to. As always, I will first acknowledge God, the one who reminds me daily of my purpose. God had my parents name me Nicole for a reason, and I am grateful that God chose me to live this unique and fulfilled life. Thank you to our publishing company, Xlibris, for their support, services, and timely responses. Thank you to our writing coach and copyeditor, Dr. Rahmatu Kassimu (who also wrote our foreword)! You are truly a gem and one of a kind. Thank you to our graphic designer, Kelly Ann (@ kagdesignco), for her amazing artwork. Thank you to Dr. Dominiqua Griffin (CEO of BlackWomenPhDs) for sharing my recruitment flier and connecting me to 24 incredible Black women– connections that, I am confident, will last forever. Lastly, I am so grateful for my ancestors, mom, dad, siblings, aunties and uncles, close (church and school) friends, family in Brooklyn, NY and family on the beautiful island of Jamaica, and all the little Black children in my life who tell me every day that they are proud to know and love me. My chapter was written with all of you in mind. - **Nicole A. Telfer**

I would like to express divine gratitude to my family for supporting me and motivating me to forge my own path. To my mother, Mufiyda, my father, Saalim, my brothers, Taariq and Joshua and their beautiful families: you all have given me the life, wisdom, and inspiration that I hope to pass on to all others who hear my voice and know my words. And to my grad school friends and BDOC, you know who you are: we have listened to each other's cries, hugged away each other's self-doubts, and fought alongside each other for the changes we wanted to see. I thank you all for being my family, community, tribe, and army. - **Munazza S. Abraham**

I would like to thank my family- my siblings who have always been there for me and who showed me the meaning of support. My mum, my human backbone who never relents, prays for me, encourages me, scolds me and loves me unconditionally. My dad, who is no longer alive but whose values and morals live on in me. Xander, the love that came into my life a few months before PhD defense and supported me in ways that I didn't even know were possible. I love you all, you encourage me to be unapologetically me through the arguments, disagreements and agreements, thank you! -**Dr. Sarah Adeyinka**

Thank the Lord and Savior Jesus Christ for allowing me the opportunity to speak on my journey. I would also like to thank Dr. Nicole for having this vision for all the women to share their experiences. To all the women and men who may read our story, thank you for taking time to read our story. I would also like to thank my family and friends for continuing to motivate me to share my story.

I hope my story will encourage anyone to keep going and never let anyone or anything stop them from achieving their goals. -**Dr. Kenyatta Aldridge**

First, I would like to thank God who has filled my life with blessings and purpose beyond anything I could have imagined for myself. Special thank you to Nicole for creating this project and inviting so many special women together to write this book. Thank you to my son whose very presence motivates me to strive for all of my biggest dreams. Thank you to my mom and dad, my brothers, all my aunties, Miracle, Dajuane, Muthoni, Felicia, Ilia, Teairah, Jas, and Jahson for being such an integral part of my life -**Chanya Anderson**

I give thanks to the land of wood and water from which I originate. To the loves of my life, my parents Colin and Jennifer Bent who have never failed in their support and love for me I extend my gratitude. You are my covering and my two heartbeats. I honor my late grandparents who saw in me greatness and did not expect me to manifest less. Their fierce faith and dedication to family travel with me to this day even as they have moved to the next life. I hope they're proud. I am blessed by the women who are wind beneath my educational wings, *Homeplace*. Those who have broken the ground I now traverse. You have inspired me, seen me, held me and helped me, and it is your example that I refer to when I feel I can't do more. Thank you to Nicole Telfer and my co-authors in this work. You are priceless and powerful! Finally, to my nieces and nephews, Auntie loves you, believes in you and holds you as sources of joy when I need it most. Shoot beyond the stars! You can do all things through The One who is your strength. - **Toneille Bent**

Thank you, God, for everything, I am nothing without you. To my parents, late grandparents, family, chosen family, and sister-friends the English language is not developed enough to describe how thankful and appreciative I am. Thank you for never letting me fall and always giving me a safe space to land. A special thanks to Nicole for being an amazing sister and allowing me the opportunity to write my truth. Lastly, to the Black women before and after me, thank you for showing up. - **Angel Boulware**

I would like to thank my immediate family who have always been very encouraging and supported me as I pursued my dreams. I also would like to thank my son Sean, granddaughters (Laila, Larena and Lauren). I pray that I make you proud and leave a legacy of compassion, activism, empathy, and success! Also, a special shout out to Andrea Whigum, Dr. Venetria Patton, Dr. Nadia Brown, Dr. Ray Fouche and Dr. Marlo David. – **Juanita Crider**

First, I would like to thank my ancestors and foremothers for their divine guidance and protection throughout this life journey. A special thank you to the family that I was born into and the one that I chose to grow old with. Mama, you have always been my guiding light, thank you for shining on me. Pops, thank you for your unwavering love and support. My siblings and sister-friends thank you for always pouring into me and showing me what it means to know unconditional love. My partner, Gary, thank you for being the wind under my wings. To my advisor, Simone, your mentorship and guidance is always right on time, thank you for always believing in me. -**Dom Garrett-Scott**

I am so grateful to have been part of this piece and am forever inspired by the Black women who have shared their stories to heal, encourage, and inspire the next generation of Black women PhD 's. Thank you to my family, friends, and community that continues to motivate and support me in my doctoral journey and in life. -**N'Dea Irvin-Choy**

First, I acknowledge my mind, body, and spirit, for having the courage to contribute to this book. Thank you, God, my Fiancé, Family, and Friends for their unwavering support of my journey. - **Elisabeth Jeffrey**

God, you have shown me that I am your favorite and there's no other position I love to be in than the apple of your eye. Your love is overwhelmingly comforting and consistent. To the parentals Artemas and Rose-Marie Julien, thank you for giving me the tools to become the God-fearing trailblazer that I am today. To my siblings, Abigail, Timothy, Chantal, Margarita, and Marisha - I hope this chapter makes you proud. Family is what makes life and I couldn't do life without you all. To my Aunt Felecia Connor, your legacy lives through me forever and always. Special thanks to my rider Lucie and Rayvon for the emotional support during the journey. To Dr. Melissa Noel, our morning prayers keep me grounded in Christ and our spiritual sisterhood thriving. To Dr. Lorna Thorpe, you have proven to be more than an advisor. You effortlessly exceed the title. - **Tabitha Esther**

First and foremost, I would like to give all praise to God. I would not be able to do anything without the blessing bestowed upon me not only by thee, but also by my angels and ancestors, who are a representation of that love. My blessings humble me, and the unconditional love I receive from my mother, sister, and daughter strengthens me even more. They are my voice of memory when I am doubtful or critical of myself. Without them, the storm of negativity and lessons needed to be learned would take longer to interpret and appreciate. I would also like to thank the entire collective for inspiring me through your stories. You are all amazing BLACK women! - **Dr. Lisa Marie Lee**

Prior to Nicole extending this opportunity, I made a promise to share my story to whomever was patient enough to listen. Since then, God has consistently provided opportunities for me to do so. So, I'm foremost thankful to God for His proven favor and consistency. I would like to express my gratitude to Nicole for granting us this transformative space to talk about our doctoral paths. The intricate process of writing and piecing together my story brought even more healing and appreciation for my journey; so, thank you! And last, but definitely not least, I want to acknowledge my family and tribe of sisters. You guys always push me to be better; thank you for consistently embracing the me that continues to blossom. -**Gaëlle Pierre**

I give all the honor, praise and glory to my Lord and Savior Jesus Christ, for His grace and mercy through-out my life. I want to thank my grandmother Wilma Burke for teaching me the importance of having an education. My sister Dr. Wilma Robinson, you encouraged me all the way through this process, you took care of me when I had cancer, prayed for me without ceasing and for being my best friend. To my entire family my sisters, brothers, aunts, uncles, cousins parents, step parents grandparents and in-laws, I thank you all for every lesson, every prayer, every hug and kiss, every text, every call, help the the kids and all the care you have shown me throughout my life. I could not have made it without you. To my girlfriends and you know who you are, thank you for being the joy during some very difficult days of my life. Justin, Ashley, Anyssa, Alyssa, Aniya and Jace, you all are the best part of my life, you inspire me to always do my best! Love you all always mommy. Damon Rentz, my love!!! Thank you for always being "Team Ivy" and all that comes with it- **Dr. Ivy Rentz**

I am my ancestors' wildest dreams! The efforts of this work were not done in isolation but with a support system out of love, support, strength and courage. Foremost, I am so thankful for God and all of his mercy and grace that he has bestowed upon me. I am grateful for my mother, Tresa, because it's by her strength, guidance, and love that I am who I am. My sister, Lilly, for being my support and strength when she least expects it. My SONshine, Calvin, I love you so much. I know that you know this, but it is because of you that I keep pushing through. My tribe! The support is always real, and I appreciate the prayers! Last but not least, Nicole!!!! You are such a blessing and truly a GEM!! Thank you for allowing me to be a part of your vision with our shared purpose. - **Kristin Robair**

I am blessed to have rich experiences and connections that have allowed me to connect with so many brilliant women that share similar journeys. Without God, that would not be possible, and I am forever thankful for the sense of community and family I have gained throughout my higher education experience. To my grandmother, who instilled in me the drive, motivation, and importance of taking care of myself, without your push I would not be here. A special thank you to the lifetime friends I've made along the way. May we all continue to prosper in the plans God has prepared for us. -**Dr. Shanel Robinson**

I'm so grateful for the opportunity to share my experiences for the purpose of helping other Black women. Thank you, Nicole, for creating this space for us to reflect, heal, and support future Black doctors. All praises to God for this opportunity. Also, special thanks to my family and friends who supported me along the doctoral journey as well as through the process of writing my chapter for this book. - **Dr. Emmanuela Stanislaus**

There is not enough time or space for me to express my gratitude to the village who have made moments and experiences like these possible. I thank God first and foremost for always positioning me for greater and granting me favor in all things through the support of my family and friends. To my mothers, fathers, family, friends, and community, thank you for believing in me and pouring into the woman I am constantly becoming. I pray that this book serves as a touchpoint for the women that read it, and that it affirms and connects you to your purpose and helps you find *you* in all things that you do. -**Deja Trammell**

The efforts that formulated this work are not mine alone but a culmination of the love, light, sacrifice, resilience, strength, dedication, and commitment of powerful Black women who paved this journey for me. This is for my mother, Annie Mae Sneed, and my mother-in-love, Pamela Payne Watkins, who are no longer physically here but whose spirits continue to run through me. This is for my other-mothers–Dr. Iris Carlton-LaNey, Ms. Bea Laney, Ms. Janet Cherry, and Ms. Wanda Reives–who were there to support my progression from hurt to healing. This is for my social work family–Dr. Trennette Goings, Mrs. Sharon Thomas, Ms. Tauchiana Williams, Dr. Travis Albritton, Dr. Michael Lambert, Dr. Kathleen Rounds, Dr. Anne Jones, Dr. Natasha Bowen, Ms. Bonita Joyce, Mrs. Amanda Hubbard, Ms. Tamsin Woolley, and many others–who were there for the ups and downs, tears of sadness, and tears of frustrations. This is for all of us. -**Dr. Charity Watkins**

Foremost, I'd like to acknowledge my Lord and Savior, Jesus Christ. You are the foundation of my purpose, and you will always order my steps. Nicole, you know I think the world of you, thank you for this dynamic opportunity. To the women who will read this book, know it is dedicated to your voices that are often silenced due to systemic marginalization in a male-dominated society. My goal is to always speak your truth in an effort to move women forward to a brighter day. -**Dr. Johniqua Williams**

Made in the USA
Las Vegas, NV
01 July 2023